MznLnx

Missing Links Exam Preps

Exam Prep for

Intermediate Accounting

Spiceland, Sepe, & Tomassini, 4th Edition

The MznLnx Exam Prep is your link from the texbook and lecture to your exams.
The MznLnx Exam Preps are unauthorized and comprehensive reviews of your textbooks.

All material provided by MznLnx and Rico Publications (c) 2010
Textbook publishers and textbook authors do not particpate in or contribute to these reviews.

MznLnx

Rico
Publications

Exam Prep for Intermediate Accounting
4th Edition
Spiceland, Sepe, & Tomassini

Publisher: Raymond Houge
Assistant Editor: Michael Rouger
Text and Cover Designer: Lisa Buckner
Marketing Manager: Sara Swagger
Project Manager, Editorial Production: Jerry Emerson
Art Director: Vernon Lowerui

Product Manager: Dave Mason
Editorial Assitant: Rachel Guzmanji
Pedagogy: Debra Long
Cover Image: Jim Reed/Getty Images
Text and Cover Printer: City Printing, Inc.
Compositor: Media Mix, Inc.

(c) 2010 Rico Publications
ALL RIGHTS RESERVED. No part of this work covered by the copyright may be reproduced or used in any form or by an means--graphic, electronic, or mechanical, including photocopying, recording, taping, Web distribution, information storage, and retrieval systems, or in any other manner--without the written permission of the publisher.

Printed in the United States
ISBN:

For more information about our products, contact us at:
Dave.Mason@RicoPublications.com

For permission to use material from this text or product, submit a request online to:
Dave.Mason@RicoPublications.com

Contents

CHAPTER 1
Environment and Theoretical Structure of Financial Accounting — 1

CHAPTER 2
Review of the Accounting Process — 23

CHAPTER 3
The Balance Sheet and Financial Disclosures — 36

CHAPTER 4
The Income Statement and Statement of Cash Flows — 53

CHAPTER 5
Income Measurement and Profitability Analysis — 68

CHAPTER 6
Time Value of Money Concepts — 79

CHAPTER 7
Cash and Receivables — 87

CHAPTER 8
Inventories: Measurement — 101

CHAPTER 9
Inventories: Additional Issues — 110

CHAPTER 10
Operational Assets: Acquisition and Disposition — 121

CHAPTER 11
Operational Assets: Utilization and Impairment — 134

CHAPTER 12
Investments — 142

CHAPTER 13
Current Liabilities and Contingencies — 154

CHAPTER 14
Bonds and Long-Term Notes — 168

CHAPTER 15
Leases — 184

CHAPTER 16
Accounting for Income Taxes — 198

CHAPTER 17
Pensions and Other Postretirement Benefits — 207

CHAPTER 18
Shareholders' Equity — 217

CHAPTER 19
Share-Based Compensation and Earnings Per Share — 232

CHAPTER 20
Accounting Changes and Error Corrections — 241

Contents (Cont.)

CHAPTER 21
  The Statement of Cash Flows Revisited   251
ANSWER KEY   272

TO THE STUDENT

COMPREHENSIVE

The *MznLnx* Exam Prep series is designed to help you pass your exams. Editors at MznLnx review your textbooks and then prepare these practice exams to help you master the textbook material. Unlike study guides, workbooks, and practice tests provided by the texbook publisher and textbook authors, *MznLnx* gives you **all** of the material in each chapter in exam form, not just samples, so you can be sure to nail your exam.

MECHANICAL

The MznLnx Exam Prep series creates exams that will help you learn the subject matter as well as test you on your understanding. Each question is designed to help you master the concept. Just working through the exams, you gain an understanding of the subject--its a simple mechanical process that produces success.

INTEGRATED STUDY GUIDE AND REVIEW

MznLnx is not just a set of exams designed to test you, its also a comprehensive review of the subject content. Each exam question is also a review of the concept, making sure that you will get the answer correct without having to go to other sources of material. You learn as you go! Its the easiest way to pass an exam.

HUMOR

Studying can be tedious and dry. MznLnx's instructional design includes moderate humor within the exam questions on occassion, to break the tedium and revitalize the brain

Chapter 1. Environment and Theoretical Structure of Financial Accounting

1. A _____ is used in research to outline possible courses of action or to present a preferred approach to an idea or thought. For example, the philosopher Isaiah Berlin used the 'hedgehogs' versus 'foxes' approach; a 'hedgehog' might approach the world in terms of a single organizing principle; a 'fox' might pursue multiple conflicting goals simultaneously. Alternatively, an empiricist might approach a subject by direct examination, whereas an intuitionist might simply intuit what's next.
   a. BNSF Railway
   b. BMC Software, Inc.
   c. 3M Company
   d. Conceptual framework

2. An _____ is a term used in behavioral economics to describe those types of behaviors that impose costs on a person in the long-run that are not taken into account when making decisions in the present. Classical Economics discourages government from creating legislation that targets internalities, because it is assumed that the consumer takes these personal costs into account when paying for the good that causes the _____. For example, cigarettes should be taxed because of the negative consumption externalities that they impose, such as second-hand smoke, not because the smoker harms him or herself by smoking.
   a. Authorised capital
   b. Inventory turnover ratio
   c. Operating budget
   d. Internality

3. _____ is concerned with the provisions and use of accounting information to managers within organizations, to provide them with the basis to make informed business decisions that will allow them to be better equipped in their management and control functions.

   In contrast to financial accountancy information, _____ information is:

   - usually confidential and used by management, instead of publicly reported;
   - forward-looking, instead of historical;
   - pragmatically computed using extensive management information systems and internal controls, instead of complying with accounting standards.

   This is because of the different emphasis: _____ information is used within an organization, typically for decision-making.

   a. Nonassurance services
   b. Grenzplankostenrechnung
   c. Governmental accounting
   d. Management accounting

4. In economics, _____ or _____ goods or real _____ refers to factors of production used to create goods or services that are not themselves significantly consumed (though they may depreciate) in the production process. _____ goods may be acquired with money or financial _____. In finance and accounting, _____ generally refers to financial wealth, especially that used to start or maintain a business.
   a. Capital
   b. Screening
   c. Vyborg Appeal
   d. Disclosure

Chapter 1. Environment and Theoretical Structure of Financial Accounting

5. _____ is the balance of the amounts of cash being received and paid by a business during a defined period of time, sometimes tied to a specific project. Measurement of _____ can be used

- to evaluate the state or performance of a business or project.
- to determine problems with liquidity. Being profitable does not necessarily mean being liquid. A company can fail because of a shortage of cash, even while profitable.
- to project rate of returns. The time of _____s into and out of projects are used as inputs to financial models such as internal rate of return, and net present value.
- to examine income or growth of a business when it is believed that accrual accounting concepts do not represent economic realities. Alternately, _____ can be used to 'validate' the net income generated by accrual accounting.

_____ as a generic term may be used differently depending on context, and certain _____ definitions may be adapted by analysts and users for their own uses. Common terms include operating _____ and free _____.

    a. Cash flow   b. Commercial paper
    c. Flow-through entity   d. Controlling interest

6. _____ is a specific term used in companies' financial reporting from the company-whole point of view. Because that use excludes the effects of changing ownership interest, an economic measure of _____ is necessary for financial analysis from the shareholders' point of view

_____ is defined by the Financial Accounting Standards Board, or FASB, as 'the change in equity [net assets] of a business enterprise during a period from transactions and other events and circumstances from nonowner sources. It includes all changes in equity during a period except those resulting from investments by owners and distributions to owners.'

_____ is the sum of net income and other items that must bypass the income statement because they have not been realized, including items like an unrealized holding gain or loss from available for sale securities and foreign currency translation gains or losses.

    a. BMC Software, Inc.   b. BNSF Railway
    c. 3M Company   d. Comprehensive income

7. _____ is a type of lease - the other being an operating lease. A _____ effectively allows a firm to finance the purchase of an asset, even if, strictly speaking, the firm never acquires the asset. Typically, a _____ will give the lessee control over an asset for a large proportion of the asset's useful life, providing them the benefits and risks of ownership.

    a. Debt ratio   b. 3M Company
    c. Profitability index   d. Finance lease

8. A _____ is any one of a variety of different systems, institutions, procedures, social relations and infrastructures whereby persons trade, and goods and services are exchanged, forming part of the economy. It is an arrangement that allows buyers and sellers to exchange things. _____s vary in size, range, geographic scale, location, types and variety of human communities, as well as the types of goods and services traded.

Chapter 1. Environment and Theoretical Structure of Financial Accounting

    a. Market Failure
    b. Perfect competition
    c. Recession
    d. Market

9. In economics, business, retail, and accounting, a _____ is the value of money that has been used up to produce something, and hence is not available for use anymore. In economics, a _____ is an alternative that is given up as a result of a decision. In business, the _____ may be one of acquisition, in which case the amount of money expended to acquire it is counted as _____.
    a. Cost allocation
    b. Prime cost
    c. Cost
    d. Cost of quality

10. _____ are formal records of a business' financial activities.

In British English, including United Kingdom company law, _____ are often referred to as accounts, although the term _____ is also used, particularly by accountants.

_____ provide an overview of a business' financial condition in both short and long term.
    a. Statement of retained earnings
    b. 3M Company
    c. Notes to the financial statements
    d. Financial statements

11. A _____ is a contract conferring a right on one person to possess property belonging to another person (called a landlord or lessor) to the exclusion of the owner landlord. It is a rental agreement between landlord and tenant. The relationship between the tenant and the landlord is called a tenancy, and the right to possession by the tenant is sometimes called a leasehold interest.
    a. Robinson-Patman Act
    b. Federal Sentencing Guidelines
    c. Model Code of Professional Responsibility
    d. Lease

12. NYSE Amex Equities, formerly known as the _____ is an _____ situated in New York. AMEX was a mutual organization, owned by its members. Until 1953 it was known as the New York Curb Exchange.
    a. AIG
    b. American Stock Exchange
    c. ABC Television Network
    d. AMEX

13. _____ is an equity (stock) exchange located at 11 Wall Street in lower Manhattan, New York, USA.) It is the largest stock exchange in the world by dollar value of its listed companies' securities. As of October 2008, the combined capitalization of all domestic _____ listed companies was US$10.1 trillion.
    a. New York Stock Exchange
    b. BNSF Railway
    c. 3M Company
    d. BMC Software, Inc.

14. _____ is a concept that denotes the precise probability of specific eventualities. Technically, the notion of _____ is independent from the notion of value and, as such, eventualities may have both beneficial and adverse consequences. However, in general usage the convention is to focus only on potential negative impact to some characteristic of value that may arise from a future event.
    a. Risk adjusted return on capital
    b. Discount factor
    c. Discounting
    d. Risk

Chapter 1. Environment and Theoretical Structure of Financial Accounting

15. The U.S. _____ is an independent agency of the United States government which holds primary responsibility for enforcing the federal securities laws and regulating the securities industry, the nation's stock and options exchanges, and other electronic securities markets. The SEC was created by section 4 of the Securities Exchange Act of 1934 (now codified as 15 U.S.C. §Â§ 78d and commonly referred to as the 1934 Act.)
   a. BMC Software, Inc.
   b. 3M Company
   c. BNSF Railway
   d. Securities and Exchange Commission

16. In economics, the concept of the _____ refers to the decision-making time frame of a firm in which at least one factor of production is fixed. Costs which are fixed in the _____ have no impact on a firms decisions. For example a firm can raise output by increasing the amount of labour through overtime.
   a. Long-run
   b. Short-run
   c. 3M Company
   d. BMC Software, Inc.

17. A _____, (formerly a securities exchange) is a corporation or mutual organization which provides 'trading' facilities for stock brokers and traders, to trade stocks and other securities. _____s also provide facilities for the issue and redemption of securities as well as other financial instruments and capital events including the payment of income and dividends. The securities traded on a _____ include: shares issued by companies, unit trusts, derivatives, pooled investment products and bonds.
   a. BMC Software, Inc.
   b. BNSF Railway
   c. Stock Exchange
   d. 3M Company

18. In finance, _____ also known as return on investment, rate of profit or sometimes just return, is the ratio of money gained or lost on an investment relative to the amount of money invested. The amount of money gained or lost may be referred to as interest, profit/loss, gain/loss, or net income/loss. The money invested may be referred to as the asset, capital, principal, or the cost basis of the investment.
   a. Theoretical ex-rights price
   b. Capital employed
   c. Debt to capital ratio
   d. Rate of return

19. _____ of something is, in finance, the adding together of interest or different investments over a period of time such as atoms (1 - the act or process of accruing; 2 - the amount that accrues.) It holds specific meanings in accounting and payroll.

   _____, in accounting, describes the accounting method known as _____ basis, whereby revenues and expenses are recognized when they are accrued, i.e. accumulated (earned or incurred), regardless when the actual cash is received or paid out.

   a. Accrual
   b. Earnings before interest, taxes, depreciation and amortization
   c. Accounts receivable
   d. Assets

20. _____ is a method of accounting whereby economic activities (rather than cash flow) of financial events are considered, because of two complementary principles, which (together) determine the point, at which expenses and revenues are recognized. According to revenue recognition principle, revenues are realized when earned, whether or not they are received in cash.

Chapter 1. Environment and Theoretical Structure of Financial Accounting

a. Accrual basis accounting

c. Accrual

b. Accrued revenue

d. Earnings before interest, taxes, depreciation and amortization

21. _____ is a method of accounting whereby cash flow of financial events is considered. The method recognizes revenues when cash is received and recognizes expenses when cash is paid out. In cash accounting, revenues and expenses are also called cash receipts and cash payments respectively.

a. Net sales

c. Treasury stock

b. Closing entries

d. Cash basis accounting

22. The _____ is a private, not-for-profit organization whose primary purpose is to develop generally accepted accounting principles (GAAP) within the United States in the public's interest. The Securities and Exchange Commission (SEC) designated the _____ as the organization responsible for setting accounting standards for public companies in the U.S. It was created in 1973, replacing the Accounting Principles Board and the Committee on Accounting Procedure of the American Institute of Certified Public Accountants. The _____'s mission is 'to establish and improve standards of financial accounting and reporting for the guidance and education of the public, including issuers, auditors, and users of financial information.'

The _____ is not a governmental body.

a. Governmental Accounting Standards Board

c. Fannie Mae

b. Public company

d. Financial Accounting Standards Board

23. In financial accounting, _____ , cash flow provided by operations or cash flow from operating activities, refers to the amount of cash a company generates from the revenues it brings in, excluding costs associated with long-term investment on capital items or investment in securities.

_____ = Cash generated from operations less taxation and interest paid, investment income received and less dividends paid gives rise to _____s per International Financial Reporting Standards.

To calculate cash generated from operations, one must calculate cash generated from customers and cash paid to suppliers.

a. AIG

c. AMEX

b. Operating cash flow

d. ABC Television Network

24. In accounting, _____ has a very specific meaning. It is an outflow of cash or other valuable assets from a person or company to another person or company. This outflow of cash is generally one side of a trade for products or services that have equal or better current or future value to the buyer than to the seller.

a. AMEX

c. ABC Television Network

b. Expense

d. AIG

25. _____ is equal to the income that a firm has after subtracting costs and expenses from the total revenue. _____ can be distributed among holders of common stock as a dividend or held by the firm as retained earnings.

The items deducted will typically include tax expense, financing expense (interest expense), and minority interest. Likewise, preferred stock dividends will be subtracted too, though they are not an expense.

a. Matching principle
b. Generally accepted accounting principles
c. Net income
d. Long-term liabilities

26. In financial accounting, a _____ or Statement of cash flows is a financial statement that shows a company's flow of cash. The money coming into the business is called cash inflow, and money going out from the business is called cash outflow. The statement shows how changes in balance sheet and income accounts affect cash and cash equivalents, and breaks the analysis down to operating, investing, and financing activities.

a. BNSF Railway
b. Cash flow statement
c. 3M Company
d. BMC Software, Inc.

27. An _____ is a practitioner of accountancy, which is the measurement, disclosure or provision of assurance about financial information that helps managers, investors, tax authorities and other decision makers make resource allocation decisions.

The word '_____' is derived from the French 'Compter' which took its origin from the Latin 'Computare'. The word was formerly written in English as 'Accomptant', but in process of time the word, which was always pronounced by dropping the 'p', became gradually changed both in pronunciation and in orthography to its present form.

a. Accountant
b. ABC Television Network
c. AMEX
d. AIG

28. The _____ is the former authoritative body of the American Institute of Certified Public Accountants (AICPA.) It was created by the American Institute of Certified Public Accountants in 1959 and issued pronouncements on accounting principles until 1973, when it was replaced by the Financial Accounting Standards Board (FASB.)

The _____ was disbanded in the hopes that the smaller, fully-independent FASB could more effectively create accounting standards.

a. American Payroll Association
b. International Federation of Accountants
c. Institute of Management Accountants
d. Accounting Principles Board

29. _____ were documents issued by the Committee on Accounting Procedure between 1938 and 1959 on various accounting problems. They were discontinued with the dissolution of the Committee in 1959 under a recommendation from the Special Committee on Research Program. In all, 51 bulletins were issued, however, the lack of binding authority over AICPA's membership reduced the influence of, and compliance with the content of the bulletins.

a. Other postemployment benefits
b. ABC Television Network
c. AIG
d. Accounting Research Bulletins

Chapter 1. Environment and Theoretical Structure of Financial Accounting

30. The _____ is the national, professional association of CPAs in the United States, with more than 330,000 members, including CPAs in business and industry, public practice, government, and education; student affiliates; and international associates. It sets ethical standards for the profession and U.S. auditing standards for audits of private companies; federal, state and local governments; and non-profit organizations.

Approximately 40% of its members are engaged in the practice of public accounting, in areas such as auditing, accounting, taxation, general business consulting, business valuation, personal financial planning and business technology.

 a. AIG
 b. ABC Television Network
 c. Other postemployment benefits
 d. American Institute of Certified Public Accountants

31. _____ is the statutory title of qualified accountants in the United States who have passed the Uniform _____ Examination and have met additional state education and experience requirements for certification as a _____. Individuals who have passed the Exam but have not either accomplished the required on-the-job experience or have previously met it but in the meantime have lapsed their continuing professional education are, in many states, permitted the designation '_____ Inactive' or an equivalent phrase. In most U.S. states, only _____s who are licensed are able to provide to the public attestation (including auditing) opinions on financial statements.

 a. Chartered Accountant
 b. Certified Public Accountant
 c. Certified General Accountant
 d. Chartered Certified Accountant

32. The _____ was a predecessor of the Accounting Principles Board, itself a predecessor to the Financial Accounting Standards Board in the United States. Its formation and activities were early efforts to rationalize and legitimize the reporting of business performance. However, it is widely regarded as having failed.

 a. Consolidated financial statements
 b. Price variance
 c. Lump sum
 d. Committee on Accounting Procedure

33. _____ is the term used to refer to the standard framework of guidelines for financial accounting used in any given jurisdiction. _____ includes the standards, conventions, and rules accountants follow in recording and summarizing transactions, and in the preparation of financial statements.

Financial accounting information must be assembled and reported objectively.

 a. Long-term liabilities
 b. Current asset
 c. Generally accepted accounting principles
 d. General ledger

34. A _____ is a fungible, negotiable instrument representing financial value. they are broadly categorized into debt securities (such as banknotes, bonds and debentures), and equity securities; e.g., common stocks. The company or other entity issuing the _____ is called the issuer.

 a. Tracking stock
 b. Security
 c. BMC Software, Inc.
 d. 3M Company

35. Congress enacted the _____, in the aftermath of the stock market crash of 1929 and during the ensuing Great Depression.

Chapter 1. Environment and Theoretical Structure of Financial Accounting

a. Sustainability measurement
b. Monte Carlo methods
c. Bookkeeping
d. Securities Act of 1933

36. The _____ of 1934 is a law governing the secondary trading of securities (stocks, bonds, and debentures) in the United States of America. The Act, 48 Stat. 881 (enacted June 6, 1934), codified at 15 U.S.C.
a. BNSF Railway
b. Securities Exchange Act
c. 3M Company
d. BMC Software, Inc.

37. The _____ is a law governing the secondary trading of securities (stocks, bonds, and debentures) in the United States of America. The Act, 48 Stat. 881 (enacted June 6, 1934), codified at 15 U.S.C.
a. BNSF Railway
b. BMC Software, Inc.
c. Securities Exchange Act of 1934
d. 3M Company

38. _____ were published by Accounting Principles Board (APB.) The board was created by American Institute of Certified Public Accountants (AICPA) in 1959 and was replaced by Financial Accounting Standards Board (FASB) in 1973. Its mission was to develop an overall conceptual framework of US generally accepted accounting principles (US GAAP.)
a. Accounting Principles Board Opinions
b. ABC Television Network
c. AMEX
d. AIG

39. The _____ is located in Norwalk, Connecticut. It is an independent, organization in the private sector that is responsible for oversight of the Financial Accounting Standards Board (FASB), the Governmental Accounting Standards Board (GASB), and their respective advisory councils.
a. BMC Software, Inc.
b. BNSF Railway
c. 3M Company
d. Financial Accounting Foundation

Chapter 1. Environment and Theoretical Structure of Financial Accounting   9

40. _____ means the giving out of information, either voluntarily or to be in compliance with legal regulations or workplace rules.

- In Computer security, full _____ means disclosing full information about vulnerabilities.
- In computing, _____ widget
- Journalism, full _____ refers to disclosing the interests of the writer which may bear on the subject being written about, for example, if the writer has worked with an interview subject in the past.

- In law:
    - The law of England and Wales, _____ refers to a process that may form part of legal proceedings, whereby parties inform to other parties the existence of any relevant documents that are, or have been, in their control. This compares with the process known as discovery in the course of legal proceedings in the United States.
    - In U.S. civil procedure (litigation rules for civil cases), _____ is a stage prior to trial. In civil cases, each party must disclose to the opposing party the following: names of witnesses which it may use to support its side, copies of documents (or mere description of these documents) in its control which it may use to support its side, computation of damages claimed, and certain insurance information. _____ is related to, but technically prior to, the discovery stage.
    - In Company law (known as 'corporate law' in the United States), _____ refers to giving out information about public or limited companies or their officers, which might be kept secret if the company was a private company or a partnership.

- In real property transactions, _____ refers to providing to a buyer information known to the seller or broker/agent concerning the condition or other aspects of real property that would affect the property's value or desirability. These rules regarding what information must be disclosed, and whether the information must be disclosed even if a buyer does not ask, vary from one jurisdiction to the next.

a. Tax harmonisation
c. Disclosure
b. Trailing
d. Controlled Foreign Corporations

41. The _____ is currently the source of generally accepted accounting principles (GAAP) used by State and Local governments in the [[United States of America]]. As with most of the entities involved in creating GAAP in the United States, it is a private, non-governmental organization.

The _____ is subject to oversight by the Financial Accounting Foundation (FAF), which selects the members of the _____ and the Financial Accounting Standards Board, and funds both organizations.

a. Governmental Accounting Standards Board
c. Fannie Mae
b. Multinational corporation
d. National Conference of Commissioners on Uniform State Laws

42. _____ is an umbrella term which refers to the various accounting systems used by various public sector entities. In the United States, for instance, there are two levels of government which follow different accounting standards set forth by independent, private sector boards. At the federal level, the Federal Accounting Standards Advisory Board (FASAB) sets forth the accounting standards to follow.

a. Product control
b. Management accounting
c. Governmental Accounting
d. Nonassurance services

43. _____ is the realization of an application idea, model, design, specification, standard, algorithm an _____ is a realization of a technical specification or algorithm as a program, software component, or other computer system. Many _____s may exist for a given specification or standard.
   a. ABC Television Network
   b. Implementation
   c. AMEX
   d. AIG

44. _____ is the process of increasing, or accounting for, an amount over a period of time. Particular instances of the term include:

   - _____, the allocation of a lump sum amount to different time periods, particularly for loans and other forms of finance, including related interest or other finance charges.
      o _____ schedule, a table detailing each periodic payment on a loan (typically a mortgage), as generated by an _____ calculator.
      o Negative _____, an _____ schedule where the loan amount actually increases through not paying the full interest
   - Amortized analysis, analyzing the execution cost of algorithms over a sequence of operations.
   - _____ of capital expenditures of certain assets under accounting rules, particularly intangible assets, in a manner analogous to depreciation.
   - _____

   a. Annuity
   b. EBIT
   c. Intangible
   d. Amortization

45. In finance, an _____ is a contract between a buyer and a seller that gives the buyer the right--but not the obligation--to buy or to sell a particular asset (the underlying asset) at a later time at an agreed price. In return for granting the _____, the seller collects a payment (the premium) from the buyer. A call _____ gives the buyer the right to buy the underlying asset; a put _____ gives the buyer of the _____ the right to sell the underlying asset.
   a. AIG
   b. ABC Television Network
   c. AMEX
   d. Option

46. _____ are defined as identifiable non-monetary assets that cannot be seen, touched or physically measured, which are created through time and/or effort and that are identifiable as a separate asset. There are two primary forms of intangibles - legal intangibles (such as trade secrets (e.g., customer lists), copyrights, patents, trademarks, and goodwill) and competitive intangibles (such as knowledge activities (know-how, knowledge), collaboration activities, leverage activities, and structural activities.) Legal intangibles are known under the generic term intellectual property and generate legal property rights defensible in a court of law.
   a. ABC Television Network
   b. Overhead
   c. AIG
   d. Intangible assets

47. _____ is any physical or virtual entity that is owned by an individual or jointly by a group of individuals. An owner of _____ has the right to consume, sell, rent, mortgage, transfer and exchange his or her _____. Important widely-recognized types of _____ include real _____, personal _____ (other physical possessions), and intellectual _____ (rights over artistic creations, inventions, etc.), although the latter is not always as widely recognized or enforced.

Chapter 1. Environment and Theoretical Structure of Financial Accounting

a. Disclosure requirement
b. Primary authority
c. Fiduciary
d. Property

48. In business and accounting, _____ are everything of value that is owned by a person or company. It is a claim on the property your income of a borrower. The balance sheet of a firm records the monetary value of the _____ owned by the firm.

a. Accrual basis accounting
b. Earnings before interest, taxes, depreciation and amortization
c. Accounts receivable
d. Assets

49. Discounting is a financial mechanism in which a debtor obtains the right to delay payments to a creditor, for a defined period of time, in exchange for a charge or fee. Essentially, the party that owes money in the present purchases the right to delay the payment until some future date. The _____, or charge, is simply the difference between the original amount owed in the present and the amount that has to be paid in the future to settle the debt.

a. Risk aversion
b. Discounting
c. Discount
d. Discount factor

50. _____ is a fee paid on borrowed assets. It is the price paid for the use of borrowed money, or, money earned by deposited funds. Assets that are sometimes lent with _____ include money, shares, consumer goods through hire purchase, major assets such as aircraft, and even entire factories in finance lease arrangements. The _____ is calculated upon the value of the assets in the same manner as upon money.

a. Interest
b. ABC Television Network
c. AIG
d. Insolvency

51. The _____ is a daily reference rate based on the interest rates at which banks borrow unsecured funds from other banks in the London wholesale money market. It is roughly comparable to the U.S. Federal funds rate.

During 1984 it became apparent that an increasing number of banks were trading actively in a variety of relatively new market instruments, notably interest rate swaps, foreign currency options and forward rate agreements.

a. London Interbank Offered Rate
b. BMC Software, Inc.
c. BNSF Railway
d. 3M Company

52. A _____ or transnational corporation (TNC) is a corporation or enterprise that manages production or delivers services in more than one country. It can also be referred to as an international corporation. The first modern _____ is generally thought to be the British East India Company, established in 1600.

a. Butterfield Bank
b. MicroStrategy
c. Multinational corporation
d. Privately held

53. In accounting, _____ are considered liabilities of the business that are to be settled in cash within the fiscal year or the operating cycle, whichever period is longer.

For example accounts payable for goods, services or supplies that were purchased for use in the operation of the business and payable within a normal period of time would be _____.

Bonds, mortgages and loans that are payable over a term exceeding one year would be fixed liabilities.

Chapter 1. Environment and Theoretical Structure of Financial Accounting

a. Treasury stock
b. Current liabilities
c. Closing entries
d. Payroll

54. An _____ is a tax levied on the financial income of people, corporations, or other legal entities. Various _____ systems exist, with varying degrees of tax incidence. Income taxation can be progressive, proportional, or regressive.
   a. Ordinary income
   b. Individual Retirement Arrangement
   c. Income tax
   d. Implied level of government service

55. In financial accounting, a _____ is defined as an obligation of an entity arising from past transactions or events, the settlement of which may result in the transfer or use of assets, provision of services or other yielding of economic benefits in the future.
   a. False Claims Act
   b. Corporate governance
   c. Liability
   d. Vested

56. The most frequent type of report is referred to as the Unqualified Opinion, and is regarded by many as the equivalent of a 'clean bill of health' to a patient, which has led many to call it the _____, but in reality it is not a clean bill of health. This type of report is issued by an auditor when the financial statements presented are free of material misstatements and are in accordance with GAAP, which in other words means that the company's financial condition, position, and operations are fairly presented in the financial statements. It is the best type of report an auditee may receive from an external auditor.
   a. Management assertions
   b. Sales Tax Audit
   c. Clean opinion
   d. Financial Instruments and Exchange Law

57. _____ are the earnings returned on the initial investment amount.

In the US, the Financial Accounting Standards Board (FASB) requires companies' income statements to report _____ for each of the major categories of the income statement: continuing operations, discontinued operations, extraordinary items, and net income.

The _____ formula does not include preferred dividends for categories outside of continued operations and net income.

   a. Earnings per share
   b. Invested capital
   c. Average accounting return
   d. Earnings yield

58. The _____ is an international organization that brings together the regulators of the world's securities and futures markets. It, along with its sister organizations, the Basel Committee on Banking Supervision and the International Association of Insurance Supervisors, together make up the Joint Forum of international financial regulators. Currently, _____ members regulate more than 90 percent of the world's securities markets.
   a. ABC Television Network
   b. AMEX
   c. AIG
   d. International Organization of Securities Commissions

59. The _____ founded on April 1, 2001 is the successor of the International Accounting Standards Committee (IASC) founded in June 1973 in London. It is responsible for developing the International Financial Reporting Standards (new name for the International Accounting Standards issued after 2001), and promoting the use and application of these standards.

The _____ is an independent, privately-funded accounting standard-setter based in London, UK.

a. Information Systems Audit and Control Association
b. International Accounting Standards Board
c. Emerging technologies
d. Institute of Management Accountants

60. _____ was founded in June 1973 in London and replaced by the International Accounting Standards Board on April 1, 2001. It was responsible for developing the International Accounting Standards and promoting the use and application of these standards.

The _____ was founded as a result of an agreement between accountancy bodies in the following countries:

- Australia (Institute of Chartered Accountants in Australia (ICAA) and the CPA Australia (formerly known as Australian Society of Certified Practising Accountants (ASCPA))

- Canada (Canadian Institute of Chartered Accountants (CICA))

- France (Ordre des Experts Comptable et des Comptables Agrees (Order of Accounting Experts and Qualified Accountants))

- Germany and the Wirtschaftsprüferkammer (WPK) (Chamber of Auditors))

- Japan Nihon Kouninkaikeishi Kyoukai)

- Mexico (Instituto Mexicano de Contadores Publicos (IMCP) (Mexican Institute of Public Accountants)) (removed from the board in 1987 due to non-payment of dues; resumed in 1995.)

- the Netherlands (Nederlands Instituut van Registeraccountants (NIVRA)

(Netherlands Institute of Registered Auditors))

- the United Kingdom and Ireland (counted as one) (Institute of Chartered Accountants in England and Wales (ICAEW), Institute of Chartered Accountants of Scotland (ICAS), Institute of Chartered Accountants in Ireland (ICAI), Association of Certified Accountants, Institute of Cost and Management Accountants, and the Institute of Municipal Treasurers and Accountants)

- the United States of America (American Institute of Certified Public Accountants (AICPA))

The Institute of Chartered Accountants of Nigeria became an associate member in 1976 and a member of the board from 1978 to 1987.

The National Council of Chartered Accountants (South Africa) became an associate member in 1974 and joined the board in 1978.

14 *Chapter 1. Environment and Theoretical Structure of Financial Accounting*

a. American Payroll Association
b. International Accounting Standards Board
c. American Accounting Association
d. International Accounting Standards Committee

61. _____ is a company's earnings per share (EPS) calculated using fully diluted shares outstanding. _____ indicates a 'worst case' scenario, one in which everyone who could have received stock without purchasing it directly for the full market value did so.

To find _____, basic EPS is calculated for each of the categories on the income statement first. Then each of the dilutive securities are ranked based on their effects, from most dilutive to least dilutive and antidilutive. Then the basic EPS number is diluted one by one by applying each one, skipping any instruments that have an antidilutive effect.

a. Diluted Earnings Per Share
b. Return on assets Du Pont
c. Cash conversion cycle
d. Financial ratio

62. _____ LLP, based in Chicago, was once one of the 'Big Five' accounting firms among PricewaterhouseCoopers, Deloitte Touche Tohmatsu, Ernst ' Young and KPMG, providing auditing, tax, and consulting services to large corporations. In 2002, the firm voluntarily surrendered its licenses to practice as Certified Public Accountants in the United States after being found guilty of criminal charges relating to the firm's handling of the auditing of Enron, the energy corporation, resulting in the loss of 85,000 jobs. Although the verdict was subsequently overturned by the Supreme Court of the United States, it has not returned as a viable business.

a. AIG
b. AMEX
c. ABC Television Network
d. Arthur Andersen

63. _____, also known as Merck Sharp ' Dohme or MSD outside the USA and Canada, is one of the largest pharmaceutical companies in the world. The headquarters of the company is located in Whitehouse Station, New Jersey, an unincorporated area in Readington Township.

a. Procter ' Gamble
b. Merck ' Co., Inc.
c. Social Security
d. Pension System

64. The term _____ usually refers to a company that is permitted to offer its registered securities (stock, bonds, etc.) for sale to the general public, typically through a stock exchange, or occasionally a company whose stock is traded over the counter (OTC) via market makers who use non-exchange quotation services.

The term '_____' may also refer to a company owned by the government.

a. MicroStrategy
b. Governmental Accounting Standards Board
c. Professional association
d. Public Company

65. The _____ (sometimes called 'Peekaboo') is a private-sector, non-profit corporation created by the Sarbanes-Oxley Act, a 2002 United States federal law, to oversee the auditors of public companies. Its stated purpose is to 'protect the interests of investors and further the public interest in the preparation of informative, fair, and independent audit reports'. Although a private entity, the _____ has many government-like regulatory functions, making it in some ways similar to the private Self Regulatory Organizations (SROs) that regulate stock markets and other aspects of the financial markets in the United States.

Chapter 1. Environment and Theoretical Structure of Financial Accounting   15

a. Financial Crimes Enforcement Network
b. 3M Company
c. Public Company Accounting Oversight Board
d. Pension Benefit Guaranty Corporation

66. The _____ of 2002 (Pub.L. 107-204, 116 Stat. 745, enacted July 30, 2002), also known as the Public Company Accounting Reform and Investor Protection Act of 2002, is a United States federal law enacted on July 30, 2002 in response to a number of major corporate and accounting scandals including those affecting Enron, Tyco International, Adelphia, Peregrine Systems and WorldCom. The legislation establishes new or enhanced standards for all U.S. public company boards, management, and public accounting firms. It does not apply to privately held companies.
   a. FCPA
   b. Lease
   c. Fair Labor Standards Act
   d. Sarbanes-Oxley Act

67. An _____ is a lease whose term is short compared to the useful life of the asset or piece of equipment (an airliner, a ship etc.) being leased. An _____ is commonly used to acquire equipment on a relatively short-term basis.
   a. Express warranty
   b. Operating lease
   c. Issued shares
   d. Employee Retirement Income Security Act

68. _____ in accounting is the process of treating equity investments, usually 20-50%, in associate companies. The investor keeps such equities as an asset. Proportional share of associate company's net income increases the investment, and proportional payment of dividends decreases it.
   a. ABC Television Network
   b. Equity method
   c. Out-of-pocket
   d. AIG

69. A _____ is a party (e.g. person, organization, company, or government) that has a claim to the services of a second party. It is a person or institution to whom money is owed. The first party, in general, has provided some property or service to the second party under the assumption (usually enforced by contract) that the second party will return an equivalent property or service.
   a. Par value
   b. Treasury company
   c. Creditor
   d. Payback period

70. In mathematics, two elements x and y of a set partially ordered by a relation ≤ are said to be _____ if and only if x ≤ y or y ≤ x if and only if x < y or y < x or y = x. For example, two sets are _____ with respect to inclusion if and only if one is a subset of the other.

In a classification of mathematical objects such as topological spaces, two criteria are said to be _____ when the objects that obey one criterion constitute a subset of the objects that obey the other one .

   a. Consumption
   b. Scientific Research and Experimental Development Tax Incentive Program
   c. Database auditing
   d. Comparable

71. _____ describes the situation when output from (or information about the result of) an event or phenomenon in the past will influence the same event/phenomenon in the present or future. When an event is part of a chain of cause-and-effect that forms a circuit or loop, then the event is said to 'feed back' into itself.

Chapter 1. Environment and Theoretical Structure of Financial Accounting

_____ is also a synonym for:

- _____ Signal; the information about the initial event that is the basis for subsequent modification of the event.
- _____ Loop; the causal path that leads from the initial generation of the _____ signal to the subsequent modification of the event.

_____ is a mechanism, process or signal that is looped back to control a system within itself. Such a loop is called a _____ loop.

a. 3M Company
b. BMC Software, Inc.
c. Controllable
d. Feedback

72. _____ is an attribute that, along with verifiability and neutrality, is among the three ingredients of reliable information. As the Securities Exchange Commission notes, 'a map's _____ may be determined by how well the map describes the coastline.' Accounting concept statement #2 defines _____ as 'correspondence or agreement between a measure or description and the phenomenon that it purports to represent.'

a. BNSF Railway
b. 3M Company
c. BMC Software, Inc.
d. Representational faithfulness

73. _____ is a term used in accounting, economics and finance to spread the cost of an asset over the span of several years.

In simple words we can say that _____ is the reduction in the value of an asset due to usage, passage of time, wear and tear, technological outdating or obsolescence, depletion, inadequacy, rot, rust, decay or other such factors.

In accounting, _____ is a term used to describe any method of attributing the historical or purchase cost of an asset across its useful life, roughly corresponding to normal wear and tear.

a. General ledger
b. Depreciation
c. Current asset
d. Net profit

74. A _____ proof is a mathematical proof that a particular theory is consistent. The early development of mathematical proof theory was driven by the desire to provide finitary _____ proofs for all of mathematics as part of Hilbert's program. Hilbert's program was strongly impacted by incompleteness theorems, which showed that sufficiently strong proof theories cannot prove their own _____

a. Daybook
b. Consumption
c. Monte Carlo methods
d. Consistency

75. In financial accounting and finance, _____ is the portion of receivables that can no longer be collected, typically from accounts receivable or loans. _____ in accounting is considered an expense.

Chapter 1. Environment and Theoretical Structure of Financial Accounting

There are two methods to account for _____:

1. Direct write off method (Non - GAAP)

A receivable which is not considered collectible is charged directly to the income statement.

1. Allowance method (GAAP)

An estimate is made at the end of each fiscal year of the amount of _____. This is then accumulated in a provision which is then used to reduce specific receivable accounts as and when necessary.

a. 3M Company
b. Total Expense Ratio
c. Bad debt
d. Tax expense

76. The term _____ describes a reduction in recognized value. In accounting terminology, it refers to recognition of the reduced or zero value of an asset. In income tax statements, it refers to a reduction of taxable income as recognition of certain expenses required to produce the income.
 a. Salvage value
 b. Write-off
 c. Current asset
 d. Payroll

77. _____ is that which is owed; usually referencing assets owed, but the term can also cover moral obligations and other interactions not requiring money. In the case of assets, _____ is a means of using future purchasing power in the present before a summation has been earned. Some companies and corporations use _____ as a part of their overall corporate finance strategy.
 a. Debenture
 b. Lender
 c. Loan
 d. Debt

78. _____ is a political and social term from the Latin verb conservare meaning to save or preserve. As the name suggests it usually indicates support for tradition and traditional values though the meaning has changed in different countries and time periods. The modern political term conservative was used by French politician Chateaubriand in 1819.
 a. Politicized issue
 b. BMC Software, Inc.
 c. 3M Company
 d. Conservatism

79. _____ are financial statements that factor the holding company's subsidiaries into its aggregated accounting figure. It is a representation of how the holding company is doing as a group. The consolidated accounts should provide a true and fair view of the financial and operating conditions of the group.
 a. Committee on Accounting Procedure
 b. Replacement cost
 c. Consolidated financial statements
 d. Redemption value

80. _____, also known as property, plant, and equipment (PP&E), is a term used in accountancy for assets and property which cannot easily be converted into cash. This can be compared with current assets such as cash or bank accounts, which are described as liquid assets. In most cases, only tangible assets are referred to as fixed.
 a. Minority interest
 b. Subledger
 c. Bankruptcy prediction
 d. Fixed asset

Chapter 1. Environment and Theoretical Structure of Financial Accounting

81. _____ is the state or fact of exclusive rights and control over property, which may be an object, land/real estate or intellectual property. An _____ right is also referred to as title.

_____ is the key building block in the development of the capitalist socio-economic system.

a. ABC Television Network
b. Ownership
c. Administrative proceeding
d. Encumbrance

82. _____ is a company's financial statement that indicates how the revenue is transformed into the net income The purpose of the _____ is to show managers and investors whether the company made or lost money during the period being reported.

The important thing to remember about an _____ is that it represents a period of time.

a. AMEX
b. ABC Television Network
c. AIG
d. Income statement

83. _____ is the value on a given date of a future payment or series of future payments, discounted to reflect the time value of money and other factors such as investment risk. _____ calculations are widely used in business and economics to provide a means to compare cash flows at different times on a meaningful 'like to like' basis.

The most commonly applied model of the time value of money is compound interest.

a. Present value
b. Net present value
c. Future value
d. 3M Company

84. _____ is generally understood in financial circles as the point at which revenue is recognized, typically through a transaction which involves the exchange of an asset, product, or service for cash or its equivalents.

This approach gives the accounting division a strictly objective basis for changing the books. For example, a homeowner may believe that his house has grown in value during a strong market, or fallen in value during a weak market, but until the house is actually sold for a specific price to a specific buyer, the change in value can only be estimated and is considered unrealized.

a. Valuation
b. Total-factor productivity
c. Merck ' Co., Inc.
d. Realization

85. The term _____ refers to government debt, expenditures and revenues, or to finance (particularly financial revenue) in general.

- _____ deficit is the budget deficit of federal or local government
- _____ policy is the discretionary spending of governments. Contrasts with monetary policy.
- _____ year and _____ quarter are reporting periods for firms and other agencies.

See also

- Procurator _____ and Crown Office and Procurator _____ Service

a. Comparable
b. Swap
c. Fiscal
d. Scientific Research and Experimental Development Tax Incentive Program

86. A _____ is a period used for calculating annual financial statements in businesses and other organizations. In many jurisdictions, regulatory laws regarding accounting and taxation require such reports once per twelve months, but do not require that the period reported on constitutes a calendar year (i.e., January through December.) _____s vary between businesses and countries.

a. Fiscal year
b. BMC Software, Inc.
c. 3M Company
d. BNSF Railway

87. A _____ is a business that functions without the intention or threat of liquidation for the foreseeable future, usually regarded as at least within 12 months.

In accounting, '_____' refers to a company's ability to continue functioning as a business entity. It is the responsibility of the directors to assess whether the _____ assumption is appropriate when preparing the financial statements.

a. Payment
b. 3M Company
c. BMC Software, Inc.
d. Going concern

88. _____ methods are means of managing inventory and financial matters involving the money a company ties up within inventory of produced goods, raw materials, parts, components, or feed stocks. FIFO stands for first-in, first-out, meaning that the oldest inventory items are recorded as sold first. LIFO stands for last-in, first-out, meaning that the most recently purchased items are recorded as sold first.

a. FIFO and LIFO accounting
b. Reorder point
c. Finished good
d. 3M Company

89. In accounting, _____ is the original monetary value of an economic item. In some circumstances, assets and liabilities may be shown at their _____, as if there had been no change in value since the date of acquisition. The balance sheet value of the item may therefore differ from the 'true' value.

a. Bottom line
b. Historical cost
c. Cost of goods sold
d. Matching principle

90. _____ is a method of evaluating an asset's worth when held in inventory, in the field of accounting. _____ is part of the Generally Accepted Accounting Principles that apply to valuing inventory, so as to not overstate or understate the value of inventory goods. Net realisable value is generally equal to the selling price of the inventory goods less the selling costs (completion and disposal).

a. 3M Company
c. BMC Software, Inc.
b. Net realizable value
d. Revenue recognition

91. _____ was a maxim coined by Josiah Warren, indicating a (prescriptive) version of the labor theory of value. Warren maintained that the just compensation for labor (or for its product) could only be an equivalent amount of labor (or a product embodying an equivalent amount.) Thus, profit, rent, and interest were considered unjust economic arrangements.

a. 3M Company
c. Politicized issue
b. BMC Software, Inc.
d. Cost the limit of price

92. In financial accounting, _____ or cost of sales includes the direct costs attributable to the production of the goods sold by a company. This amount includes the materials cost used in creating the goods along with the direct labor costs used to produce the good. It excludes indirect expenses such as distribution costs and sales force costs.

a. 3M Company
c. Reorder point
b. FIFO and LIFO accounting
d. Cost of goods sold

93. _____ is a cornerstone of accrual accounting together with the revenue recognition principle. They both determine the accounting period, in which revenues and expenses are recognized. According to the principle, expenses are recognized when obligations are (1) incurred (usually when goods are transferred or services rendered, e.g. sold), and (2) offset against recognized revenues, which were generated from those expenses (related on the cause-and-effect basis), no matter when cash is paid out.

a. Payroll
c. Matching principle
b. Net sales
d. Current liabilities

94. _____ refers to services paid for in advance. Examples include tolls, pay as you go cell phones, and stored-value cards such as gift cards and preloaded credit cards. _____ accounts are assets, and they are increased by debiting the account(s.)

a. BNSF Railway
c. Prepaid
b. BMC Software, Inc.
d. 3M Company

95. _____ principle is a cornerstone of accrual accounting together with matching principle. They both determine the accounting period, in which revenues and expenses are recognized. According to the principle, revenues are recognized when they are (1) realized or realizable, and are (2) earned (usually when goods are transferred or services rendered), no matter when cash is received.

a. Net realizable value
c. BMC Software, Inc.
b. 3M Company
d. Revenue recognition

96. A _____ is the transfer of wealth from one party (such as a person or company) to another. A _____ is usually made in exchange for the provision of goods, services or both, or to fulfill a legal obligation.

The simplest and oldest form of _____ is barter, the exchange of one good or service for another.

a. BMC Software, Inc.
c. Payment
b. Payee
d. 3M Company

Chapter 1. Environment and Theoretical Structure of Financial Accounting

97. In tax accounting the _____ is the default applicable convention used for federal income tax purposes. Like other conventions, the _____ affects the depreciation deduction computation in the year in which the property is placed into service. Using the _____, a taxpayer claims a half of a year's depreciation for the first taxable year, regardless of when the property was actually put into service.

   a. Revenue Procedures
   b. Taxable income
   c. Reverse Morris trust
   d. Half-year convention

98. The general definition of an _____ is an evaluation of a person, organization, system, process, project or product. _____s are performed to ascertain the validity and reliability of information; also to provide an assessment of a system's internal control. The goal of an _____ is to express an opinion on the person/organization/system (etc) in question, under evaluation based on work done on a test basis.

   a. Audit regime
   b. Assurance service
   c. Institute of Chartered Accountants of India
   d. Audit

99. Established in 1941, The _____ is internationally recognized as a trustworthy guidance-setting body. Serving members in 165 countries, The IIA is the internal audit profession's global voice, chief advocate, recognized authority, acknowledged leader, and principal educator, with global headquarters in Altamonte Springs, Fla., United States.

   The stated mission of The _____ is to provide dynamic leadership for the global profession of internal auditing.

   a. Audit regime
   b. Event data
   c. Auditor independence
   d. Institute of Internal Auditors

100. The _____ is a professional organization headquartered in Montvale, New Jersey consisting of over 70,000 members worldwide. The IMA is dedicated to advancing the role of the management accountant and financial manager within the business organization, and provides relevant professional certification.

   The IMA awards the Certified Management Accountant (CMA) designation in the United States.

   a. Emerging technologies
   b. Institute of Management Accountants
   c. International Accounting Standards Committee
   d. American Accounting Association

101. Internal auditing is a profession and activity involved in helping organisations achieve their stated objectives. It does this by utilizing a systematic methodology for analyzing business processes, procedures and activities with the goal of highlighting organizational problems and recommending solutions. Professionals called _____ are employed by organizations to perform the internal auditing activity.

   a. Auditing Standards Board
   b. Internal auditors
   c. Internal Auditing
   d. Auditor independence

102. The _____ of a company or public agency is the corporate officer primarily responsible for managing the financial risks of the business or agency. This officer is also responsible for financial planning and record-keeping, as well as financial reporting to higher management. (In recent years, however, the role has expanded to encompass communicating financial performance and forecasts to the analyst community.)

a. Merck ' Co., Inc.
c. Chief executive officer
b. NASDAQ
d. Chief financial officer

Chapter 2. Review of the Accounting Process

1. In accounting/accountancy, _____ are journal entries usually made at the end of an accounting period to allocate income and expenditure to the period in which they actually occurred. The revenue recognition principle is the basis of making _____ that pertain to unearned and accrued revenues under accrual-basis accounting. They are sometimes called Balance Day adjustments because they are made on balance day.

   a. Accrued expense
   b. Earnings before interest, taxes, depreciation and amortization
   c. Accrual
   d. Adjusting entries

2. _____ is application software that records and processes accounting transactions within functional modules such as accounts payable, accounts receivable, payroll, and trial balance. It functions as an accounting information system. It may be developed in-house by the company or organization using it, may be purchased from a third party, or may be a combination of a third-party application software package with local modifications.

   a. Amgen
   b. Economic value added
   c. AIG
   d. Accounting Software

3. The basic _____ is the foundation for the double-entry bookkeeping system. It shows how assets were financed: either by borrowing money from someone (liability) or by paying your own money (shareholders' equity.)

   Assets = Liabilities + (Shareholders or Owners equity)

   For example: A student buys a computer for $945.

   a. Accounting equation
   b. AIG
   c. ABC Television Network
   d. AMEX

4. _____ is a company-wide computer software system used to manage and coordinate all the resources, information, and functions of a business from shared data stores.

   An _____ system has a service-oriented architecture with modular hardware and software units or 'services' that communicate on a local area network. The modular design allows a business to add or reconfigure modules (perhaps from different vendors) while preserving data integrity in one shared database that may be centralized or distributed.

   a. AMEX
   b. ABC Television Network
   c. AIG
   d. Enterprise resource planning

5. An _____ is a term used in behavioral economics to describe those types of behaviors that impose costs on a person in the long-run that are not taken into account when making decisions in the present. Classical Economics discourages government from creating legislation that targets internalities, because it is assumed that the consumer takes these personal costs into account when paying for the good that causes the _____. For example, cigarettes should be taxed because of the negative consumption externalities that they impose, such as second-hand smoke, not because the smoker harms him or herself by smoking.

   a. Inventory turnover ratio
   b. Authorised capital
   c. Operating budget
   d. Internality

6. _____ refers to a business or organization attempting to acquire goods or services to accomplish the goals of the enterprise. Though there are several organizations that attempt to set standards in the _____ process, processes can vary greatly between organizations. Typically the word e;_____e; is not used interchangeably with the word e;procuremente;, since procurement typically includes Expediting, Supplier Quality, and Traffic and Logistics (T'L) in addition to _____.
   a. Supply chain
   b. Free port
   c. Purchasing
   d. Consignor

7. In business and accounting, _____ are everything of value that is owned by a person or company. It is a claim on the property your income of a borrower. The balance sheet of a firm records the monetary value of the _____ owned by the firm.
   a. Accrual basis accounting
   b. Accounts receivable
   c. Assets
   d. Earnings before interest, taxes, depreciation and amortization

8. In financial accounting, a _____ is defined as an obligation of an entity arising from past transactions or events, the settlement of which may result in the transfer or use of assets, provision of services or other yielding of economic benefits in the future.
   a. Vested
   b. Corporate governance
   c. Liability
   d. False Claims Act

9. _____ is any physical or virtual entity that is owned by an individual or jointly by a group of individuals. An owner of _____ has the right to consume, sell, rent, mortgage, transfer and exchange his or her _____. Important widely-recognized types of _____ include real _____, personal _____ (other physical possessions), and intellectual _____ (rights over artistic creations, inventions, etc.), although the latter is not always as widely recognized or enforced.
   a. Fiduciary
   b. Primary authority
   c. Property
   d. Disclosure requirement

10. _____, also known as property, plant, and equipment (PP&E), is a term used in accountancy for assets and property which cannot easily be converted into cash. This can be compared with current assets such as cash or bank accounts, which are described as liquid assets. In most cases, only tangible assets are referred to as fixed.
    a. Minority interest
    b. Subledger
    c. Fixed asset
    d. Bankruptcy prediction

11. In economics, _____ or _____ goods or real _____ refers to factors of production used to create goods or services that are not themselves significantly consumed (though they may depreciate) in the production process. _____ goods may be acquired with money or financial _____. In finance and accounting, _____ generally refers to financial wealth, especially that used to start or maintain a business.
    a. Capital
    b. Vyborg Appeal
    c. Disclosure
    d. Screening

12. _____ is a specific term used in companies' financial reporting from the company-whole point of view. Because that use excludes the effects of changing ownership interest, an economic measure of _____ is necessary for financial analysis from the shareholders' point of view

Chapter 2. Review of the Accounting Process

_____ is defined by the Financial Accounting Standards Board, or FASB, as 'the change in equity [net assets] of a business enterprise during a period from transactions and other events and circumstances from nonowner sources. It includes all changes in equity during a period except those resulting from investments by owners and distributions to owners.'

_____ is the sum of net income and other items that must bypass the income statement because they have not been realized, including items like an unrealized holding gain or loss from available for sale securities and foreign currency translation gains or losses.

- a. 3M Company
- b. BMC Software, Inc.
- c. BNSF Railway
- d. Comprehensive income

13. _____ is one of a series of accounting transactions dealing with the billing of customers who owe money to a person, company or organization for goods and services that have been provided to the customer. In most business entities this is typically done by generating an invoice and mailing or electronically delivering it to the customer, who in turn must pay it within an established timeframe called credit or payment terms.

An example of a common payment term is Net 30, meaning payment is due in the amount of the invoice 30 days from the date of invoice.

- a. Accounts receivable
- b. Accrued revenue
- c. Accrual
- d. Adjusting entries

14. In accounting, _____ are considered liabilities of the business that are to be settled in cash within the fiscal year or the operating cycle, whichever period is longer.

For example accounts payable for goods, services or supplies that were purchased for use in the operation of the business and payable within a normal period of time would be _____.

Bonds, mortgages and loans that are payable over a term exceeding one year would be fixed liabilities.

- a. Current liabilities
- b. Closing entries
- c. Payroll
- d. Treasury stock

15. _____ and credit are formal bookkeeping and accounting terms. They are the most fundamental concepts in accounting, representing the two records that one party in a transaction makes on its records, transferring a money balance from one account to another, one representing a reduction of liability or increase in asset, and the other representing a balancing increase in liability or reduction of asset.

Introduction

_____s and credits are a system of notation used in accounting to keep track of money movements (transactions) into and out of an account.

a. Bookkeeping
b. Debit
c. Cookie jar accounting
d. Debit and credit

16. _____, in accrual accounting, is any account where the asset or liability is not realized until a future date (accounting period), e.g. annuities, charges, taxes, income, etc. The _____ item may be carried, dependent on type of deferral, as either an asset or liability.
   a. Cash basis accounting
   b. Payroll
   c. Pro forma
   d. Deferred

17. _____ is an accounting concept, meaning a future tax liability or asset, resulting from temporary differences between book (accounting) value of assets and liabilities and their tax value, or timing differences between the recognition of gains and losses in financial statements and their recognition in a tax computation.

Temporary differences are differences between the carrying amount of an asset or liability recognised in the balance sheet and the amount attributed to that asset or liability for tax purposes (the tax base.)

   a. Deferred tax
   b. Tax refund
   c. Deficit
   d. Federal tax revenue by state

18. The _____, sometimes known as the nominal ledger, is the main accounting record of a business which uses double-entry bookkeeping. It will usually include accounts for such items as current assets, fixed assets, liabilities, revenue and expense items, gains and losses.

The _____ is a collection of the group of accounts that supports the items shown in the major financial statements.

   a. General journal
   b. Sales journal
   c. Journal entry
   d. General ledger

19. The term _____, derived from the distinctive T shape, is frequently used when discussing or analyzing accounting or business transactions. _____s are used to represent general ledger accounts.

Typically one or more Ts are drawn on a white board or blank piece of paper. A general ledger account name or number is then written above each T. Debit entries are recorded on the left side of the 'T' and credit entries are recorded on the right side of the 'T'.

   a. BNSF Railway
   b. T account
   c. 3M Company
   d. BMC Software, Inc.

20. A _____, in business matters, is an entity that is controlled by a bigger and more powerful entity. The controlled entity is called a company, corporation, or limited liability company, and the controlling entity is called its parent (or the parent company.) The reason for this distinction is that a lone company cannot be a _____ of any organization; only an entity representing a legal fiction as a separate entity can be a _____.
   a. Parent company
   b. 3M Company
   c. BMC Software, Inc.
   d. Subsidiary

Chapter 2. Review of the Accounting Process

21. The _____ is a subset of the general ledger used in accounting. The _____ shows detail for part of the accounting records such as property and equipment, prepaid expenses, etc. The detail would include such items as date the item was purchased or expense incurred, a description of the item, the original balance, and the net book value.

   a. Minority interest
   b. Subledger
   c. Credit memo
   d. Remittance advice

22. _____ of something is, in finance, the adding together of interest or different investments over a period of time such as atoms (1 - the act or process of accruing; 2 - the amount that accrues.) It holds specific meanings in accounting and payroll.

   _____, in accounting, describes the accounting method known as _____ basis, whereby revenues and expenses are recognized when they are accrued, i.e. accumulated (earned or incurred), regardless when the actual cash is received or paid out.

   a. Accrual
   b. Accounts receivable
   c. Assets
   d. Earnings before interest, taxes, depreciation and amortization

23. The _____ is where double entry bookkeeping entries are recorded by debiting one account and crediting another account with the same amount. The amount debited and the amount credited should always be equal, thereby ensuring the accounting equation is maintained.

   Depending on the business's accounting information system, specialized journals may be used in conjunction with the _____ for record-keeping.

   a. General ledger
   b. General journal
   c. Journal entry
   d. Sales journal

24. A _____ has several related meanings:

   - a daily record of events or business; a private _____ is usually referred to as a diary.
   - a newspaper or other periodical, in the literal sense of one published each day;
   - many publications issued at stated intervals, such as magazines, or scholarly academic _____s, or the record of the transactions of a society, are often called _____s. Although _____ is sometimes used, erroneously, as a synonym for 'magazine,' in academic use, a _____ refers to a serious, scholarly publication, most often peer-reviewed. A non-scholarly magazine written for an educated audience about an industry or an area of professional activity is usually called a professional magazine.

   The word 'journalist' for one whose business is writing for the public press has been in use since the end of the 17th century.

   Open access _____s are scholarly _____s that are available to the reader without financial or other barrier other than access to the internet itself. Some are subsidized, and some require payment on behalf of the author. Subsidized _____s are financed by an academic institution or a government information center.

a. Journal
b. BMC Software, Inc.
c. BNSF Railway
d. 3M Company

25. A _____ is the pinnacle activity involved in selling products or services in return for money or other compensation. It is an act of completion of a commercial activity.

A _____ is completed by the seller, the owner of the goods.

a. High yield stock
b. Tertiary sector of economy
c. Sale
d. Maturity

26. A _____ is a specialized accounting journal used in an accounting system to keep track of the sales of items that customers have purchased by changing them to their accounts-receivable account.

a. General journal
b. General ledger
c. Journal entry
d. Sales journal

27. _____ is a form of corporation equity ownership represented in the securities. It is a stock whose dividends are based on market fluctuations. It is dangerous in comparison to preferred shares and some other investment options, in that in the event of bankruptcy, _____ investors receive their funds after preferred stock holders, bondholders, creditors, etc. On the other hand, common shares on average perform better than preferred shares or bonds over time.

a. Stock split
b. Common stock
c. 3M Company
d. Growth investing

28. A _____, also referred to as a note payable in accounting, is a contract where one party (the maker or issuer) makes an unconditional promise in writing to pay a sum of money to the other (the payee), either at a fixed or determinable future time or on demand of the payee, under specific terms. They differ from IOUs in that they contain a specific promise to pay, rather than simply acknowledging that a debt exists.

The terms of a note typically include the principal amount, the interest rate if any, and the maturity date.

a. Promissory note
b. 3M Company
c. BNSF Railway
d. BMC Software, Inc.

29. _____ refers to services paid for in advance. Examples include tolls, pay as you go cell phones, and stored-value cards such as gift cards and preloaded credit cards. _____ accounts are assets, and they are increased by debiting the account(s).

a. BNSF Railway
b. BMC Software, Inc.
c. Prepaid
d. 3M Company

30. A _____ is the transfer of wealth from one party (such as a person or company) to another. A _____ is usually made in exchange for the provision of goods, services or both, or to fulfill a legal obligation.

The simplest and oldest form of _____ is barter, the exchange of one good or service for another.

Chapter 2. Review of the Accounting Process

a. 3M Company
b. BMC Software, Inc.
c. Payee
d. Payment

31. _____ is the process of increasing, or accounting for, an amount over a period of time. Particular instances of the term include:

- _____, the allocation of a lump sum amount to different time periods, particularly for loans and other forms of finance, including related interest or other finance charges.
  - _____ schedule, a table detailing each periodic payment on a loan (typically a mortgage), as generated by an _____ calculator.
  - Negative _____, an _____ schedule where the loan amount actually increases through not paying the full interest
- Amortized analysis, analyzing the execution cost of algorithms over a sequence of operations.
- _____ of capital expenditures of certain assets under accounting rules, particularly intangible assets, in a manner analogous to depreciation.
- _____

a. EBIT
b. Intangible
c. Annuity
d. Amortization

32. A _____ is like a lottery bond issued by the United Kingdom government's National Savings and Investments scheme. The government promises to buy back the bond, on request, for its original price.

_____s were introduced by the government in 1956, with the aim of encouraging saving and controlling inflation, with the first bonds going on sale on 1 November of that year.

a. Callable bond
b. Zero-coupon bond
c. Revenue bonds
d. Premium bond

33. In finance, a _____ is a debt security, in which the authorized issuer owes the holders a debt and, depending on the terms of the _____, is obliged to pay interest (the coupon) and/or to repay the principal at a later date, termed maturity. It is a formal contract to repay borrowed money with interest at fixed intervals.

Thus a _____ is like a loan: the issuer is the borrower, the _____ holder is the lender, and the coupon is the interest.

a. Zero-coupon bond
b. Bond
c. Revenue bonds
d. Coupon rate

34. _____ are payments made by a corporation to its shareholder members. It is the portion of corporate profits paid out to stockholders. When a corporation earns a profit or surplus, that money can be put to two uses: it can either be re-invested in the business (called retained earnings), or it can be paid to the shareholders as a dividend.

a. Dividend payout ratio
b. Dividends
c. Dividend yield
d. Dividend stripping

Chapter 2. Review of the Accounting Process

35. In accounting, the _____ is a worksheet listing the balance at a certain date, of each ledger account in two columns, namely debit and credit. Under the double-entry system, in any transaction the total of any debits must equal the total of any credits, so in a _____ the total of the debit side should always be equal to the total of the credit side. The _____ thus serves as a tool to detect errors, which can result in the totals not being equal.
   a. Depreciation
   b. Current asset
   c. Bottom line
   d. Trial balance

36. _____ is a method of accounting whereby economic activities (rather than cash flow) of financial events are considered, because of two complementary principles, which (together) determine the point, at which expenses and revenues are recognized. According to revenue recognition principle, revenues are realized when earned, whether or not they are received in cash.
   a. Accrual
   b. Accrual basis accounting
   c. Accrued revenue
   d. Earnings before interest, taxes, depreciation and amortization

37. _____ is a cornerstone of accrual accounting together with the revenue recognition principle. They both determine the accounting period, in which revenues and expenses are recognized. According to the principle, expenses are recognized when obligations are (1) incurred (usually when goods are transferred or services rendered, e.g. sold), and (2) offset against recognized revenues, which were generated from those expenses (related on the cause-and-effect basis), no matter when cash is paid out.
   a. Current liabilities
   b. Net sales
   c. Payroll
   d. Matching principle

38. _____ is generally understood in financial circles as the point at which revenue is recognized, typically through a transaction which involves the exchange of an asset, product, or service for cash or its equivalents.

This approach gives the accounting division a strictly objective basis for changing the books. For example, a homeowner may believe that his house has grown in value during a strong market, or fallen in value during a weak market, but until the house is actually sold for a specific price to a specific buyer, the change in value can only be estimated and is considered unrealized.

   a. Valuation
   b. Total-factor productivity
   c. Merck ' Co., Inc.
   d. Realization

39. In accounting, _____ has a very specific meaning. It is an outflow of cash or other valuable assets from a person or company to another person or company. This outflow of cash is generally one side of a trade for products or services that have equal or better current or future value to the buyer than to the seller.
   a. AMEX
   b. Expense
   c. ABC Television Network
   d. AIG

40. _____ is a term used in accounting, economics and finance to spread the cost of an asset over the span of several years.

In simple words we can say that _____ is the reduction in the value of an asset due to usage, passage of time, wear and tear, technological outdating or obsolescence, depletion, inadequacy, rot, rust, decay or other such factors.

Chapter 2. Review of the Accounting Process

In accounting, _____ is a term used to describe any method of attributing the historical or purchase cost of an asset across its useful life, roughly corresponding to normal wear and tear.

a. Depreciation
c. Net profit
b. Current asset
d. General ledger

41. _____, in accrual accounting, (e.g. advance payment received from a client) is, according to revenue recognition, revenue not earned until the delivery of goods or services, which until then, is still owed to the payer, hence remaining a liability.

_____, sometimes referred to as deferred revenue or unearned revenue, shares characteristics with accrued expense with the difference that a liability to be covered latter is cash received FROM a counterpart, while goods or services are to be delivered in a latter period, when such income item is earned, the related revenue item is recognized, and the same amount is deducted from deferred revenues.

a. Treasury stock
c. Gross sales
b. Matching principle
d. Deferred income

42. _____ are liabilities which have occurred, but have not been paid or logged under accounts payable during an accounting period; in other words, obligations for goods and services provided to a company for which invoices have not yet been received. Examples would include accrued wages payable, accrued sales tax payable, and accrued rent payable.

There are two general types of _____:

- Routine and recurring
- Infrequent or non-routine

Most companies pay their employees on a predetermined schedule. Let's say that the 'Imaginary company Ltd.' pays its employees each Friday for the hours worked that week.

a. Accrued liabilities
c. AIG
b. ABC Television Network
d. AMEX

43. _____ is a fee paid on borrowed assets. It is the price paid for the use of borrowed money, or, money earned by deposited funds .Assets that are sometimes lent with _____ include money, shares, consumer goods through hire purchase, major assets such as aircraft, and even entire factories in finance lease arrangements. The _____ is calculated upon the value of the assets in the same manner as upon money.

a. AIG
c. ABC Television Network
b. Insolvency
d. Interest

44. An _____ is the price a borrower pays for the use of money they do not own, for instance a small company might borrow from a bank to kick start their business, and the return a lender receives for deferring the use of funds, by lending it to the borrower. _____s are normally expressed as a percentage rate over the period of one year.

_____s targets are also a vital tool of monetary policy and are used to control variables like investment, inflation, and unemployment.

   a. AMEX
   c. ABC Television Network
   b. AIG
   d. Interest rate

45. In financial accounting and finance, _____ is the portion of receivables that can no longer be collected, typically from accounts receivable or loans. _____ in accounting is considered an expense.

There are two methods to account for _____:

   1. Direct write off method (Non - GAAP)

A receivable which is not considered collectible is charged directly to the income statement.

   1. Allowance method (GAAP)

An estimate is made at the end of each fiscal year of the amount of _____. This is then accumulated in a provision which is then used to reduce specific receivable accounts as and when necessary.

   a. Total Expense Ratio
   c. Bad debt
   b. Tax expense
   d. 3M Company

46. _____ are formal bookkeeping and accounting terms. They are the most fundamental concepts in accounting, representing the two records that one party in a transaction makes on its records, transferring a money balance from one account to another, one representing a reduction of liability or increase in asset, and the other representing a balancing increase in liability or reduction of asset.

Debits and credits are a system of notation used in accounting to keep track of money movements (transactions) into and out of an account.

   a. Bookkeeping
   c. Controlling account
   b. Debit and credit
   d. Cookie jar accounting

47. _____ is that which is owed; usually referencing assets owed, but the term can also cover moral obligations and other interactions not requiring money. In the case of assets, _____ is a means of using future purchasing power in the present before a summation has been earned. Some companies and corporations use _____ as a part of their overall corporate finance strategy.
   a. Lender
   c. Debenture
   b. Loan
   d. Debt

48. _____ is a company's financial statement that indicates how the revenue is transformed into the net income The purpose of the _____ is to show managers and investors whether the company made or lost money during the period being reported.

Chapter 2. Review of the Accounting Process

The important thing to remember about an _____ is that it represents a period of time.

a. Income statement
c. ABC Television Network
b. AIG
d. AMEX

49. In financial accounting, a _____ or statement of financial position is a summary of a person's or organization's balances. Assets, liabilities and ownership equity are listed as of a specific date, such as the end of its financial year. A _____ is often described as a snapshot of a company's financial condition.

a. Financial statements
c. 3M Company
b. Statement of retained earnings
d. Balance sheet

50. In accounting, a _____ is an asset on the balance sheet which is expected to be sold or otherwise used up in the near future, usually within one year, or one business cycle - whichever is longer. Typical _____s include cash, cash equivalents, accounts receivable, inventory, the portion of prepaid accounts which will be used within a year, and short-term investments.

On the balance sheet, assets will typically be classified into _____s and long-term assets.

a. Current asset
c. Pro forma
b. Deferred
d. General ledger

51. Discounting is a financial mechanism in which a debtor obtains the right to delay payments to a creditor, for a defined period of time, in exchange for a charge or fee. Essentially, the party that owes money in the present purchases the right to delay the payment until some future date. The _____, or charge, is simply the difference between the original amount owed in the present and the amount that has to be paid in the future to settle the debt.

a. Risk aversion
c. Discounting
b. Discount factor
d. Discount

52. In economic models, the _____ time frame assumes no fixed factors of production. Firms can enter or leave the marketplace, and the cost (and availability) of land, labor, raw materials, and capital goods can be assumed to vary. In contrast, in the short-run time frame, certain factors are assumed to be fixed, because there is not sufficient time for them to change.

a. Long-run
c. Short-run
b. 3M Company
d. BMC Software, Inc.

53. _____ are liabilities with a future benefit over one year, such as notes payable that mature greater than one year.

In accounting, the _____ are shown on the right wing of the balance-sheet representing the sources of funds, which are generally bounded in form of capital assets.

Examples of _____ are debentures, mortgage loans and other bank loans (note: not all bank loans are long term as not all are paid over a period greater than a year, the example is bridging loan.)

Chapter 2. Review of the Accounting Process

a. Long-term liabilities
b. Book value
c. Gross sales
d. Cash basis accounting

54. _____ is the balance of the amounts of cash being received and paid by a business during a defined period of time, sometimes tied to a specific project. Measurement of _____ can be used

- to evaluate the state or performance of a business or project.
- to determine problems with liquidity. Being profitable does not necessarily mean being liquid. A company can fail because of a shortage of cash, even while profitable.
- to project rate of returns. The time of _____s into and out of projects are used as inputs to financial models such as internal rate of return, and net present value.
- to examine income or growth of a business when it is believed that accrual accounting concepts do not represent economic realities. Alternately, _____ can be used to 'validate' the net income generated by accrual accounting.

_____ as a generic term may be used differently depending on context, and certain _____ definitions may be adapted by analysts and users for their own uses. Common terms include operating _____ and free _____.

a. Flow-through entity
b. Controlling interest
c. Cash flow
d. Commercial paper

55. In financial accounting, a _____ or Statement of cash flows is a financial statement that shows a company's flow of cash. The money coming into the business is called cash inflow, and money going out from the business is called cash outflow. The statement shows how changes in balance sheet and income accounts affect cash and cash equivalents, and breaks the analysis down to operating, investing, and financing activities.

a. Cash flow statement
b. BMC Software, Inc.
c. 3M Company
d. BNSF Railway

56. _____ is a method of accounting whereby cash flow of financial events is considered. The method recognizes revenues when cash is received and recognizes expenses when cash is paid out. In cash accounting, revenues and expenses are also called cash receipts and cash payments respectively.

a. Closing entries
b. Net sales
c. Cash basis accounting
d. Treasury stock

57. _____, in law and economics, is a form of risk management primarily used to hedge against the risk of a contingent loss. _____ is defined as the equitable transfer of the risk of a loss, from one entity to another, in exchange for a premium, and can be thought of as a guaranteed small loss to prevent a large, possibly devastating loss. An insurer is a company selling the _____; an insured is the person or entity buying the _____.

a. AMEX
b. AIG
c. ABC Television Network
d. Insurance

58. In financial accounting, _____ , cash flow provided by operations or cash flow from operating activities, refers to the amount of cash a company generates from the revenues it brings in, excluding costs associated with long-term investment on capital items or investment in securities.

_____ = Cash generated from operations less taxation and interest paid, investment income received and less dividends paid gives rise to _____s per International Financial Reporting Standards.

To calculate cash generated from operations, one must calculate cash generated from customers and cash paid to suppliers.

- a. Operating cash flow
- b. ABC Television Network
- c. AMEX
- d. AIG

59. A _____ is a piece of paper, often preprinted in a way designed to help organize material for learning or clear understanding. Students in a school may have 'fill-in-the-blank' sheets of questions, diagrams or maps to help them with their exercises. Students will often use _____s to review what has been taught in class.

- a. 3M Company
- b. BMC Software, Inc.
- c. Value based pricing
- d. Worksheet

Chapter 3. The Balance Sheet and Financial Disclosures

1. In financial accounting, a _____ or statement of financial position is a summary of a person's or organization's balances. Assets, liabilities and ownership equity are listed as of a specific date, such as the end of its financial year. A _____ is often described as a snapshot of a company's financial condition.
   - a. 3M Company
   - b. Financial statements
   - c. Balance sheet
   - d. Statement of retained earnings

2. _____ is a legally declared inability or impairment of ability of an individual or organization to pay its creditors. Creditors may file a _____ petition against a debtor ('involuntary _____') in an effort to recoup a portion of what they are owed or initiate a restructuring. In the majority of cases, however, _____ is initiated by the debtor (a 'voluntary _____' that is filed by the bankrupt individual or organization.)
   - a. BMC Software, Inc.
   - b. Bankruptcy
   - c. 3M Company
   - d. Bankruptcy protection

3. A _____ is any one of a variety of different systems, institutions, procedures, social relations and infrastructures whereby persons trade, and goods and services are exchanged, forming part of the economy. It is an arrangement that allows buyers and sellers to exchange things. _____s vary in size, range, geographic scale, location, types and variety of human communities, as well as the types of goods and services traded.
   - a. Market Failure
   - b. Market
   - c. Recession
   - d. Perfect competition

4. _____ is the price at which an asset would trade in a competitive Walrasian auction setting. _____ is often used interchangeably with open _____, fair value or fair _____, although these terms have distinct definitions in different standards, and may differ in some circumstances.

   International Valuation Standards defines _____ as 'the estimated amount for which a property should exchange on the date of valuation between a willing buyer and a willing seller in an arme;s-length transaction after proper marketing wherein the parties had each acted knowledgeably, prudently, and without compulsion.'

   _____ is a concept distinct from market price, which is e;the price at which one can transacte;, while _____ is e;the true underlying valuee; according to theoretical standards.
   - a. Debtor
   - b. Market value
   - c. Sinking fund
   - d. Segregated portfolio company

5. _____ is any physical or virtual entity that is owned by an individual or jointly by a group of individuals. An owner of _____ has the right to consume, sell, rent, mortgage, transfer and exchange his or her _____. Important widely-recognized types of _____ include real _____, personal _____ (other physical possessions), and intellectual _____ (rights over artistic creations, inventions, etc.), although the latter is not always as widely recognized or enforced.
   - a. Fiduciary
   - b. Property
   - c. Primary authority
   - d. Disclosure requirement

6. _____, also known as property, plant, and equipment (PP&E), is a term used in accountancy for assets and property which cannot easily be converted into cash. This can be compared with current assets such as cash or bank accounts, which are described as liquid assets. In most cases, only tangible assets are referred to as fixed.
   - a. Minority interest
   - b. Subledger
   - c. Bankruptcy prediction
   - d. Fixed asset

Chapter 3. The Balance Sheet and Financial Disclosures

7. In finance, a _____ is a debt security, in which the authorized issuer owes the holders a debt and, depending on the terms of the _____, is obliged to pay interest (the coupon) and/or to repay the principal at a later date, termed maturity. It is a formal contract to repay borrowed money with interest at fixed intervals.

Thus a _____ is like a loan: the issuer is the borrower, the _____ holder is the lender, and the coupon is the interest.

a. Zero-coupon bond
b. Coupon rate
c. Bond
d. Revenue bonds

8. _____ is the balance of the amounts of cash being received and paid by a business during a defined period of time, sometimes tied to a specific project. Measurement of _____ can be used

- to evaluate the state or performance of a business or project.
- to determine problems with liquidity. Being profitable does not necessarily mean being liquid. A company can fail because of a shortage of cash, even while profitable.
- to project rate of returns. The time of _____s into and out of projects are used as inputs to financial models such as internal rate of return, and net present value.
- to examine income or growth of a business when it is believed that accrual accounting concepts do not represent economic realities. Alternately, _____ can be used to 'validate' the net income generated by accrual accounting.

_____ as a generic term may be used differently depending on context, and certain _____ definitions may be adapted by analysts and users for their own uses. Common terms include operating _____ and free _____.

a. Controlling interest
b. Commercial paper
c. Cash flow
d. Flow-through entity

9. In financial accounting, a _____ or Statement of cash flows is a financial statement that shows a company's flow of cash. The money coming into the business is called cash inflow, and money going out from the business is called cash outflow. The statement shows how changes in balance sheet and income accounts affect cash and cash equivalents, and breaks the analysis down to operating, investing, and financing activities.

a. BMC Software, Inc.
b. 3M Company
c. BNSF Railway
d. Cash flow statement

10. In accounting, _____ or carrying value is the value of an asset according to its balance sheet account balance. For assets, the value is based on the original cost of the asset less any depreciation, amortization or impairment costs made against the asset. Traditionally, a company's _____ is its total assets minus intangible assets and liabilities.

a. Book value
b. Matching principle
c. Depreciation
d. Generally accepted accounting principles

11. _____ is a business, economics or investment term that refers to an asset's ability to be easily converted through an act of buying or selling without causing a significant movement in the price and with minimum loss of value. Money, or cash on hand, is the most liquid asset. An act of exchange of a less liquid asset with a more liquid asset is called liquidation.

a. Transfer agent
b. Spot rate
c. Market liquidity
d. Financial instruments

12. In economic models, the _____ time frame assumes no fixed factors of production. Firms can enter or leave the marketplace, and the cost (and availability) of land, labor, raw materials, and capital goods can be assumed to vary. In contrast, in the short-run time frame, certain factors are assumed to be fixed, because there is not sufficient time for them to change.
   a. 3M Company
   b. BMC Software, Inc.
   c. Short-run
   d. Long-run

13. In finance, or business _____ is the ability of an entity to pay its debts with available cash. _____ can also be described as the ability of a corporation to meet its long-term fixed expenses and to accomplish long-term expansion and growth. The better a company's _____, the better it is financially.
   a. BMC Software, Inc.
   b. Capital asset
   c. 3M Company
   d. Solvency

14. _____ is one of a series of accounting transactions dealing with the billing of customers who owe money to a person, company or organization for goods and services that have been provided to the customer. In most business entities this is typically done by generating an invoice and mailing or electronically delivering it to the customer, who in turn must pay it within an established timeframe called credit or payment terms.

An example of a common payment term is Net 30, meaning payment is due in the amount of the invoice 30 days from the date of invoice.

   a. Accrued revenue
   b. Adjusting entries
   c. Accounts receivable
   d. Accrual

15. In business and accounting, _____ are everything of value that is owned by a person or company. It is a claim on the property your income of a borrower. The balance sheet of a firm records the monetary value of the _____ owned by the firm.
   a. Earnings before interest, taxes, depreciation and amortization
   b. Accrual basis accounting
   c. Accounts receivable
   d. Assets

16. _____ are the most liquid assets found within the asset portion of a company's balance sheet. Cash equivalents are assets that are readily convertible into cash, such as money market holdings, short-term government bonds or Treasury bills, marketable securities and commercial paper. _____ are distinguished from other investments through their short-term existence; they mature within 3 months whereas short-term investments are 12 months or less, and long-term investments are any investments that mature in excess of 12 months.
   a. Payback period
   b. Debtor
   c. Par value
   d. Cash and cash equivalents

17. In accounting, a _____ is an asset on the balance sheet which is expected to be sold or otherwise used up in the near future, usually within one year, or one business cycle - whichever is longer. Typical _____s include cash, cash equivalents, accounts receivable, inventory, the portion of prepaid accounts which will be used within a year, and short-term investments.

Chapter 3. The Balance Sheet and Financial Disclosures

On the balance sheet, assets will typically be classified into _____s and long-term assets.

a. General ledger
c. Current asset
b. Deferred
d. Pro forma

18. In economics, the concept of the _____ refers to the decision-making time frame of a firm in which at least one factor of production is fixed. Costs which are fixed in the _____ have no impact on a firms decisions. For example a firm can raise output by increasing the amount of labour through overtime.

a. Long-run
c. Short-run
b. 3M Company
d. BMC Software, Inc.

19. In financial accounting, a _____ is defined as an obligation of an entity arising from past transactions or events, the settlement of which may result in the transfer or use of assets, provision of services or other yielding of economic benefits in the future.

a. Vested
c. Corporate governance
b. False Claims Act
d. Liability

20. _____ represents claims for which formal instruments of credit are issued as evidence of debt, such as a promissory note. The credit instrument normally requires the debtor to pay interest and extends for time periods of 60-90 days or longer.

a. Public offering
c. Moving average
b. Restricted stock
d. Notes receivable

21. A _____ is a fungible, negotiable instrument representing financial value. they are broadly categorized into debt securities (such as banknotes, bonds and debentures), and equity securities; e.g., common stocks. The company or other entity issuing the _____ is called the issuer.

a. Security
c. Tracking stock
b. BMC Software, Inc.
d. 3M Company

22. _____s are goods that have completed the manufacturing process but have not yet been sold or distributed to the end user.

Manufacturing has three classes of inventory:

1. Raw material
2. Work in process
3. _____s

A good purchased as a 'raw material' goes into the manufacture of a product. A good only partially completed during the manufacturing process is called 'work in process'. When the good is completed as to manufacturing but not yet sold or distributed to the end-user is called a '_____'.

a. Finished good
c. Reorder point
b. FIFO and LIFO accounting
d. 3M Company

23. _____ are defined as identifiable non-monetary assets that cannot be seen, touched or physically measured, which are created through time and/or effort and that are identifiable as a separate asset. There are two primary forms of intangibles - legal intangibles (such as trade secrets (e.g., customer lists), copyrights, patents, trademarks, and goodwill) and competitive intangibles (such as knowledge activities (know-how, knowledge), collaboration activities, leverage activities, and structural activities.) Legal intangibles are known under the generic term intellectual property and generate legal property rights defensible in a court of law.
  a. ABC Television Network
  b. Overhead
  c. AIG
  d. Intangible assets

24. _____ refers to services paid for in advance. Examples include tolls, pay as you go cell phones, and stored-value cards such as gift cards and preloaded credit cards. _____ accounts are assets, and they are increased by debiting the account(s.)
  a. BNSF Railway
  b. 3M Company
  c. Prepaid
  d. BMC Software, Inc.

25. _____, in accrual accounting, is any account where the asset or liability is not realized until a future date (accounting period), e.g. annuities, charges, taxes, income, etc. The _____ item may be carried, dependent on type of deferral, as either an asset or liability.
  a. Payroll
  b. Pro forma
  c. Cash basis accounting
  d. Deferred

26. A _____ is something that is acted upon or used by or by human labour or industry, for use as a building material to create some product or structure. Often the term is used to denote material that came from nature and is in an unprocessed or minimally processed state. Iron ore, logs, and crude oil, would be examples.
  a. 3M Company
  b. BMC Software, Inc.
  c. BNSF Railway
  d. Raw material

27. _____ consists of the sale of goods or merchandise from a fixed location, such as a department store, boutique or kiosk in small or individual lots for direct consumption by the purchaser. _____ may include subordinated services, such as delivery. Purchasers may be individuals or businesses.
  a. Retailing
  b. BNSF Railway
  c. 3M Company
  d. BMC Software, Inc.

28. _____ or in-process inventory includes the set at large of unfinished items for products in a production process. These items are not yet completed but either just being fabricated or waiting in a queue for further processing or in a buffer storage. The term is used in production and supply chain management.
  a. BMC Software, Inc.
  b. BNSF Railway
  c. 3M Company
  d. Work in process

29. In accounting, _____ has a very specific meaning. It is an outflow of cash or other valuable assets from a person or company to another person or company. This outflow of cash is generally one side of a trade for products or services that have equal or better current or future value to the buyer than to the seller.
  a. AIG
  b. ABC Television Network
  c. AMEX
  d. Expense

Chapter 3. The Balance Sheet and Financial Disclosures

30. _____ is a demonstration of a process -- such as a variable, term, or object -- relative in terms of the specific process or set of validation tests used to determine its presence and quantity. Properties described in this manner must be sufficiently accessible, so that persons other than the definer may independently measure or test for them at will. An _____ is generally designed to model a conceptual definition.

    a. AIG
    b. Operational definition
    c. ABC Television Network
    d. AMEX

31. A _____ is a contract conferring a right on one person to possess property belonging to another person (called a landlord or lessor) to the exclusion of the owner landlord. It is a rental agreement between landlord and tenant. The relationship between the tenant and the landlord is called a tenancy, and the right to possession by the tenant is sometimes called a leasehold interest.

    a. Robinson-Patman Act
    b. Model Code of Professional Responsibility
    c. Federal Sentencing Guidelines
    d. Lease

32. _____ is a file or account that contains money that a person or company owes to suppliers, but has not paid yet (a form of debt.) When you receive an invoice you add it to the file, and then you remove it when you pay. Thus, the A/P is a form of credit that suppliers offer to their purchasers by allowing them to pay for a product or service after it has already been received.

    a. Accounts receivable
    b. Accrual
    c. Earnings before interest, taxes, depreciation and amortization
    d. Accounts payable

33. _____ are liabilities which have occurred, but have not been paid or logged under accounts payable during an accounting period; in other words, obligations for goods and services provided to a company for which invoices have not yet been received. Examples would include accrued wages payable, accrued sales tax payable, and accrued rent payable.

There are two general types of _____:

- Routine and recurring
- Infrequent or non-routine

Most companies pay their employees on a predetermined schedule. Let's say that the 'Imaginary company Ltd.' pays its employees each Friday for the hours worked that week.

    a. AIG
    b. ABC Television Network
    c. AMEX
    d. Accrued liabilities

34. In accounting, _____ are considered liabilities of the business that are to be settled in cash within the fiscal year or the operating cycle, whichever period is longer.

For example accounts payable for goods, services or supplies that were purchased for use in the operation of the business and payable within a normal period of time would be _____.

Bonds, mortgages and loans that are payable over a term exceeding one year would be fixed liabilities.

Chapter 3. The Balance Sheet and Financial Disclosures

a. Closing entries
b. Payroll
c. Current liabilities
d. Treasury stock

35. A _____ is a type of debt Like all debt instruments, a _____ entails the redistribution of financial assets over time, between the lender and the borrower.
   a. Loan
   b. Debenture
   c. Loan to value
   d. Lender

36. A _____ is the transfer of an interest in property (or the equivalent in law - a charge) to a lender as a security for a debt - usually a loan of money. While a _____ in itself is not a debt, it is the lender's security for a debt. It is a transfer of an interest in land (or the equivalent) from the owner to the _____ lender, on the condition that this interest will be returned to the owner when the terms of the _____ have been satisfied or performed.
   a. BMC Software, Inc.
   b. 3M Company
   c. BNSF Railway
   d. Mortgage

37. A _____, also referred to as a note payable in accounting, is a contract where one party (the maker or issuer) makes an unconditional promise in writing to pay a sum of money to the other (the payee), either at a fixed or determinable future time or on demand of the payee, under specific terms. They differ from IOUs in that they contain a specific promise to pay, rather than simply acknowledging that a debt exists.

The terms of a note typically include the principal amount, the interest rate if any, and the maturity date.

   a. Promissory note
   b. 3M Company
   c. BNSF Railway
   d. BMC Software, Inc.

38. _____, in accrual accounting, (e.g. advance payment received from a client) is, according to revenue recognition, revenue not earned until the delivery of goods or services, which until then, is still owed to the payer, hence remaining a liability.

_____, sometimes referred to as deferred revenue or unearned revenue, shares characteristics with accrued expense with the difference that a liability to be covered latter is cash received FROM a counterpart, while goods or services are to be delivered in a latter period, when such income item is earned, the related revenue item is recognized, and the same amount is deducted from deferred revenues.

   a. Deferred income
   b. Gross sales
   c. Matching principle
   d. Treasury stock

39. _____ are liabilities with a future benefit over one year, such as notes payable that mature greater than one year.

In accounting, the _____ are shown on the right wing of the balance-sheet representing the sources of funds, which are generally bounded in form of capital assets.

Examples of _____ are debentures, mortgage loans and other bank loans (note: not all bank loans are long term as not all are paid over a period greater than a year, the example is bridging loan.)

Chapter 3. The Balance Sheet and Financial Disclosures 43

    a. Book value   b. Gross sales
    c. Long-term liabilities   d. Cash basis accounting

40. _____, is a liability with an uncertain timing or amount, but where the uncertainty is not significant enough to qualify it as a provision. An example is an unpaid obligation to pay for goods or services received FROM a counterpart, while cash for them is to be paid out in a latter accounting period when its amount is deducted from _____s.

    a. Accounts receivable   b. Accrued expense
    c. Assets   d. Accrual basis accounting

41. In economics, _____ or _____ goods or real _____ refers to factors of production used to create goods or services that are not themselves significantly consumed (though they may depreciate) in the production process. _____ goods may be acquired with money or financial _____. In finance and accounting, _____ generally refers to financial wealth, especially that used to start or maintain a business.

    a. Vyborg Appeal   b. Disclosure
    c. Screening   d. Capital

42. _____ is that which is owed; usually referencing assets owed, but the term can also cover moral obligations and other interactions not requiring money. In the case of assets, _____ is a means of using future purchasing power in the present before a summation has been earned. Some companies and corporations use _____ as a part of their overall corporate finance strategy.

    a. Loan   b. Debenture
    c. Debt   d. Lender

43. _____ is a specific term used in companies' financial reporting from the company-whole point of view. Because that use excludes the effects of changing ownership interest, an economic measure of _____ is necessary for financial analysis from the shareholders' point of view

_____ is defined by the Financial Accounting Standards Board, or FASB, as 'the change in equity [net assets] of a business enterprise during a period from transactions and other events and circumstances from nonowner sources. It includes all changes in equity during a period except those resulting from investments by owners and distributions to owners.'

_____ is the sum of net income and other items that must bypass the income statement because they have not been realized, including items like an unrealized holding gain or loss from available for sale securities and foreign currency translation gains or losses.

    a. Comprehensive income   b. 3M Company
    c. BNSF Railway   d. BMC Software, Inc.

44. In accounting, the _____ is a worksheet listing the balance at a certain date, of each ledger account in two columns, namely debit and credit. Under the double-entry system, in any transaction the total of any debits must equal the total of any credits, so in a _____ the total of the debit side should always be equal to the total of the credit side. The _____ thus serves as a tool to detect errors, which can result in the totals not being equal.

    a. Bottom line   b. Depreciation
    c. Current asset   d. Trial balance

Chapter 3. The Balance Sheet and Financial Disclosures

45. _____ means the giving out of information, either voluntarily or to be in compliance with legal regulations or workplace rules.

- In Computer security, full _____ means disclosing full information about vulnerabilities.
- In computing, _____ widget
- Journalism, full _____ refers to disclosing the interests of the writer which may bear on the subject being written about, for example, if the writer has worked with an interview subject in the past.

- In law:
    - The law of England and Wales, _____ refers to a process that may form part of legal proceedings, whereby parties inform to other parties the existence of any relevant documents that are, or have been, in their control. This compares with the process known as discovery in the course of legal proceedings in the United States.
    - In U.S. civil procedure (litigation rules for civil cases), _____ is a stage prior to trial. In civil cases, each party must disclose to the opposing party the following: names of witnesses which it may use to support its side, copies of documents (or mere description of these documents) in its control which it may use to support its side, computation of damages claimed, and certain insurance information. _____ is related to, but technically prior to, the discovery stage.
    - In Company law (known as 'corporate law' in the United States), _____ refers to giving out information about public or limited companies or their officers, which might be kept secret if the company was a private company or a partnership.

- In real property transactions, _____ refers to providing to a buyer information known to the seller or broker/agent concerning the condition or other aspects of real property that would affect the property's value or desirability. These rules regarding what information must be disclosed, and whether the information must be disclosed even if a buyer does not ask, vary from one jurisdiction to the next.

    a. Tax harmonisation
    b. Trailing
    c. Controlled Foreign Corporations
    d. Disclosure

46. _____ is a fee paid on borrowed assets. It is the price paid for the use of borrowed money , or, money earned by deposited funds .Assets that are sometimes lent with _____ include money, shares, consumer goods through hire purchase, major assets such as aircraft, and even entire factories in finance lease arrangements. The _____ is calculated upon the value of the assets in the same manner as upon money.
   a. Insolvency
   b. ABC Television Network
   c. AIG
   d. Interest

47. _____ relates to the cost of borrowing money. It is the price that a lender charges a borrower for the use of the lender's money. _____ is different from OPEX and CAPEX, for it relates to the capital structure of a company.
   a. Interest
   b. AIG
   c. Interest expense
   d. ABC Television Network

48. _____ is the process of comparing the cost, cycle time, productivity, or quality of a specific process or method to another that is widely considered to be an industry standard or best practice. Essentially, _____ provides a snapshot of the performance of your business and helps you understand where you are in relation to a particular standard. The result is often a business case for making changes in order to make improvements.

a. Strategic business unit
c. BMC Software, Inc.
b. 3M Company
d. Benchmarking

49. The _____ of 1977 (15 U.S.C. §§ 78dd-1, et seq.) is a United States federal law known primarily for two of its main provisions, one that addresses accounting transparency requirements under the Securities Exchange Act of 1934 and another concerning bribery of foreign officials.
   a. Foreign Corrupt Practices Act
   c. Competition law
   b. Pre-emption right
   d. Lease

50. _____ are generally defined as increases (decreases) in the replacement costs of the assets held during a given period. _____ and losses accrue to the owners of assets and liabilities purely as a result of holding the assets or liabilities over time, without transforming them in any way.

For example, if a company holds bottles of wine in its inventory and that specific wine becomes more expensive on the market, the replacement cost of the wine in the inventory increases as it has become more expensive for the company to replace its current stock of wine.

   a. Par value
   c. Fair market value
   b. Net worth
   d. Holding gains

51. _____ are standards and interpretations adopted by the International Accounting Standards Board (IASB.)

Many of the standards forming part of _____ are known by the older name of International Accounting Standards (IAS.) IAS were issued between 1973 and 2001 by the board of the International Accounting Standards Committee (IASC.)

   a. International Financial Reporting Standards
   c. Out-of-pocket
   b. ABC Television Network
   d. AIG

52. _____ methods are means of managing inventory and financial matters involving the money a company ties up within inventory of produced goods, raw materials, parts, components, or feed stocks. FIFO stands for first-in, first-out, meaning that the oldest inventory items are recorded as sold first. LIFO stands for last-in, first-out, meaning that the most recently purchased items are recorded as sold first.
   a. FIFO and LIFO accounting
   c. 3M Company
   b. Reorder point
   d. Finished good

53. In law, _____ refers to the process by which a company (or part of a company) is brought to an end, and the assets and property of the company redistributed. _____ can also be referred to as winding-up or dissolution, although dissolution technically refers to the last stage of _____. The process of _____ also arises when customs, an authority or agency in a country responsible for collecting and safeguarding customs duties, determines the final computation or ascertainment of the duties or drawback accruing on an entry.
   a. Bankruptcy protection
   c. BMC Software, Inc.
   b. 3M Company
   d. Liquidation

Chapter 3. The Balance Sheet and Financial Disclosures

54. An _____ is a practitioner of accountancy, which is the measurement, disclosure or provision of assurance about financial information that helps managers, investors, tax authorities and other decision makers make resource allocation decisions.

The word '_____' is derived from the French 'Compter' which took its origin from the Latin 'Computare'. The word was formerly written in English as 'Accomptant', but in process of time the word, which was always pronounced by dropping the 'p', became gradually changed both in pronunciation and in orthography to its present form.

a. ABC Television Network
b. AIG
c. AMEX
d. Accountant

55. The _____ is the national, professional association of CPAs in the United States, with more than 330,000 members, including CPAs in business and industry, public practice, government, and education; student affiliates; and international associates. It sets ethical standards for the profession and U.S. auditing standards for audits of private companies; federal, state and local governments; and non-profit organizations.

Approximately 40% of its members are engaged in the practice of public accounting, in areas such as auditing, accounting, taxation, general business consulting, business valuation, personal financial planning and business technology.

a. AIG
b. ABC Television Network
c. Other postemployment benefits
d. American Institute of Certified Public Accountants

56. _____ is the statutory title of qualified accountants in the United States who have passed the Uniform _____ Examination and have met additional state education and experience requirements for certification as a _____. Individuals who have passed the Exam but have not either accomplished the required on-the-job experience or have previously met it but in the meantime have lapsed their continuing professional education are, in many states, permitted the designation '_____ Inactive' or an equivalent phrase. In most U.S. states, only _____s who are licensed are able to provide to the public attestation (including auditing) opinions on financial statements.

a. Chartered Accountant
b. Certified Public Accountant
c. Certified General Accountant
d. Chartered Certified Accountant

57. The term _____ usually refers to a company that is permitted to offer its registered securities (stock, bonds, etc.) for sale to the general public, typically through a stock exchange, or occasionally a company whose stock is traded over the counter (OTC) via market makers who use non-exchange quotation services.

The term '_____' may also refer to a company owned by the government.

a. MicroStrategy
b. Governmental Accounting Standards Board
c. Public Company
d. Professional association

Chapter 3. The Balance Sheet and Financial Disclosures

58. The _____ (sometimes called 'Peekaboo') is a private-sector, non-profit corporation created by the Sarbanes-Oxley Act, a 2002 United States federal law, to oversee the auditors of public companies. Its stated purpose is to 'protect the interests of investors and further the public interest in the preparation of informative, fair, and independent audit reports'. Although a private entity, the _____ has many government-like regulatory functions, making it in some ways similar to the private Self Regulatory Organizations (SROs) that regulate stock markets and other aspects of the financial markets in the United States.
   a. Public Company Accounting Oversight Board
   b. Pension Benefit Guaranty Corporation
   c. Financial Crimes Enforcement Network
   d. 3M Company

59. The _____ of 2002 (Pub.L. 107-204, 116 Stat. 745, enacted July 30, 2002), also known as the Public Company Accounting Reform and Investor Protection Act of 2002, is a United States federal law enacted on July 30, 2002 in response to a number of major corporate and accounting scandals including those affecting Enron, Tyco International, Adelphia, Peregrine Systems and WorldCom. The legislation establishes new or enhanced standards for all U.S. public company boards, management, and public accounting firms. It does not apply to privately held companies.
   a. Fair Labor Standards Act
   b. FCPA
   c. Lease
   d. Sarbanes-Oxley Act

60. _____ refers to the confirmation of certain characteristics of an object, person, or organization. This confirmation is often, but not always, provided by some form of external review, education, or assessment. One of the most common types of _____ in modern society is professional _____, where a person is certified as being able to competently complete a job or task, usually by the passing of an examination.
   a. 3M Company
   b. Certification
   c. BMC Software, Inc.
   d. BNSF Railway

61. _____ are formal records of a business' financial activities.

In British English, including United Kingdom company law, _____ are often referred to as accounts, although the term _____ is also used, particularly by accountants.

_____ provide an overview of a business' financial condition in both short and long term.

   a. Statement of retained earnings
   b. Financial statements
   c. 3M Company
   d. Notes to the financial statements

62. A _____ is a business that functions without the intention or threat of liquidation for the foreseeable future, usually regarded as at least within 12 months.

In accounting, '_____' refers to a company's ability to continue functioning as a business entity. It is the responsibility of the directors to assess whether the _____ assumption is appropriate when preparing the financial statements.

   a. Payment
   b. BMC Software, Inc.
   c. 3M Company
   d. Going concern

63. The U.S. _____ is an independent agency of the United States government which holds primary responsibility for enforcing the federal securities laws and regulating the securities industry, the nation's stock and options exchanges, and other electronic securities markets. The SEC was created by section 4 of the Securities Exchange Act of 1934 (now codified as 15 U.S.C. §§ 78d and commonly referred to as the 1934 Act.)
   a. BNSF Railway
   b. Securities and Exchange Commission
   c. 3M Company
   d. BMC Software, Inc.

64. In finance, an _____ is a contract between a buyer and a seller that gives the buyer the right--but not the obligation--to buy or to sell a particular asset (the underlying asset) at a later time at an agreed price. In return for granting the _____, the seller collects a payment (the premium) from the buyer. A call _____ gives the buyer the right to buy the underlying asset; a put _____ gives the buyer of the _____ the right to sell the underlying asset.
   a. ABC Television Network
   b. AIG
   c. AMEX
   d. Option

65. Most patent law systems require that a patent application disclose a claimed invention in sufficient detail for the notional person skilled in the art to carry out that claimed invention. This requirement is often known as sufficiency of disclosure or enablement, depending on the jurisdiction.

The _____ lies at the heart and origin of patent law. A state or government grants an inventor, or the inventor's assignee, a monopoly for a given period of time in exchange for the inventor disclosing to the public how to make or practice his or her invention. If a patent fails to contain such information, then the bargain is violated, and the patent is unenforceable.

   a. Tax patent
   b. Disclosure requirement
   c. Pre-emption right
   d. False Claims Act

66. _____ is a concept that denotes the precise probability of specific eventualities. Technically, the notion of _____ is independent from the notion of value and, as such, eventualities may have both beneficial and adverse consequences. However, in general usage the convention is to focus only on potential negative impact to some characteristic of value that may arise from a future event.
   a. Risk adjusted return on capital
   b. Discounting
   c. Risk
   d. Discount factor

67. In mathematics _____s are numbers or other things that get multiplied. In particular, see:

   - Factorization, the decomposition of an object into a product of other objects
   - Integer factorization, the process of breaking down a composite number into smaller non-trivial divisors
   - A coefficient
   - A divisor of a particular number, or of an element of a monoid
   - A von Neumann algebra with a trivial center

In statistics

   - _____ analysis is the study of how _____s or certain variables affect variables.

In technology:

- Human _____ s, a profession that focuses on how people interact with products, tools, or procedures
- 'Functionality, Application domain, Conditions, Technology, Objects and Responsibility;', In object-oriented programming

In computer science and information technology:

- Authentication _____, a piece of information used to verify a person's identity for security purposes
- _____, a Unix command for numbers factorization
- _____ (programming language), an experimental Forth-like programming language

In television:

- The O'Reilly _____, an American talk show hosted by Bill O'Reilly on Fox News.
- The Krypton _____, a British game show hosted by Gordon Burns, formally on ITV. Also had an American version.

a. The Goodyear Tire ' Rubber Company
b. Merck ' Co., Inc.
c. Valuation
d. Factor

68. In finance, the _____ or quick ratio or liquid ratio measures the ability of a company to use its near cash or quick assets to immediately extinguish or retire its current liabilities. Quick assets include those current assets that presumably can be quickly converted to cash at close to their book values.

$$\text{Quick (Acid Test) Ratio} = \frac{\text{Cash} + \text{Marketable Securities} + \text{Accounts Receivables}}{\text{Current Liabilities}}$$

Generally, the acid test ratio should be 1:1 or better, however this varies widely by industry.

a. Earnings per share
b. Invested capital
c. Inventory turnover
d. Acid-test

69. The _____ is a financial ratio that measures whether or not a firm has enough resources to pay its debts over the next 12 months. It compares a firm's current assets to its current liabilities. It is expressed as follows:

$$\text{Current ratio} = \frac{\text{Current Assets}}{\text{Current Liabilities}}$$

For example, if WXY Company's current assets are $50,000,000 and its current liabilities are $40,000,000, then its _____ would be $50,000,000 divided by $40,000,000, which equals 1.25.

a. Times interest earned
b. Current ratio
c. Return on capital
d. Net Interest Income

70. _____ is a financial metric which represents operating liquidity available to a business. Along with fixed assets such as plant and equipment, _____ is considered a part of operating capital. It is calculated as current assets minus current liabilities.
   a. 3M Company
   b. BMC Software, Inc.
   c. Working capital management
   d. Working capital

71. In finance, a _____ or accounting ratio is a ratio of two selected numerical values taken from an enterprise's financial statements. There are many standard ratios used to try to evaluate the overall financial condition of a corporation or other organization. _____s may be used by managers within a firm, by current and potential shareholders (owners) of a firm, and by a firm's creditors.
   a. Return of capital
   b. Current ratio
   c. Price/cash flow ratio
   d. Financial ratio

72. The _____ is a financial ratio indicating the relative proportion of equity to all used to finance a company's assets. The two components are often taken from the firm's balance sheet or statement of financial position (so-called book value), but the ratio may also be calculated using market values for both, if the company's equities are publicly traded.

The _____ is especially in Central Europe a very common financial ratio while in the US the debt to _____ is more often used in financial (research) reports.

   a. Average accounting return
   b. Efficiency ratio
   c. Earnings yield
   d. Equity ratio

73. _____ or interest coverage ratio is a measure of a company's ability to honor its debt payments. It may be calculated as either EBIT or EBITDA divided by the total interest payable.

   a. Return of capital
   b. Yield Gap
   c. Times interest earned
   d. Capital recovery factor

74. A _____, also client, buyer or purchaser is the buyer or user of the paid products of an individual or organization, mostly called the supplier or seller. This is typically through purchasing or renting goods or services.
   a. Customer
   b. BNSF Railway
   c. 3M Company
   d. BMC Software, Inc.

75. _____ was founded in June 1973 in London and replaced by the International Accounting Standards Board on April 1, 2001. It was responsible for developing the International Accounting Standards and promoting the use and application of these standards.

Chapter 3. The Balance Sheet and Financial Disclosures   51

The _____ was founded as a result of an agreement between accountancy bodies in the following countries:

- Australia (Institute of Chartered Accountants in Australia (ICAA) and the CPA Australia (formerly known as Australian Society of Certified Practising Accountants (ASCPA))

- Canada (Canadian Institute of Chartered Accountants (CICA))

- France (Ordre des Experts Comptable et des Comptables Agrees (Order of Accounting Experts and Qualified Accountants))

- Germany and the Wirtschaftsprüferkammer (WPK) (Chamber of Auditors))

- Japan Nihon Kouninkaikeishi Kyoukai)

- Mexico (Instituto Mexicano de Contadores Publicos (IMCP) (Mexican Institute of Public Accountants)) (removed from the board in 1987 due to non-payment of dues; resumed in 1995.)

- the Netherlands (Nederlands Instituut van Registeraccountants (NIVRA)

(Netherlands Institute of Registered Auditors))

- the United Kingdom and Ireland (counted as one) (Institute of Chartered Accountants in England and Wales (ICAEW), Institute of Chartered Accountants of Scotland (ICAS), Institute of Chartered Accountants in Ireland (ICAI), Association of Certified Accountants, Institute of Cost and Management Accountants, and the Institute of Municipal Treasurers and Accountants)

- the United States of America (American Institute of Certified Public Accountants (AICPA))

The Institute of Chartered Accountants of Nigeria became an associate member in 1976 and a member of the board from 1978 to 1987.

The National Council of Chartered Accountants (South Africa) became an associate member in 1974 and joined the board in 1978.

  a. American Payroll Association
  c. American Accounting Association
  b. International Accounting Standards Board
  d. International Accounting Standards Committee

   76. Procter is a surname, and may also refer to:

- Bryan Waller Procter (pseud. Barry Cornwall), English poet
- Goodwin Procter, American law firm
- _____, consumer products multinational

a. Welfare
b. Screening
c. Markup
d. Procter ' Gamble

Chapter 4. The Income Statement and Statement of Cash Flows

1. _____ is a term used with respect to a retailed product, indicating that the product is in the end of its product lifetime and a vendor will no longer be marketing, selling, or promoting a particular product and may also be limiting or ending support for the product. In the specific case of product sales, the term end-of-sale (EOS) has also been used. The term lifetime, after the last production date, depends on the product and is related to a customer's expected product lifetime.

   a. End-of-life
   b. AIG
   c. ABC Television Network
   d. AMEX

2. _____ is a specific term used in companies' financial reporting from the company-whole point of view. Because that use excludes the effects of changing ownership interest, an economic measure of _____ is necessary for financial analysis from the shareholders' point of view

   _____ is defined by the Financial Accounting Standards Board, or FASB, as 'the change in equity [net assets] of a business enterprise during a period from transactions and other events and circumstances from nonowner sources. It includes all changes in equity during a period except those resulting from investments by owners and distributions to owners.'

   _____ is the sum of net income and other items that must bypass the income statement because they have not been realized, including items like an unrealized holding gain or loss from available for sale securities and foreign currency translation gains or losses.

   a. 3M Company
   b. Comprehensive income
   c. BNSF Railway
   d. BMC Software, Inc.

3. _____ is a company's financial statement that indicates how the revenue is transformed into the net income The purpose of the _____ is to show managers and investors whether the company made or lost money during the period being reported.

   The important thing to remember about an _____ is that it represents a period of time.

   a. AMEX
   b. Income statement
   c. ABC Television Network
   d. AIG

4. _____ is the difference between operating revenues and operating expenses, but it is also sometimes used as a synonym for EBIT and operating profit. This is true if the firm has no non-_____.

   A professional investor contemplating a change to the capital structure of a firm first evaluates a firm's fundamental earnings potential (reflected by Earnings Before Interest, Taxes, Depreciation and Amortization EBITDA and EBIT), and then determines the optimal use of debt vs. equity.

   a. Operating income
   b. ABC Television Network
   c. AMEX
   d. AIG

5. The phrase _____, according to the Organization for Economic Co-operation and Development, refers to 'creative work undertaken on a systematic basis in order to increase the stock of knowledge, including knowledge of man, culture and society, and the use of this stock of knowledge to devise new applications [sic]'

54 *Chapter 4. The Income Statement and Statement of Cash Flows*

New product design and development is more than often a crucial factor in the survival of a company. In an industry that is fast changing, firms must continually revise their design and range of products. This is necessary due to continuous technology change and development as well as other competitors and the changing preference of customers.

a. BMC Software, Inc.
b. 3M Company
c. Research and development
d. BNSF Railway

6. _____ is the corporate management term for the act of partially dismantling or otherwise reorganizing a company for the purpose of making it more profitable. Also known as corporate _____, debt _____ and financial _____.

_____ is often done as part of a bankruptcy or of a strategic takeover by another firm, such as a leveraged buyout by a private equity firm.

a. Fair market value
b. Net worth
c. Payback period
d. Restructuring

7. In economics, business, retail, and accounting, a _____ is the value of money that has been used up to produce something, and hence is not available for use anymore. In economics, a _____ is an alternative that is given up as a result of a decision. In business, the _____ may be one of acquisition, in which case the amount of money expended to acquire it is counted as _____.

a. Prime cost
b. Cost allocation
c. Cost
d. Cost of quality

8. In financial accounting, a _____ or Statement of cash flows is a financial statement that shows a company's flow of cash. The money coming into the business is called cash inflow, and money going out from the business is called cash outflow. The statement shows how changes in balance sheet and income accounts affect cash and cash equivalents, and breaks the analysis down to operating, investing, and financing activities.

a. BMC Software, Inc.
b. BNSF Railway
c. 3M Company
d. Cash flow statement

9. _____ is the balance of the amounts of cash being received and paid by a business during a defined period of time, sometimes tied to a specific project. Measurement of _____ can be used

- to evaluate the state or performance of a business or project.
- to determine problems with liquidity. Being profitable does not necessarily mean being liquid. A company can fail because of a shortage of cash, even while profitable.
- to project rate of returns. The time of _____s into and out of projects are used as inputs to financial models such as internal rate of return, and net present value.
- to examine income or growth of a business when it is believed that accrual accounting concepts do not represent economic realities. Alternately, _____ can be used to 'validate' the net income generated by accrual accounting.

_____ as a generic term may be used differently depending on context, and certain _____ definitions may be adapted by analysts and users for their own uses. Common terms include operating _____ and free _____.

a. Commercial paper
b. Controlling interest
c. Flow-through entity
d. Cash flow

10. _____, in accrual accounting, is any account where the asset or liability is not realized until a future date (accounting period), e.g. annuities, charges, taxes, income, etc. The _____ item may be carried, dependent on type of deferral, as either an asset or liability.
   a. Pro forma
   b. Deferred
   c. Cash basis accounting
   d. Payroll

11. _____ in accounting is the process of treating equity investments, usually 20-50%, in associate companies. The investor keeps such equities as an asset. Proportional share of associate company's net income increases the investment, and proportional payment of dividends decreases it.
   a. Equity method
   b. AIG
   c. Out-of-pocket
   d. ABC Television Network

12. _____, also called fair price (in a commonplace conflation of the two distinct concepts), is a concept used in finance and economics, defined as a rational and unbiased estimate of the potential market price of a good, service, or asset, taking into account such objective factors as:

   - acquisition/production/distribution costs, replacement costs, or costs of close substitutes
   - actual utility at a given level of development of social productive capability
   - supply vs. demand

and subjective factors such as

   - risk characteristics
   - cost of capital
   - individually perceived utility

In accounting, _____ is used as an estimate of the market value of an asset (or liability) for which a market price cannot be determined (usually because there is no established market for the asset.) Under GAAP (FAS 157), _____ is the amount at which the asset could be bought or sold in a current transaction between willing parties, or transferred to an equivalent party, other than in a liquidation sale. This is used for assets whose carrying value is based on mark-to-market valuations; for assets carried at historical cost, the _____ of the asset is not used. One example of where _____ is an issue is a College kitchen with a cost of $2 million which was built 5 years ago.

   a. 3M Company
   b. BNSF Railway
   c. BMC Software, Inc.
   d. Fair value

13. _____ are generally defined as increases (decreases) in the replacement costs of the assets held during a given period. _____ and losses accrue to the owners of assets and liabilities purely as a result of holding the assets or liabilities over time, without transforming them in any way.

For example, if a company holds bottles of wine in its inventory and that specific wine becomes more expensive on the market, the replacement cost of the wine in the inventory increases as it has become more expensive for the company to replace its current stock of wine.

a. Par value
b. Holding gains
c. Fair market value
d. Net worth

14. _____ is the process of increasing, or accounting for, an amount over a period of time. Particular instances of the term include:

- _____, the allocation of a lump sum amount to different time periods, particularly for loans and other forms of finance, including related interest or other finance charges.
    - _____ schedule, a table detailing each periodic payment on a loan (typically a mortgage), as generated by an _____ calculator.
    - Negative _____, an _____ schedule where the loan amount actually increases through not paying the full interest
- Amortized analysis, analyzing the execution cost of algorithms over a sequence of operations.
- _____ of capital expenditures of certain assets under accounting rules, particularly intangible assets, in a manner analogous to depreciation.
- _____

a. EBIT
b. Annuity
c. Amortization
d. Intangible

15. In business and accounting, _____ are everything of value that is owned by a person or company. It is a claim on the property your income of a borrower. The balance sheet of a firm records the monetary value of the _____ owned by the firm.

a. Assets
b. Accrual basis accounting
c. Earnings before interest, taxes, depreciation and amortization
d. Accounts receivable

16. A _____ is a hedge of the exposure to the variability of cash flow that

1. is attributable to a particular risk associated with a recognized asset or liability. Such as all or some future interest payments on variable rate debt or a highly probable forecast transaction and
2. could affect profit or loss

a. Credit risk
b. Currency risk
c. 3M Company
d. Cash flow hedge

Chapter 4. The Income Statement and Statement of Cash Flows

17. In monetary economics _____ can refer either to a particular _____, for example British Pounds or United States Dollars, or, to the coins and banknotes of a particular _____, which actually form only a small part of the monetary base of a nation's money supply. The other part of a nation's money supply consists of money deposited in banks (sometimes called deposit money), ownership of which can be transferred by means of checks (cheques in the United Kingdom and Australia) or other forms of money transfer such as credit and debit cards. Deposit money and _____ are 'money' in the sense that both are acceptable as a means of exchange, but money need not necessarily be '_____'.
   a. 3M Company
   b. BNSF Railway
   c. BMC Software, Inc.
   d. Currency

18. In financial accounting, a _____ is defined as an obligation of an entity arising from past transactions or events, the settlement of which may result in the transfer or use of assets, provision of services or other yielding of economic benefits in the future.
   a. Vested
   b. False Claims Act
   c. Corporate governance
   d. Liability

19. _____ or fair value accounting refers to the accounting standards of assigning a value to a position held in a financial instrument based on the current fair market price for the instrument or similar instruments. Fair value accounting has been a part of US Generally Accepted Accounting Principles (GAAP) since the early 1990s. The use of fair value measurements has increased steadily over the past decade, primarily in response to investor demand for relevant and timely financial statements that will aid in making better informed decisions.
   a. Transfer agent
   b. Financial instruments
   c. Market liquidity
   d. Mark-to-market

20. The term _____ or superannuation refers to a pension granted upon retirement. They may be set up by employers, insurance companies, the government or other institutions such as employer associations or trade unions.
   a. BMC Software, Inc.
   b. 3M Company
   c. Wage
   d. Retirement plan

21. A _____ is a fungible, negotiable instrument representing financial value. they are broadly categorized into debt securities (such as banknotes, bonds and debentures), and equity securities; e.g., common stocks. The company or other entity issuing the _____ is called the issuer.
   a. BMC Software, Inc.
   b. Security
   c. Tracking stock
   d. 3M Company

22. A _____ is a computer application that simulates a paper worksheet. It displays multiple cells that together make up a grid consisting of rows and columns, each cell containing either alphanumeric text or numeric values. A _____ cell may alternatively contain a formula that defines how the contents of that cell is to be calculated from the contents of any other cell (or combination of cells) each time any cell is updated.
   a. Spreadsheet
   b. Linear regression
   c. Merck ' Co., Inc.
   d. Mutual fund

23. _____ is generally understood in financial circles as the point at which revenue is recognized, typically through a transaction which involves the exchange of an asset, product, or service for cash or its equivalents.

This approach gives the accounting division a strictly objective basis for changing the books. For example, a homeowner may believe that his house has grown in value during a strong market, or fallen in value during a weak market, but until the house is actually sold for a specific price to a specific buyer, the change in value can only be estimated and is considered unrealized.

- a. Total-factor productivity
- b. Merck ' Co., Inc.
- c. Valuation
- d. Realization

24. _____ is a subsection in equity where 'other comprehensive income' is accumulated (summed or 'aggregated'.)

The balance of _____ is presented in the Equity section of the Balance Sheet as is the Retained Earnings balance, which aggregates past and current Earnings, and past and current Dividends.

Other comprehensive income is the difference between net income and comprehensive income and represents the certain gains and losses of the enterprise.

- a. Authorised capital
- b. Operating budget
- c. Inventory turnover ratio
- d. Accumulated other comprehensive income

25. _____ is an accounting concept, meaning a future tax liability or asset, resulting from temporary differences between book (accounting) value of assets and liabilities and their tax value, or timing differences between the recognition of gains and losses in financial statements and their recognition in a tax computation.

Temporary differences are differences between the carrying amount of an asset or liability recognised in the balance sheet and the amount attributed to that asset or liability for tax purposes (the tax base.)

- a. Federal tax revenue by state
- b. Tax refund
- c. Deferred tax
- d. Deficit

26. In accounting, _____ has a very specific meaning. It is an outflow of cash or other valuable assets from a person or company to another person or company. This outflow of cash is generally one side of a trade for products or services that have equal or better current or future value to the buyer than to the seller.
- a. AIG
- b. ABC Television Network
- c. AMEX
- d. Expense

27. An _____ is a tax levied on the financial income of people, corporations, or other legal entities. Various _____ systems exist, with varying degrees of tax incidence. Income taxation can be progressive, proportional, or regressive.
- a. Implied level of government service
- b. Ordinary income
- c. Income tax
- d. Individual Retirement Arrangement

28. _____, in law and economics, is a form of risk management primarily used to hedge against the risk of a contingent loss. _____ is defined as the equitable transfer of the risk of a loss, from one entity to another, in exchange for a premium, and can be thought of as a guaranteed small loss to prevent a large, possibly devastating loss. An insurer is a company selling the _____; an insured is the person or entity buying the _____.

Chapter 4. The Income Statement and Statement of Cash Flows

a. ABC Television Network
c. AMEX

b. AIG
d. Insurance

29. _____ is a cornerstone of accrual accounting together with the revenue recognition principle. They both determine the accounting period, in which revenues and expenses are recognized. According to the principle, expenses are recognized when obligations are (1) incurred (usually when goods are transferred or services rendered, e.g. sold), and (2) offset against recognized revenues, which were generated from those expenses (related on the cause-and-effect basis), no matter when cash is paid out.

a. Current liabilities
c. Payroll

b. Matching principle
d. Net sales

30. _____ principle is a cornerstone of accrual accounting together with matching principle. They both determine the accounting period, in which revenues and expenses are recognized. According to the principle, revenues are recognized when they are (1) realized or realizable, and are (2) earned (usually when goods are transferred or services rendered), no matter when cash is received.

a. BMC Software, Inc.
c. Net realizable value

b. 3M Company
d. Revenue recognition

31. At its simplest, a company's _____ as it sometimes called, is computed in by multiplying the income before tax number, as reported to shareholders, by the appropriate tax rate. In reality, the computation is typically considerably more complex due to things such as expenses considered not deductible by taxing authorities ('add backs'), the range of tax rates applicable to various levels of income, different tax rates in different jurisdictions, multiple layers of tax on income, and other issues.

Historically, in many places, a revenue-expense method was used, in which the income statement was seen as primary, and the balance sheet as secondary.

a. 3M Company
c. Total Expense Ratio

b. Tax expense
d. Payroll

32. _____ is the portion of income that is the subject of taxation according to the laws that determine what is income and the taxation rate for that income. Generally, _____ refers to an individual's (or corporation's) gross income, adjusted for various deductions allowable by statute. The main questions put by most individuals in any jurisdiction are 'what makes up my _____' and what tax rates should be applied such that I can work out my tax liability to the state.

a. Reverse Morris trust
c. Half-year convention

b. SUTA dumping
d. Taxable income

33. In economics, _____ or _____ goods or real _____ refers to factors of production used to create goods or services that are not themselves significantly consumed (though they may depreciate) in the production process. _____ goods may be acquired with money or financial _____. In finance and accounting, _____ generally refers to financial wealth, especially that used to start or maintain a business.

a. Disclosure
c. Screening

b. Vyborg Appeal
d. Capital

34. A _____ has several related meanings:

- a daily record of events or business; a private _____ is usually referred to as a diary.
- a newspaper or other periodical, in the literal sense of one published each day;
- many publications issued at stated intervals, such as magazines, or scholarly academic _____s, or the record of the transactions of a society, are often called _____s. Although _____ is sometimes used, erroneously, as a synonym for 'magazine,' in academic use, a _____ refers to a serious, scholarly publication, most often peer-reviewed. A non-scholarly magazine written for an educated audience about an industry or an area of professional activity is usually called a professional magazine.

The word 'journalist' for one whose business is writing for the public press has been in use since the end of the 17th century.

Open access _____s are scholarly _____s that are available to the reader without financial or other barrier other than access to the internet itself. Some are subsidized, and some require payment on behalf of the author. Subsidized _____s are financed by an academic institution or a government information center.

a. BMC Software, Inc.
b. BNSF Railway
c. 3M Company
d. Journal

35. The U.S. _____ is an independent agency of the United States government which holds primary responsibility for enforcing the federal securities laws and regulating the securities industry, the nation's stock and options exchanges, and other electronic securities markets. The SEC was created by section 4 of the Securities Exchange Act of 1934 (now codified as 15 U.S.C. ÂÂ§ 78d and commonly referred to as the 1934 Act.)

a. 3M Company
b. Securities and Exchange Commission
c. BMC Software, Inc.
d. BNSF Railway

36. In financial accounting, a _____ or statement of financial position is a summary of a person's or organization's balances. Assets, liabilities and ownership equity are listed as of a specific date, such as the end of its financial year. A _____ is often described as a snapshot of a company's financial condition.

a. Balance sheet
b. 3M Company
c. Financial statements
d. Statement of retained earnings

Chapter 4. The Income Statement and Statement of Cash Flows

37. _____ means the giving out of information, either voluntarily or to be in compliance with legal regulations or workplace rules.

- In Computer security, full _____ means disclosing full information about vulnerabilities.
- In computing, _____ widget
- Journalism, full _____ refers to disclosing the interests of the writer which may bear on the subject being written about, for example, if the writer has worked with an interview subject in the past.

- In law:
    - The law of England and Wales, _____ refers to a process that may form part of legal proceedings, whereby parties inform to other parties the existence of any relevant documents that are, or have been, in their control. This compares with the process known as discovery in the course of legal proceedings in the United States.
    - In U.S. civil procedure (litigation rules for civil cases), _____ is a stage prior to trial. In civil cases, each party must disclose to the opposing party the following: names of witnesses which it may use to support its side, copies of documents (or mere description of these documents) in its control which it may use to support its side, computation of damages claimed, and certain insurance information. _____ is related to, but technically prior to, the discovery stage.
    - In Company law (known as 'corporate law' in the United States), _____ refers to giving out information about public or limited companies or their officers, which might be kept secret if the company was a private company or a partnership.

- In real property transactions, _____ refers to providing to a buyer information known to the seller or broker/agent concerning the condition or other aspects of real property that would affect the property's value or desirability. These rules regarding what information must be disclosed, and whether the information must be disclosed even if a buyer does not ask, vary from one jurisdiction to the next.

a. Tax harmonisation
b. Controlled Foreign Corporations
c. Trailing
d. Disclosure

38. _____ is a term in both law and accounting that is based on the economics term of 'market value.' It is also a common basis for assessing damages to be awarded for the loss of or damage to the property, generally in a claim under tort or a contract of insurance.

A _____ is often an estimate of what a willing buyer would pay to a willing seller, both in a free market, for an asset or any piece of property. If such a transaction actually occurs, then the actual transaction price is usually the _____.

a. Disposal tax effect
b. Cash and cash equivalents
c. Shares authorized
d. Fair market value

39. A _____ is any one of a variety of different systems, institutions, procedures, social relations and infrastructures whereby persons trade, and goods and services are exchanged, forming part of the economy. It is an arrangement that allows buyers and sellers to exchange things. _____s vary in size, range, geographic scale, location, types and variety of human communities, as well as the types of goods and services traded.

a. Market
b. Perfect competition
c. Market Failure
d. Recession

40. _____ is the price at which an asset would trade in a competitive Walrasian auction setting. _____ is often used interchangeably with open _____, fair value or fair _____, although these terms have distinct definitions in different standards, and may differ in some circumstances.

International Valuation Standards defines _____ as 'the estimated amount for which a property should exchange on the date of valuation between a willing buyer and a willing seller in an arme;s-length transaction after proper marketing wherein the parties had each acted knowledgeably, prudently, and without compulsion.'

_____ is a concept distinct from market price, which is e;the price at which one can transacte;, while _____ is e;the true underlying valuee; according to theoretical standards.

a. Debtor
b. Sinking fund
c. Segregated portfolio company
d. Market value

41. In physics, and more specifically kinematics, _____ is the change in velocity over time. Because velocity is a vector, it can change in two ways: a change in magnitude and/or a change in direction. In one dimension, _____ is the rate at which something speeds up or slows down.

a. ABC Television Network
b. AMEX
c. AIG
d. Acceleration

42. The term _____ describes a reduction in recognized value. In accounting terminology, it refers to recognition of the reduced or zero value of an asset. In income tax statements, it refers to a reduction of taxable income as recognition of certain expenses required to produce the income.

a. Salvage value
b. Payroll
c. Current asset
d. Write-off

43. The term _____ is a term applied to practices that are perfunctory, or seek to satisfy the minimum requirements or to conform to a convention or doctrine. It has different meanings in different fields.

In accounting, _____ earnings are those earnings of companies in addition to actual earnings calculated under the Generally Accepted Accounting Principles (GAAP) in their quarterly and yearly financial reports.

a. Treasury stock
b. Bottom line
c. Payroll
d. Pro forma

44. An _____ is generally a 'disposition of property where at least 1 payment is to be received after the close of the taxable year in which the disposition occurs.'

If a taxpayer realizes income (e.g., gain) from an _____, the income generally must be reported by the taxpayer under the 'installment method.' The 'installment method' is defined as 'a method under which the income recognized for any taxable year [.

Chapter 4. The Income Statement and Statement of Cash Flows 63

a. ABC Television Network
c. AIG
b. Installment sale
d. AMEX

45. A _____ is the pinnacle activity involved in selling products or services in return for money or other compensation. It is an act of completion of a commercial activity.

A _____ is completed by the seller, the owner of the goods.

a. Sale
c. High yield stock
b. Maturity
d. Tertiary sector of economy

46. The _____ is the current method of accelerated asset depreciation required by the United States income tax code. Under _____, all assets are divided into classes which dictate the number of years over which an asset's cost will be recovered.

Prior to the Accelerated Cost Recovery System (ACRS), most capital purchases were depreciated using a straight line technique, that allowed for the depreciation of the asset over its useful life.

a. BMC Software, Inc.
c. Modified Accelerated Cost Recovery System
b. Categorical grants
d. 3M Company

47. An _____ is the buying of one company by another. An _____ may be friendly or hostile. In the former case, the companies cooperate in negotiations; in the latter case, the takeover target is unwilling to be bought or the target's board has no prior knowledge of the offer. _____ usually refers to a purchase of a smaller firm by a larger one. Sometimes, however, a smaller firm will acquire management control of a larger or longer established company and keep its name for the combined entity. This is known as a reverse takeover.

a. AIG
c. ABC Television Network
b. AMEX
d. Acquisition

48. Discounting is a financial mechanism in which a debtor obtains the right to delay payments to a creditor, for a defined period of time, in exchange for a charge or fee. Essentially, the party that owes money in the present purchases the right to delay the payment until some future date. The _____, or charge, is simply the difference between the original amount owed in the present and the amount that has to be paid in the future to settle the debt.

a. Discounting
c. Risk aversion
b. Discount factor
d. Discount

49. A _____ or reacquired stock is stock which is bought back by the issuing company, reducing the amount of outstanding stock on the open market ('open market' including insiders' holdings).

Stock repurchases are often used as a tax-efficient method to put cash into shareholders' hands, rather than pay dividends. Sometimes, companies do this when they feel that their stock is undervalued on the open market.

a. Matching principle
c. Net profit
b. Treasury stock
d. Cost of goods sold

Chapter 4. The Income Statement and Statement of Cash Flows

50. The _____ is an independent agency of the United States government, established in 1914 by the _____ Act. Its principal mission is the promotion of 'consumer protection' and the elimination and prevention of what regulators perceive to be harmfully 'anti-competitive' business practices, such as coercive monopoly.

The _____ Act was one of President Wilson's major acts against trusts.

a. 3M Company
b. BMC Software, Inc.
c. BNSF Railway
d. Federal Trade Commission

51. _____ methods are means of managing inventory and financial matters involving the money a company ties up within inventory of produced goods, raw materials, parts, components, or feed stocks. FIFO stands for first-in, first-out, meaning that the oldest inventory items are recorded as sold first. LIFO stands for last-in, first-out, meaning that the most recently purchased items are recorded as sold first.

a. Reorder point
b. FIFO and LIFO accounting
c. Finished good
d. 3M Company

52. In law, _____ refers to the process by which a company (or part of a company) is brought to an end, and the assets and property of the company redistributed. _____ can also be referred to as winding-up or dissolution, although dissolution technically refers to the last stage of _____. The process of _____ also arises when customs, an authority or agency in a country responsible for collecting and safeguarding customs duties, determines the final computation or ascertainment of the duties or drawback accruing on an entry.

a. Liquidation
b. BMC Software, Inc.
c. Bankruptcy protection
d. 3M Company

53. _____ refers to any one of several methods by which a company, for 'financial accounting' and/or tax purposes, depreciates a fixed asset in such a way that the amount of depreciation taken each year is higher during the earlier years of an assete;s life. For financial accounting purposes, _____ is generally used when an asset is expected to be much more productive during its early years, so that depreciation expense will more accurately represent how much of an assete;s usefulness is being used up each year. For tax purposes, _____ provides a way of deferring corporate income taxes by reducing taxable income in current years, in exchange for increased taxable income in future years.

a. User charge
b. Effective marginal tax rates
c. Accelerated depreciation
d. Indirect tax

54. _____ is an acronym for First In, First Out, an abstraction in ways of organizing and manipulation of data relative to time and prioritization. This expression describes the principle of a queue processing technique or servicing conflicting demands by ordering process by first-come, first-served (FCFS) behaviour: what comes in first is handled first, what comes in next waits until the first is finished, etc.

Thus it is analogous to the behaviour of persons queueing (or 'standing in line', in common American parlance), where the persons leave the queue in the order they arrive, or waiting one's turn at a traffic control signal.

a. Kanban
b. FIFO
c. Risk management
d. Trademark

55. _____ is a term used in accounting, economics and finance to spread the cost of an asset over the span of several years.

Chapter 4. The Income Statement and Statement of Cash Flows

In simple words we can say that _____ is the reduction in the value of an asset due to usage, passage of time, wear and tear, technological outdating or obsolescence, depletion, inadequacy, rot, rust, decay or other such factors.

In accounting, _____ is a term used to describe any method of attributing the historical or purchase cost of an asset across its useful life, roughly corresponding to normal wear and tear.

   a. General ledger
   b. Net profit
   c. Depreciation
   d. Current asset

56. An _____ is a term used in behavioral economics to describe those types of behaviors that impose costs on a person in the long-run that are not taken into account when making decisions in the present. Classical Economics discourages government from creating legislation that targets internalities, because it is assumed that the consumer takes these personal costs into account when paying for the good that causes the _____. For example, cigarettes should be taxed because of the negative consumption externalities that they impose, such as second-hand smoke, not because the smoker harms him or herself by smoking.

   a. Inventory turnover ratio
   b. Authorised capital
   c. Operating budget
   d. Internality

57. In accounting and organizational theory, _____ is defined as a process effected by an organization's structure, work and authority flows, people and management information systems, designed to help the organization accomplish specific goals or objectives. It is a means by which an organization's resources are directed, monitored, and measured. It plays an important role in preventing and detecting fraud and protecting the organization's resources, both physical (e.g., machinery and property) and intangible (e.g., reputation or intellectual property such as trademarks.)

   a. Audit committee
   b. Auditor independence
   c. Audit risk
   d. Internal control

58. _____ are the earnings returned on the initial investment amount.

In the US, the Financial Accounting Standards Board (FASB) requires companies' income statements to report _____ for each of the major categories of the income statement: continuing operations, discontinued operations, extraordinary items, and net income.

The _____ formula does not include preferred dividends for categories outside of continued operations and net income.

   a. Invested capital
   b. Earnings yield
   c. Average accounting return
   d. Earnings per share

59. _____ is a company's earnings per share (EPS) calculated using fully diluted shares outstanding. _____ indicates a 'worst case' scenario, one in which everyone who could have received stock without purchasing it directly for the full market value did so.

To find _____, basic EPS is calculated for each of the categories on the income statement first. Then each of the dilutive securities are ranked based on their effects, from most dilutive to least dilutive and antidilutive. Then the basic EPS number is diluted one by one by applying each one, skipping any instruments that have an antidilutive effect.

a. Financial ratio
b. Return on assets Du Pont
c. Cash conversion cycle
d. Diluted Earnings Per Share

60. _____ is a demonstration of a process -- such as a variable, term, or object -- relative in terms of the specific process or set of validation tests used to determine its presence and quantity. Properties described in this manner must be sufficiently accessible, so that persons other than the definer may independently measure or test for them at will. An _____ is generally designed to model a conceptual definition.

a. ABC Television Network
b. AIG
c. AMEX
d. Operational definition

61. In accounting, _____ are considered liabilities of the business that are to be settled in cash within the fiscal year or the operating cycle, whichever period is longer.

For example accounts payable for goods, services or supplies that were purchased for use in the operation of the business and payable within a normal period of time would be _____.

Bonds, mortgages and loans that are payable over a term exceeding one year would be fixed liabilities.

a. Closing entries
b. Current liabilities
c. Treasury stock
d. Payroll

62. _____ are the most liquid assets found within the asset portion of a company's balance sheet. Cash equivalents are assets that are readily convertible into cash, such as money market holdings, short-term government bonds or Treasury bills, marketable securities and commercial paper. _____ are distinguished from other investments through their short-term existence; they mature within 3 months whereas short-term investments are 12 months or less, and long-term investments are any investments that mature in excess of 12 months.

a. Par value
b. Debtor
c. Payback period
d. Cash and cash equivalents

63. _____ of something is, in finance, the adding together of interest or different investments over a period of time such as atoms (1 - the act or process of accruing; 2 - the amount that accrues.) It holds specific meanings in accounting and payroll.

_____, in accounting, describes the accounting method known as _____ basis, whereby revenues and expenses are recognized when they are accrued, i.e. accumulated (earned or incurred), regardless when the actual cash is received or paid out.

a. Accounts receivable

b. Earnings before interest, taxes, depreciation and amortization

c. Assets

d. Accrual

64. _____ is a method of accounting whereby economic activities (rather than cash flow) of financial events are considered, because of two complementary principles, which (together) determine the point, at which expenses and revenues are recognized. According to revenue recognition principle, revenues are realized when earned, whether or not they are received in cash.

a. Accrued revenue

b. Accrual basis accounting

c. Earnings before interest, taxes, depreciation and amortization

d. Accrual

Chapter 5. Income Measurement and Profitability Analysis

1. _____ is generally understood in financial circles as the point at which revenue is recognized, typically through a transaction which involves the exchange of an asset, product, or service for cash or its equivalents.

This approach gives the accounting division a strictly objective basis for changing the books. For example, a homeowner may believe that his house has grown in value during a strong market, or fallen in value during a weak market, but until the house is actually sold for a specific price to a specific buyer, the change in value can only be estimated and is considered unrealized.

- a. Valuation
- b. Realization
- c. Merck ' Co., Inc.
- d. Total-factor productivity

2. _____ principle is a cornerstone of accrual accounting together with matching principle. They both determine the accounting period, in which revenues and expenses are recognized. According to the principle, revenues are recognized when they are (1) realized or realizable, and are (2) earned (usually when goods are transferred or services rendered), no matter when cash is received.
- a. 3M Company
- b. BMC Software, Inc.
- c. Net realizable value
- d. Revenue recognition

3. _____ means the giving out of information, either voluntarily or to be in compliance with legal regulations or workplace rules.

- In Computer security, full _____ means disclosing full information about vulnerabilities.
- In computing, _____ widget
- Journalism, full _____ refers to disclosing the interests of the writer which may bear on the subject being written about, for example, if the writer has worked with an interview subject in the past.

- In law:
    - The law of England and Wales, _____ refers to a process that may form part of legal proceedings, whereby parties inform to other parties the existence of any relevant documents that are, or have been, in their control. This compares with the process known as discovery in the course of legal proceedings in the United States.
    - In U.S. civil procedure (litigation rules for civil cases), _____ is a stage prior to trial. In civil cases, each party must disclose to the opposing party the following: names of witnesses which it may use to support its side, copies of documents (or mere description of these documents) in its control which it may use to support its side, computation of damages claimed, and certain insurance information. _____ is related to, but technically prior to, the discovery stage.
    - In Company law (known as 'corporate law' in the United States), _____ refers to giving out information about public or limited companies or their officers, which might be kept secret if the company was a private company or a partnership.

- In real property transactions, _____ refers to providing to a buyer information known to the seller or broker/agent concerning the condition or other aspects of real property that would affect the property's value or desirability. These rules regarding what information must be disclosed, and whether the information must be disclosed even if a buyer does not ask, vary from one jurisdiction to the next.

Chapter 5. Income Measurement and Profitability Analysis

a. Disclosure
b. Controlled Foreign Corporations
c. Trailing
d. Tax harmonisation

4. The _____ founded on April 1, 2001 is the successor of the International Accounting Standards Committee (IASC) founded in June 1973 in London. It is responsible for developing the International Financial Reporting Standards (new name for the International Accounting Standards issued after 2001), and promoting the use and application of these standards.

The _____ is an independent, privately-funded accounting standard-setter based in London, UK.

a. International Accounting Standards Board
b. Information Systems Audit and Control Association
c. Emerging technologies
d. Institute of Management Accountants

5. _____ is a specific term used in companies' financial reporting from the company-whole point of view. Because that use excludes the effects of changing ownership interest, an economic measure of _____ is necessary for financial analysis from the shareholders' point of view

_____ is defined by the Financial Accounting Standards Board, or FASB, as 'the change in equity [net assets] of a business enterprise during a period from transactions and other events and circumstances from nonowner sources. It includes all changes in equity during a period except those resulting from investments by owners and distributions to owners.'

_____ is the sum of net income and other items that must bypass the income statement because they have not been realized, including items like an unrealized holding gain or loss from available for sale securities and foreign currency translation gains or losses.

a. 3M Company
b. Comprehensive income
c. BNSF Railway
d. BMC Software, Inc.

6. In economics, business, retail, and accounting, a _____ is the value of money that has been used up to produce something, and hence is not available for use anymore. In economics, a _____ is an alternative that is given up as a result of a decision. In business, the _____ may be one of acquisition, in which case the amount of money expended to acquire it is counted as _____.

a. Cost allocation
b. Cost of quality
c. Prime cost
d. Cost

7. In financial accounting, _____ or cost of sales includes the direct costs attributable to the production of the goods sold by a company. This amount includes the materials cost used in creating the goods along with the direct labor costs used to produce the good. It excludes indirect expenses such as distribution costs and sales force costs.

a. 3M Company
b. FIFO and LIFO accounting
c. Cost of goods sold
d. Reorder point

8. _____ or international commercial terms are a series of international sales terms widely used throughout the world. They are used to divide transaction costs and responsibilities between buyer and seller and reflect state-of-the-art transportation practices. They closely correspond to the U.N. Convention on Contracts for the International Sale of Goods.

Chapter 5. Income Measurement and Profitability Analysis

a. ABC Television Network
b. Incoterms
c. AIG
d. AMEX

9. _____ of something is, in finance, the adding together of interest or different investments over a period of time such as atoms (1 - the act or process of accruing; 2 - the amount that accrues.) It holds specific meanings in accounting and payroll.

_____, in accounting, describes the accounting method known as _____ basis, whereby revenues and expenses are recognized when they are accrued, i.e. accumulated (earned or incurred), regardless when the actual cash is received or paid out.

a. Assets
b. Accounts receivable
c. Earnings before interest, taxes, depreciation and amortization
d. Accrual

10. _____ is a method of accounting whereby economic activities (rather than cash flow) of financial events are considered, because of two complementary principles, which (together) determine the point, at which expenses and revenues are recognized. According to revenue recognition principle, revenues are realized when earned, whether or not they are received in cash.

a. Earnings before interest, taxes, depreciation and amortization
b. Accrual
c. Accrual basis accounting
d. Accrued revenue

11. In accounting, _____ or sales profit is the difference between revenue and the cost of making a product or providing a service, before deducting overhead, payroll, taxation, and interest payments. Note that this is different from operating profit (earnings before interest and taxes.)

Net sales are calculated:

Net sales = Sales - Sales returns and allowances.

a. Commercial paper
b. Capital structure
c. Participating preferred stock
d. Gross profit

12. An _____ is generally a 'disposition of property where at least 1 payment is to be received after the close of the taxable year in which the disposition occurs.'

If a taxpayer realizes income (e.g., gain) from an _____, the income generally must be reported by the taxpayer under the 'installment method.' The 'installment method' is defined as 'a method under which the income recognized for any taxable year [.

a. AIG
b. AMEX
c. ABC Television Network
d. Installment sale

13. A _____ is the pinnacle activity involved in selling products or services in return for money or other compensation. It is an act of completion of a commercial activity.

Chapter 5. Income Measurement and Profitability Analysis 71

A _____ is completed by the seller, the owner of the goods.

a. Maturity
c. Sale

b. Tertiary sector of economy
d. High yield stock

14. _____ are formal bookkeeping and accounting terms. They are the most fundamental concepts in accounting, representing the two records that one party in a transaction makes on its records, transferring a money balance from one account to another, one representing a reduction of liability or increase in asset, and the other representing a balancing increase in liability or reduction of asset.

Debits and credits are a system of notation used in accounting to keep track of money movements (transactions) into and out of an account.

a. Bookkeeping
c. Controlling account

b. Cookie jar accounting
d. Debit and credit

15. _____, in accrual accounting, is any account where the asset or liability is not realized until a future date (accounting period), e.g. annuities, charges, taxes, income, etc. The _____ item may be carried, dependent on type of deferral, as either an asset or liability.

a. Deferred
c. Pro forma

b. Cash basis accounting
d. Payroll

16. _____ is the process of increasing, or accounting for, an amount over a period of time. Particular instances of the term include:

- _____, the allocation of a lump sum amount to different time periods, particularly for loans and other forms of finance, including related interest or other finance charges.
    - _____ schedule, a table detailing each periodic payment on a loan (typically a mortgage), as generated by an _____ calculator.
    - Negative _____, an _____ schedule where the loan amount actually increases through not paying the full interest
- Amortized analysis, analyzing the execution cost of algorithms over a sequence of operations.
- _____ of capital expenditures of certain assets under accounting rules, particularly intangible assets, in a manner analogous to depreciation.
- _____

a. EBIT
c. Intangible

b. Annuity
d. Amortization

17. In financial accounting and finance, _____ is the portion of receivables that can no longer be collected, typically from accounts receivable or loans. _____ in accounting is considered an expense.

Chapter 5. Income Measurement and Profitability Analysis

There are two methods to account for _____:

1. Direct write off method (Non - GAAP)

A receivable which is not considered collectible is charged directly to the income statement.

1. Allowance method (GAAP)

An estimate is made at the end of each fiscal year of the amount of _____. This is then accumulated in a provision which is then used to reduce specific receivable accounts as and when necessary.

a. Tax expense
c. 3M Company
b. Bad debt
d. Total Expense Ratio

18. In accounting, _____ are considered liabilities of the business that are to be settled in cash within the fiscal year or the operating cycle, whichever period is longer.

For example accounts payable for goods, services or supplies that were purchased for use in the operation of the business and payable within a normal period of time would be _____.

Bonds, mortgages and loans that are payable over a term exceeding one year would be fixed liabilities.

a. Current liabilities
c. Treasury stock
b. Payroll
d. Closing entries

19. _____ is that which is owed; usually referencing assets owed, but the term can also cover moral obligations and other interactions not requiring money. In the case of assets, _____ is a means of using future purchasing power in the present before a summation has been earned. Some companies and corporations use _____ as a part of their overall corporate finance strategy.
a. Lender
c. Debt
b. Loan
d. Debenture

20. In financial accounting, a _____ is defined as an obligation of an entity arising from past transactions or events, the settlement of which may result in the transfer or use of assets, provision of services or other yielding of economic benefits in the future.
a. Liability
c. Vested
b. Corporate governance
d. False Claims Act

21. A _____ is the transfer of wealth from one party (such as a person or company) to another. A _____ is usually made in exchange for the provision of goods, services or both, or to fulfill a legal obligation.

The simplest and oldest form of _____ is barter, the exchange of one good or service for another.

Chapter 5. Income Measurement and Profitability Analysis

a. Payment
c. Payee
b. 3M Company
d. BMC Software, Inc.

22. In economic models, the _____ time frame assumes no fixed factors of production. Firms can enter or leave the marketplace, and the cost (and availability) of land, labor, raw materials, and capital goods can be assumed to vary. In contrast, in the short-run time frame, certain factors are assumed to be fixed, because there is not sufficient time for them to change.
a. Short-run
c. Long-run
b. 3M Company
d. BMC Software, Inc.

23. The _____ of 2002 (Pub.L. 107-204, 116 Stat. 745, enacted July 30, 2002), also known as the Public Company Accounting Reform and Investor Protection Act of 2002, is a United States federal law enacted on July 30, 2002 in response to a number of major corporate and accounting scandals including those affecting Enron, Tyco International, Adelphia, Peregrine Systems and WorldCom. The legislation establishes new or enhanced standards for all U.S. public company boards, management, and public accounting firms. It does not apply to privately held companies.
a. Sarbanes-Oxley Act
c. Lease
b. Fair Labor Standards Act
d. FCPA

24. The term _____ is a term applied to practices that are perfunctory, or seek to satisfy the minimum requirements or to conform to a convention or doctrine. It has different meanings in different fields.

In accounting, _____ earnings are those earnings of companies in addition to actual earnings calculated under the Generally Accepted Accounting Principles (GAAP) in their quarterly and yearly financial reports.

a. Treasury stock
c. Payroll
b. Pro forma
d. Bottom line

25. In financial accounting, a _____ or statement of financial position is a summary of a person's or organization's balances. Assets, liabilities and ownership equity are listed as of a specific date, such as the end of its financial year. A _____ is often described as a snapshot of a company's financial condition.
a. Balance sheet
c. Statement of retained earnings
b. 3M Company
d. Financial statements

26. A _____ or reacquired stock is stock which is bought back by the issuing company, reducing the amount of outstanding stock on the open market ('open market' including insiders' holdings).

Stock repurchases are often used as a tax-efficient method to put cash into shareholders' hands, rather than pay dividends. Sometimes, companies do this when they feel that their stock is undervalued on the open market.

a. Cost of goods sold
c. Matching principle
b. Treasury stock
d. Net profit

Chapter 5. Income Measurement and Profitability Analysis

27. A _____ has several related meanings:

- a daily record of events or business; a private _____ is usually referred to as a diary.
- a newspaper or other periodical, in the literal sense of one published each day;
- many publications issued at stated intervals, such as magazines, or scholarly academic _____s, or the record of the transactions of a society, are often called _____s. Although _____ is sometimes used, erroneously, as a synonym for 'magazine,' in academic use, a _____ refers to a serious, scholarly publication, most often peer-reviewed. A non-scholarly magazine written for an educated audience about an industry or an area of professional activity is usually called a professional magazine.

The word 'journalist' for one whose business is writing for the public press has been in use since the end of the 17th century.

Open access _____s are scholarly _____s that are available to the reader without financial or other barrier other than access to the internet itself. Some are subsidized, and some require payment on behalf of the author. Subsidized _____s are financed by an academic institution or a government information center.

a. BNSF Railway
b. BMC Software, Inc.
c. 3M Company
d. Journal

28. Discounting is a financial mechanism in which a debtor obtains the right to delay payments to a creditor, for a defined period of time, in exchange for a charge or fee. Essentially, the party that owes money in the present purchases the right to delay the payment until some future date. The _____, or charge, is simply the difference between the original amount owed in the present and the amount that has to be paid in the future to settle the debt.

a. Discounting
b. Risk aversion
c. Discount
d. Discount factor

29. _____, in accrual accounting, (e.g. advance payment received from a client) is, according to revenue recognition, revenue not earned until the delivery of goods or services, which until then, is still owed to the payer, hence remaining a liability.

_____, sometimes referred to as deferred revenue or unearned revenue, shares characteristics with accrued expense with the difference that a liability to be covered latter is cash received FROM a counterpart, while goods or services are to be delivered in a latter period, when such income item is earned, the related revenue item is recognized, and the same amount is deducted from deferred revenues.

a. Matching principle
b. Deferred income
c. Treasury stock
d. Gross sales

30. In business and accounting, _____ are everything of value that is owned by a person or company. It is a claim on the property your income of a borrower. The balance sheet of a firm records the monetary value of the _____ owned by the firm.

a. Accrual basis accounting
b. Earnings before interest, taxes, depreciation and amortization
c. Accounts receivable
d. Assets

31. _____ is a financial ratio that measures the efficiency of a company's use of its assets in generating sales revenue or sales income to the company.

$$Asset\ Turnover = \frac{Sales}{Average\ Total\ Assets}$$

- 'Sales' is the value of 'Net Sales' or 'Sales' from the company's income statement
- 'Average Total Assets' is the value of 'Total assets' from the company's balance sheet in the beginning and the end of the fiscal period divided by 2.

a. Average propensity to consume
b. Asset turnover
c. Information ratio
d. Enterprise Value/Sales

32. The _____ is an equation that equals the cost of goods sold divided by the average inventory. Average inventory equals beginning inventory plus ending inventory divided by 2.

The formula for _____:

$$Inventory\ Turnover = \frac{Cost\ of\ Goods\ Sold}{Average\ Inventory}$$

The formula for average inventory:

$$Average\ Inventory = \frac{Beginning\ inventory + Ending\ inventory}{2}$$

A low turnover rate may point to overstocking, obsolescence, or deficiencies in the product line or marketing effort.

a. Upside potential ratio
b. Earnings per share
c. Enterprise Value/Sales
d. Inventory turnover

33. _____ is one of the Accounting Liquidity ratios, a financial ratio. This ratio measures the number of times, on average, the inventory is sold during the period. Its purpose is to measure the liquidity of the inventory.

a. ABC Television Network
b. Inventory turnover ratio
c. AIG
d. Ending inventory

34. _____ is one of the accounting liquidity ratios, a financial ratio. This ratio measures the number of times, on average, receivables (e.g. Accounts Receivable) are collected during the period. A popular variant of the _____ is to convert it into an Average Collection Period in terms of days.

a. Price-to-sales ratio
b. Receivable turnover ratio
c. Capital
d. Shrinkage

Chapter 5. Income Measurement and Profitability Analysis

35. _____ consists of the sale of goods or merchandise from a fixed location, such as a department store, boutique or kiosk in small or individual lots for direct consumption by the purchaser. _____ may include subordinated services, such as delivery. Purchasers may be individuals or businesses.
   - a. BNSF Railway
   - b. BMC Software, Inc.
   - c. 3M Company
   - d. Retailing

36. _____ is the calculated approximation of a result which is usable even if input data may be incomplete or uncertain.

In statistics, see _____ theory, estimator.

In mathematics, approximation or _____ typically means finding upper or lower bounds of a quantity that cannot readily be computed precisely and is also an educated guess.

   - a. ABC Television Network
   - b. AIG
   - c. AMEX
   - d. Estimation

37. _____, net margin, net _____ or net profit ratio all refer to a measure of profitability. It is calculated by finding the net profit as a percentage of the revenue.

$$\text{Net profit margin} = \frac{\text{Net profit (after taxes)}}{\text{Revenue}} \times 100$$

The _____ is mostly used for internal comparison.

   - a. Profit margin
   - b. BNSF Railway
   - c. 3M Company
   - d. BMC Software, Inc.

38. The _____ percentage shows how profitable a company's assets are in generating revenue.

_____ can be computed as:

$$\text{ROA} = \frac{\text{Net Income - Interest Expense - Interest Tax savings}}{\text{Average Total Assets}}$$

This number tells you what the company can do with what it has, i.e. how many dollars of earnings they derive from each dollar of assets they control. Its a useful number for comparing competing companies in the same industry.

   - a. Statutory Liquidity Ratio
   - b. Return on sales
   - c. Capital employed
   - d. Return on assets

39. The _____ is a financial ratio indicating the relative proportion of equity to all used to finance a company's assets. The two components are often taken from the firm's balance sheet or statement of financial position (so-called book value), but the ratio may also be calculated using market values for both, if the company's equities are publicly traded.

Chapter 5. Income Measurement and Profitability Analysis 77

The _____ is especially in Central Europe a very common financial ratio while in the US the debt to _____ is more often used in financial (research) reports.

a. Average accounting return
b. Earnings yield
c. Efficiency ratio
d. Equity ratio

40. _____, in finance and accounting, means stated value or face value. From this comes the expressions at par (at the _____), over par (over _____) and under par (under _____).

_____ is a nominal value of a security which is determined by an issuer company at a minimum price. _____ of an equity (a stock) is a somewhat archaic concept. The _____ of a stock was the share price upon initial offering; the issuing company promised not to issue further shares below _____, so investors could be confident that no one else was receiving a more favorable issue price. This was far more important in unregulated equity markets than in the regulated markets that exist today.

a. Restructuring
b. Creditor
c. Net worth
d. Par value

41. _____, also known as Merck Sharp ' Dohme or MSD outside the USA and Canada, is one of the largest pharmaceutical companies in the world. The headquarters of the company is located in Whitehouse Station, New Jersey, an unincorporated area in Readington Township.

a. Social Security
b. Pension System
c. Procter ' Gamble
d. Merck ' Co., Inc.

42. The U.S. _____ is an independent agency of the United States government which holds primary responsibility for enforcing the federal securities laws and regulating the securities industry, the nation's stock and options exchanges, and other electronic securities markets. The SEC was created by section 4 of the Securities Exchange Act of 1934 (now codified as 15 U.S.C. §Â§ 78d and commonly referred to as the 1934 Act).

a. Securities and Exchange Commission
b. BNSF Railway
c. 3M Company
d. BMC Software, Inc.

43. In accounting, _____ has a very specific meaning. It is an outflow of cash or other valuable assets from a person or company to another person or company. This outflow of cash is generally one side of a trade for products or services that have equal or better current or future value to the buyer than to the seller.

a. Expense
b. AIG
c. AMEX
d. ABC Television Network

44. _____ are the earnings returned on the initial investment amount.

In the US, the Financial Accounting Standards Board (FASB) requires companies' income statements to report _____ for each of the major categories of the income statement: continuing operations, discontinued operations, extraordinary items, and net income.

The _____ formula does not include preferred dividends for categories outside of continued operations and net income.

a. Earnings per share
c. Average accounting return
b. Invested capital
d. Earnings yield

45. _____ is a company's earnings per share (EPS) calculated using fully diluted shares outstanding. _____ indicates a 'worst case' scenario, one in which everyone who could have received stock without purchasing it directly for the full market value did so.

To find _____, basic EPS is calculated for each of the categories on the income statement first. Then each of the dilutive securities are ranked based on their effects, from most dilutive to least dilutive and antidilutive. Then the basic EPS number is diluted one by one by applying each one, skipping any instruments that have an antidilutive effect.

a. Return on assets Du Pont
c. Cash conversion cycle
b. Diluted Earnings Per Share
d. Financial ratio

Chapter 6. Time Value of Money Concepts

1. Simply put, _____ is the value of money figuring in a given amount of interest for a given amount of time. For example 100 dollars of todays money held for a year at 5 percent interest is worth 105 dollars, therefore 100 dollars paid now or 105 dollars paid exactly one year from now is the same amount of payment of money with that given intersest at that given amount of time. This notion dates at least to Martín de Azpilcueta of the School of Salamanca.
   a. Competition law
   b. Collusion
   c. Merck ' Co., Inc.
   d. Time value of money

2. _____ is the concept of adding accumulated interest back to the principal, so that interest is earned on interest from that moment on. The act of declaring interest to be principal is called compounding (i.e., interest is compounded.) A loan, for example, may have its interest compounded every month: in this case, a loan with $100 principal and 1% interest per month would have a balance of $101 at the end of the first month.
   a. Risk management
   b. Trademark
   c. Compound interest
   d. Kanban

3. _____ is a fee paid on borrowed assets. It is the price paid for the use of borrowed money , or, money earned by deposited funds .Assets that are sometimes lent with _____ include money, shares, consumer goods through hire purchase, major assets such as aircraft, and even entire factories in finance lease arrangements. The _____ is calculated upon the value of the assets in the same manner as upon money.
   a. Insolvency
   b. ABC Television Network
   c. AIG
   d. Interest

4. _____ is interest calculated only on the principal amount, or on that portion of the principal amount which remains unpaid.

The amount of _____ is calculated according to the following formula:

$$I_{simp} = (r \cdot B_0) \cdot m$$

where r is the period interest rate , B_0 the initial balance and m the number of time periods elapsed.

   a. BMC Software, Inc.
   b. Line of credit
   c. 3M Company
   d. Simple interest

5. _____ are the most liquid assets found within the asset portion of a company's balance sheet. Cash equivalents are assets that are readily convertible into cash, such as money market holdings, short-term government bonds or Treasury bills, marketable securities and commercial paper. _____ are distinguished from other investments through their short-term existence; they mature within 3 months whereas short-term investments are 12 months or less, and long-term investments are any investments that mature in excess of 12 months.
   a. Debtor
   b. Payback period
   c. Par value
   d. Cash and cash equivalents

6. _____ measures the nominal future sum of money that a given sum of money is 'worth' at a specified time in the future assuming a certain interest rate rate of return; it is the present value multiplied by the accumulation function.

The value does not include corrections for inflation or other factors that affect the true value of money in the future. This is used in time value of money calculations.

Chapter 6. Time Value of Money Concepts

a. 3M Company
b. Present value
c. Net present value
d. Future value

7. An _____ is the price a borrower pays for the use of money they do not own, for instance a small company might borrow from a bank to kick start their business, and the return a lender receives for deferring the use of funds, by lending it to the borrower. _____s are normally expressed as a percentage rate over the period of one year.

_____s targets are also a vital tool of monetary policy and are used to control variables like investment, inflation, and unemployment.

a. Interest rate
b. AMEX
c. ABC Television Network
d. AIG

8. The term _____ is used in finance theory to refer to any terminating stream of fixed payments over a specified period of time. This usage is most commonly seen in academic discussions of finance, usually in connection with the valuation of the stream of payments, taking into account time value of money concepts such as interest rate and future value.

Examples of these are regular deposits to a savings account, monthly home mortgage payments and monthly insurance payments.

a. Annuity
b. Appropriation
c. Intangible
d. Improvement

9. _____ is the balance of the amounts of cash being received and paid by a business during a defined period of time, sometimes tied to a specific project. Measurement of _____ can be used

- to evaluate the state or performance of a business or project.
- to determine problems with liquidity. Being profitable does not necessarily mean being liquid. A company can fail because of a shortage of cash, even while profitable.
- to project rate of returns. The time of _____s into and out of projects are used as inputs to financial models such as internal rate of return, and net present value.
- to examine income or growth of a business when it is believed that accrual accounting concepts do not represent economic realities. Alternately, _____ can be used to 'validate' the net income generated by accrual accounting.

_____ as a generic term may be used differently depending on context, and certain _____ definitions may be adapted by analysts and users for their own uses. Common terms include operating _____ and free _____.

a. Commercial paper
b. Controlling interest
c. Flow-through entity
d. Cash flow

10. In finance, the term _____ describes the amount in cash that returns to the owners of a security. Normally it does not include the price variations, at the difference of the total return. _____ applies to various stated rates of return on stocks (common and preferred, and convertible), fixed income instruments (bonds, notes, bills, strips, zero coupon), and some other investment type insurance products (e.g. annuities.)

Chapter 6. Time Value of Money Concepts

a. Residence trusts
c. Disclosure
b. Pension System
d. Yield

11. _____ is the value on a given date of a future payment or series of future payments, discounted to reflect the time value of money and other factors such as investment risk. _____ calculations are widely used in business and economics to provide a means to compare cash flows at different times on a meaningful 'like to like' basis.

The most commonly applied model of the time value of money is compound interest.

a. Net present value
c. Future value
b. 3M Company
d. Present value

12. A _____ is a computer application that simulates a paper worksheet. It displays multiple cells that together make up a grid consisting of rows and columns, each cell containing either alphanumeric text or numeric values. A _____ cell may alternatively contain a formula that defines how the contents of that cell is to be calculated from the contents of any other cell (or combination of cells) each time any cell is updated.

a. Merck ' Co., Inc.
c. Mutual fund
b. Linear regression
d. Spreadsheet

13. In mathematics _____s are numbers or other things that get multiplied. In particular, see:

- Factorization, the decomposition of an object into a product of other objects
- Integer factorization, the process of breaking down a composite number into smaller non-trivial divisors
- A coefficient
- A divisor of a particular number, or of an element of a monoid
- A von Neumann algebra with a trivial center

In statistics

- _____ analysis is the study of how _____s or certain variables affect variables.

In technology:

- Human _____s, a profession that focuses on how people interact with products, tools, or procedures
- 'Functionality, Application domain, Conditions, Technology, Objects and Responsibility;', In object-oriented programming

In computer science and information technology:

- Authentication _____, a piece of information used to verify a person's identity for security purposes
- _____, a Unix command for numbers factorization
- _____ (programming language), an experimental Forth-like programming language

In television:

- The O'Reilly _____, an American talk show hosted by Bill O'Reilly on Fox News.
- The Krypton _____, a British game show hosted by Gordon Burns, formally on ITV. Also had an American version.

a. Merck ' Co., Inc.
b. The Goodyear Tire ' Rubber Company
c. Valuation
d. Factor

14. _____, in accrual accounting, is any account where the asset or liability is not realized until a future date (accounting period), e.g. annuities, charges, taxes, income, etc. The _____ item may be carried, dependent on type of deferral, as either an asset or liability.

a. Cash basis accounting
b. Deferred
c. Pro forma
d. Payroll

15. _____ is an accounting concept, meaning a future tax liability or asset, resulting from temporary differences between book (accounting) value of assets and liabilities and their tax value, or timing differences between the recognition of gains and losses in financial statements and their recognition in a tax computation.

Temporary differences are differences between the carrying amount of an asset or liability recognised in the balance sheet and the amount attributed to that asset or liability for tax purposes (the tax base.)

a. Deferred tax
b. Tax refund
c. Deficit
d. Federal tax revenue by state

16. _____ are defined as identifiable non-monetary assets that cannot be seen, touched or physically measured, which are created through time and/or effort and that are identifiable as a separate asset. There are two primary forms of intangibles - legal intangibles (such as trade secrets (e.g., customer lists), copyrights, patents, trademarks, and goodwill) and competitive intangibles (such as knowledge activities (know-how, knowledge), collaboration activities, leverage activities, and structural activities.) Legal intangibles are known under the generic term intellectual property and generate legal property rights defensible in a court of law.

a. Overhead
b. ABC Television Network
c. AIG
d. Intangible assets

17. A _____ is a contract conferring a right on one person to possess property belonging to another person (called a landlord or lessor) to the exclusion of the owner landlord. It is a rental agreement between landlord and tenant. The relationship between the tenant and the landlord is called a tenancy, and the right to possession by the tenant is sometimes called a leasehold interest.

a. Robinson-Patman Act
b. Model Code of Professional Responsibility
c. Federal Sentencing Guidelines
d. Lease

18. In business and accounting, _____ are everything of value that is owned by a person or company. It is a claim on the property your income of a borrower. The balance sheet of a firm records the monetary value of the _____ owned by the firm.

Chapter 6. Time Value of Money Concepts

    a. Assets

    b. Accounts receivable

    c. Accrual basis accounting

    d. Earnings before interest, taxes, depreciation and amortization

19. In financial accounting, a _____ is defined as an obligation of an entity arising from past transactions or events, the settlement of which may result in the transfer or use of assets, provision of services or other yielding of economic benefits in the future.

    a. Corporate governance

    b. Vested

    c. False Claims Act

    d. Liability

20. In economic models, the _____ time frame assumes no fixed factors of production. Firms can enter or leave the marketplace, and the cost (and availability) of land, labor, raw materials, and capital goods can be assumed to vary. In contrast, in the short-run time frame, certain factors are assumed to be fixed, because there is not sufficient time for them to change.

    a. 3M Company

    b. Short-run

    c. BMC Software, Inc.

    d. Long-run

21. In finance, _____ is the process of estimating the potential market value of a financial asset or liability. They can be done on assets (for example, investments in marketable securities such as stocks, options, business enterprises, or intangible assets such as patents and trademarks) or on liabilities (e.g., Bonds issued by a company.) A _____ is required in many contexts including investment analysis, capital budgeting, merger and acquisition transactions, financial reporting, taxable events to determine the proper tax liability, and in litigation.

    a. Vyborg Appeal

    b. Disclosure

    c. Valuation

    d. Daybook

22. An _____ is a derivative in which one party exchanges a stream of interest payments for another party's stream of cash flows. They can be used by hedgers to manage their fixed or floating assets and liabilities. They can also be used by speculators to replicate unfunded bond exposures to profit from changes in interest rates.

    a. AMEX

    b. AIG

    c. ABC Television Network

    d. Interest rate swap

23. A _____ is the transfer of wealth from one party (such as a person or company) to another. A _____ is usually made in exchange for the provision of goods, services or both, or to fulfill a legal obligation.

The simplest and oldest form of _____ is barter, the exchange of one good or service for another.

    a. Payee

    b. 3M Company

    c. Payment

    d. BMC Software, Inc.

24. In finance, a _____ is a derivative in which two counterparties agree to exchange one stream of cash flow against another stream. These streams are called the legs of the _____.

The cash flows are calculated over a notional principal amount, which is usually not exchanged between counterparties.

Chapter 6. Time Value of Money Concepts

a. Controlled Foreign Corporations
b. Total-factor productivity
c. Swap
d. Department of the Treasury

25. Discounting is a financial mechanism in which a debtor obtains the right to delay payments to a creditor, for a defined period of time, in exchange for a charge or fee. Essentially, the party that owes money in the present purchases the right to delay the payment until some future date. The _____, or charge, is simply the difference between the original amount owed in the present and the amount that has to be paid in the future to settle the debt.

a. Discount
b. Discount factor
c. Discounting
d. Risk aversion

26. A _____ is a bond bought at a price lower than its face value, with the face value repaid at the time of maturity. It does not make periodic interest payments, or so-called 'coupons,' hence the term _____. Investors earn return from the compounded interest all paid at maturity plus the difference between the discounted price of the bond and its par value.

a. Callable bond
b. Municipal bond
c. Zero-coupon bond
d. Premium bond

27. _____s are cash, evidence of an ownership interest in an entity or deliver, cash or another _____.

_____s can be categorized by form depending on whether they are cash instruments or derivative instruments:

- Cash instruments are _____s whose value is determined directly by markets. They can be divided into securities, which are readily transferable, and other cash instruments such as loans and deposits, where both borrower and lender have to agree on a transfer.
- Derivative instruments are _____s which derive their value from the value and characteristics of one or more underlying assets. They can be divided into exchange-traded derivatives and over-the-counter (OTC) derivatives.

Alternatively, _____s can be categorized by 'asset class' depending on whether they are equity based (reflecting ownership of the issuing entity) or debt based (reflecting a loan the investor has made to the issuing entity.) If it is debt, it can be further categorised into short term (less than one year) or long term.

Foreign Exchange instruments and transactions are neither debt nor equity based and belong in their own category.

a. Mark-to-market
b. Market price
c. Financial instruments
d. Financial instrument

28. _____ are cash, evidence of an ownership interest in an entity, or a contractual right to receive, or deliver, cash or another financial instrument.

Chapter 6. Time Value of Money Concepts 85

_____ can be categorized by form depending on whether they are cash instruments or derivative instruments:

- Cash instruments are _____ whose value is determined directly by markets. They can be divided into securities, which are readily transferable, and other cash instruments such as loans and deposits, where both borrower and lender have to agree on a transfer.
- Derivative instruments are _____ which derive their value from the value and characteristics of one or more underlying assets. They can be divided into exchange-traded derivatives and over-the-counter (OTC) derivatives.

Alternatively, _____ can be categorized by 'asset class' depending on whether they are equity based (reflecting ownership of the issuing entity) or debt based (reflecting a loan the investor has made to the issuing entity.) If it is debt, it can be further categorised into short term (less than one year) or long term.

Foreign Exchange instruments and transactions are neither debt nor equity based and belong in their own category.

a. Market liquidity
c. Spot rate
b. Transfer agent
d. Financial instruments

29. A _____ is any one of a variety of different systems, institutions, procedures, social relations and infrastructures whereby persons trade, and goods and services are exchanged, forming part of the economy. It is an arrangement that allows buyers and sellers to exchange things. _____s vary in size, range, geographic scale, location, types and variety of human communities, as well as the types of goods and services traded.

a. Market Failure
c. Recession
b. Market
d. Perfect competition

30. A _____ is like a lottery bond issued by the United Kingdom government's National Savings and Investments scheme. The government promises to buy back the bond, on request, for its original price.

_____s were introduced by the government in 1956, with the aim of encouraging saving and controlling inflation, with the first bonds going on sale on 1 November of that year.

a. Premium bond
c. Callable bond
b. Revenue bonds
d. Zero-coupon bond

31. In finance, a _____ is a debt security, in which the authorized issuer owes the holders a debt and, depending on the terms of the _____, is obliged to pay interest (the coupon) and/or to repay the principal at a later date, termed maturity. It is a formal contract to repay borrowed money with interest at fixed intervals.

Thus a _____ is like a loan: the issuer is the borrower, the _____ holder is the lender, and the coupon is the interest.

Chapter 6. Time Value of Money Concepts

a. Bond
c. Coupon rate
b. Revenue bonds
d. Zero-coupon bond

32. A _____ is a time deposit, a financial product commonly offered to consumers by banks, thrift institutions, and credit unions.

They are similar to savings accounts in that they are insured and thus virtually risk-free; they are 'money in the bank' (_____s are insured by the FDIC for banks or by the NCUA for credit unions.) They are different from savings accounts in that the _____ has a specific, fixed term (often three months, six months, or one to five years), and, usually, a fixed interest rate.

a. Certificate of deposit
c. Transactional account
b. Reserve requirement
d. Prime rate

33. The _____ is an interest rate a central bank charges depository institutions that borrow reserves from it.

The term _____ has two meanings:

- the same as interest rate; the term 'discount' does not refer to the meaning of the word, but to the purpose of using the quantity, such as computations of present value, e.g. net present value or discounted cash flow

- the annual effective _____, which is the annual interest divided by the capital including that interest; this rate is lower than the interest rate; it corresponds to using the value after a year as the nominal value, and seeing the initial value as the nominal value minus a discount; it is used for Treasury Bills and similar financial instruments

The annual effective _____ is the annual interest divided by the capital including that interest, which is the interest rate divided by 100% plus the interest rate. It is the annual discount factor to be applied to the future cash flow, to find the discount, subtracted from a future value to find the value one year earlier.

For example, suppose there is a government bond that sells for $95 and pays $100 in a year's time.

a. Process time
c. Discount rate
b. Convertible bond
d. Municipal bond

Chapter 7. Cash and Receivables

1. In financial accounting and finance, _____ is the portion of receivables that can no longer be collected, typically from accounts receivable or loans. _____ in accounting is considered an expense.

There are two methods to account for _____:

   1. Direct write off method (Non - GAAP)

A receivable which is not considered collectible is charged directly to the income statement.

   1. Allowance method (GAAP)

An estimate is made at the end of each fiscal year of the amount of _____. This is then accumulated in a provision which is then used to reduce specific receivable accounts as and when necessary.

   a. Total Expense Ratio
   c. 3M Company
   b. Tax expense
   d. Bad debt

2. _____ is that which is owed; usually referencing assets owed, but the term can also cover moral obligations and other interactions not requiring money. In the case of assets, _____ is a means of using future purchasing power in the present before a summation has been earned. Some companies and corporations use _____ as a part of their overall corporate finance strategy.
   a. Loan
   c. Lender
   b. Debt
   d. Debenture

3. _____ are the most liquid assets found within the asset portion of a company's balance sheet. Cash equivalents are assets that are readily convertible into cash, such as money market holdings, short-term government bonds or Treasury bills, marketable securities and commercial paper. _____ are distinguished from other investments through their short-term existence; they mature within 3 months whereas short-term investments are 12 months or less, and long-term investments are any investments that mature in excess of 12 months.
   a. Debtor
   c. Par value
   b. Payback period
   d. Cash and cash equivalents

4. _____ means the giving out of information, either voluntarily or to be in compliance with legal regulations or workplace rules.

- In Computer security, full _____ means disclosing full information about vulnerabilities.
- In computing, _____ widget
- Journalism, full _____ refers to disclosing the interests of the writer which may bear on the subject being written about, for example, if the writer has worked with an interview subject in the past.

- In law:
    - The law of England and Wales, _____ refers to a process that may form part of legal proceedings, whereby parties inform to other parties the existence of any relevant documents that are, or have been, in their control. This compares with the process known as discovery in the course of legal proceedings in the United States.
    - In U.S. civil procedure (litigation rules for civil cases), _____ is a stage prior to trial. In civil cases, each party must disclose to the opposing party the following: names of witnesses which it may use to support its side, copies of documents (or mere description of these documents) in its control which it may use to support its side, computation of damages claimed, and certain insurance information. _____ is related to, but technically prior to, the discovery stage.
    - In Company law (known as 'corporate law' in the United States), _____ refers to giving out information about public or limited companies or their officers, which might be kept secret if the company was a private company or a partnership.

- In real property transactions, _____ refers to providing to a buyer information known to the seller or broker/agent concerning the condition or other aspects of real property that would affect the property's value or desirability. These rules regarding what information must be disclosed, and whether the information must be disclosed even if a buyer does not ask, vary from one jurisdiction to the next.

a. Tax harmonisation
c. Trailing
b. Controlled Foreign Corporations
d. Disclosure

5. An _____ is a term used in behavioral economics to describe those types of behaviors that impose costs on a person in the long-run that are not taken into account when making decisions in the present. Classical Economics discourages government from creating legislation that targets internalities, because it is assumed that the consumer takes these personal costs into account when paying for the good that causes the _____. For example, cigarettes should be taxed because of the negative consumption externalities that they impose, such as second-hand smoke, not because the smoker harms him or herself by smoking.

a. Inventory turnover ratio
c. Internality
b. Authorised capital
d. Operating budget

6. In accounting and organizational theory, _____ is defined as a process effected by an organization's structure, work and authority flows, people and management information systems, designed to help the organization accomplish specific goals or objectives. It is a means by which an organization's resources are directed, monitored, and measured. It plays an important role in preventing and detecting fraud and protecting the organization's resources, both physical (e.g., machinery and property) and intangible (e.g., reputation or intellectual property such as trademarks).

a. Auditor independence
b. Audit committee
c. Audit risk
d. Internal control

7. The _____ of 2002 (Pub.L. 107-204, 116 Stat. 745, enacted July 30, 2002), also known as the Public Company Accounting Reform and Investor Protection Act of 2002, is a United States federal law enacted on July 30, 2002 in response to a number of major corporate and accounting scandals including those affecting Enron, Tyco International, Adelphia, Peregrine Systems and WorldCom. The legislation establishes new or enhanced standards for all U.S. public company boards, management, and public accounting firms. It does not apply to privately held companies.
   a. FCPA
   b. Fair Labor Standards Act
   c. Lease
   d. Sarbanes-Oxley Act

8. A _____ is a fund established by a government agency or business for the purpose of reducing debt.

The _____ was first used in Great Britain in the 18th century to reduce national debt. While used by Robert Walpole in 1716 and effectively in the 1720s and early 1730s, it originated in the commercial tax syndicates of the Italian peninsula of the 14th century to retire redeemable public debt of those cities.

   a. Treasury company
   b. Sinking fund
   c. Payback period
   d. Segregated portfolio company

9. A _____ is a fungible, negotiable instrument representing financial value. they are broadly categorized into debt securities (such as banknotes, bonds and debentures), and equity securities; e.g., common stocks. The company or other entity issuing the _____ is called the issuer.
   a. BMC Software, Inc.
   b. 3M Company
   c. Tracking stock
   d. Security

10. In finance, the _____ or quick ratio or liquid ratio measures the ability of a company to use its near cash or quick assets to immediately extinguish or retire its current liabilities. Quick assets include those current assets that presumably can be quickly converted to cash at close to their book values.

$$\text{Quick (Acid Test) Ratio} = \frac{\text{Cash} + \text{Marketable Securities} + \text{Accounts Receivables}}{\text{Current Liabilities}}$$

Generally, the acid test ratio should be 1:1 or better, however this varies widely by industry.

   a. Inventory turnover
   b. Invested capital
   c. Acid-test
   d. Earnings per share

11. The _____ is a financial ratio that measures whether or not a firm has enough resources to pay its debts over the next 12 months. It compares a firm's current assets to its current liabilities. It is expressed as follows:

$$\text{Current ratio} = \frac{\text{Current Assets}}{\text{Current Liabilities}}$$

For example, if WXY Company's current assets are $50,000,000 and its current liabilities are $40,000,000, then its _____ would be $50,000,000 divided by $40,000,000, which equals 1.25.

    a. Return on capital
    b. Net Interest Income
    c. Times interest earned
    d. Current ratio

12. A _____ is a contract conferring a right on one person to possess property belonging to another person (called a landlord or lessor) to the exclusion of the owner landlord. It is a rental agreement between landlord and tenant. The relationship between the tenant and the landlord is called a tenancy, and the right to possession by the tenant is sometimes called a leasehold interest.
    a. Model Code of Professional Responsibility
    b. Robinson-Patman Act
    c. Federal Sentencing Guidelines
    d. Lease

13. _____ is a business, economics or investment term that refers to an asset's ability to be easily converted through an act of buying or selling without causing a significant movement in the price and with minimum loss of value. Money, or cash on hand, is the most liquid asset. An act of exchange of a less liquid asset with a more liquid asset is called liquidation.
    a. Market liquidity
    b. Transfer agent
    c. Spot rate
    d. Financial instruments

14. In business and accounting, _____ are everything of value that is owned by a person or company. It is a claim on the property your income of a borrower. The balance sheet of a firm records the monetary value of the _____ owned by the firm.
    a. Earnings before interest, taxes, depreciation and amortization
    b. Accrual basis accounting
    c. Accounts receivable
    d. Assets

15. _____ is one of a series of accounting transactions dealing with the billing of customers who owe money to a person, company or organization for goods and services that have been provided to the customer. In most business entities this is typically done by generating an invoice and mailing or electronically delivering it to the customer, who in turn must pay it within an established timeframe called credit or payment terms.

An example of a common payment term is Net 30, meaning payment is due in the amount of the invoice 30 days from the date of invoice.

    a. Accrued revenue
    b. Accounts receivable
    c. Accrual
    d. Adjusting entries

16. Discounting is a financial mechanism in which a debtor obtains the right to delay payments to a creditor, for a defined period of time, in exchange for a charge or fee. Essentially, the party that owes money in the present purchases the right to delay the payment until some future date. The _____, or charge, is simply the difference between the original amount owed in the present and the amount that has to be paid in the future to settle the debt.
    a. Discounting
    b. Risk aversion
    c. Discount factor
    d. Discount

Chapter 7. Cash and Receivables

17. _____ represents claims for which formal instruments of credit are issued as evidence of debt, such as a promissory note. The credit instrument normally requires the debtor to pay interest and extends for time periods of 60-90 days or longer.
    a. Moving average
    b. Restricted stock
    c. Public offering
    d. Notes receivable

18. _____ is generally understood in financial circles as the point at which revenue is recognized, typically through a transaction which involves the exchange of an asset, product, or service for cash or its equivalents.

This approach gives the accounting division a strictly objective basis for changing the books. For example, a homeowner may believe that his house has grown in value during a strong market, or fallen in value during a weak market, but until the house is actually sold for a specific price to a specific buyer, the change in value can only be estimated and is considered unrealized.

   a. Valuation
   b. Total-factor productivity
   c. Merck ' Co., Inc.
   d. Realization

19. In finance, _____ is the process of estimating the potential market value of a financial asset or liability. They can be done on assets (for example, investments in marketable securities such as stocks, options, business enterprises, or intangible assets such as patents and trademarks) or on liabilities (e.g., Bonds issued by a company.) A _____ is required in many contexts including investment analysis, capital budgeting, merger and acquisition transactions, financial reporting, taxable events to determine the proper tax liability, and in litigation.
    a. Disclosure
    b. Vyborg Appeal
    c. Daybook
    d. Valuation

20. _____ are reductions to a basic price of goods or services. They can occur anywhere in the distribution channel, modifying either the manufacturer's list price (determined by the manufacturer and often printed on the package), the retail price (set by the retailer and often attached to the product with a sticker), or the list price (which is quoted to a potential buyer, usually in written form.) The market price (also called effective price) is the amount actually paid.
    a. Pricing
    b. Resale price maintenance
    c. Target costing
    d. Discounts and allowances

21. A _____ is the pinnacle activity involved in selling products or services in return for money or other compensation. It is an act of completion of a commercial activity.

A _____ is completed by the seller, the owner of the goods.

   a. High yield stock
   b. Tertiary sector of economy
   c. Maturity
   d. Sale

22. _____ are formal bookkeeping and accounting terms. They are the most fundamental concepts in accounting, representing the two records that one party in a transaction makes on its records, transferring a money balance from one account to another, one representing a reduction of liability or increase in asset, and the other representing a balancing increase in liability or reduction of asset.

Debits and credits are a system of notation used in accounting to keep track of money movements (transactions) into and out of an account.

   a. Controlling account
   b. Cookie jar accounting
   c. Bookkeeping
   d. Debit and credit

23. _____ methods are means of managing inventory and financial matters involving the money a company ties up within inventory of produced goods, raw materials, parts, components, or feed stocks. FIFO stands for first-in, first-out, meaning that the oldest inventory items are recorded as sold first. LIFO stands for last-in, first-out, meaning that the most recently purchased items are recorded as sold first.
   a. Finished good
   b. Reorder point
   c. 3M Company
   d. FIFO and LIFO accounting

24. _____ principle is a cornerstone of accrual accounting together with matching principle. They both determine the accounting period, in which revenues and expenses are recognized. According to the principle, revenues are recognized when they are (1) realized or realizable, and are (2) earned (usually when goods are transferred or services rendered), no matter when cash is received.
   a. 3M Company
   b. Net realizable value
   c. BMC Software, Inc.
   d. Revenue recognition

25. An _____ allows a company to provide a monetary value for items that make up their inventory. Inventories are usually the largest current asset of a business, and proper measurement of them is necessary to assure accurate financial statements. If inventory is not properly measured, expenses and revenues cannot be properly matched and a company could make poor business decisions.
   a. ABC Television Network
   b. AIG
   c. Inventory valuation
   d. AMEX

26. _____ is an approach to valuing and reporting inventory. Normally ending inventory is stated at historical cost (what was paid to obtain it) but there are times when the original cost of the ending inventory is greater than the cost of replacement thus the inventory has lost value. If the inventory has decreased in value below historical cost then its carrying value is reduced and reported on the balance sheet.
   a. Bankruptcy prediction
   b. Certified Practising Accountant
   c. Remittance advice
   d. Lower of cost or market

27. In economics, business, retail, and accounting, a _____ is the value of money that has been used up to produce something, and hence is not available for use anymore. In economics, a _____ is an alternative that is given up as a result of a decision. In business, the _____ may be one of acquisition, in which case the amount of money expended to acquire it is counted as _____.
   a. Prime cost
   b. Cost allocation
   c. Cost of quality
   d. Cost

28. A _____ is any one of a variety of different systems, institutions, procedures, social relations and infrastructures whereby persons trade, and goods and services are exchanged, forming part of the economy. It is an arrangement that allows buyers and sellers to exchange things. _____s vary in size, range, geographic scale, location, types and variety of human communities, as well as the types of goods and services traded.

a. Recession
b. Market
c. Perfect competition
d. Market Failure

29. _____ is a company's financial statement that indicates how the revenue is transformed into the net income The purpose of the _____ is to show managers and investors whether the company made or lost money during the period being reported.

The important thing to remember about an _____ is that it represents a period of time.

a. AIG
b. ABC Television Network
c. Income statement
d. AMEX

30. In accounting, _____ has a very specific meaning. It is an outflow of cash or other valuable assets from a person or company to another person or company. This outflow of cash is generally one side of a trade for products or services that have equal or better current or future value to the buyer than to the seller.

a. AIG
b. Expense
c. AMEX
d. ABC Television Network

31. In financial accounting, a _____ or statement of financial position is a summary of a person's or organization's balances. Assets, liabilities and ownership equity are listed as of a specific date, such as the end of its financial year. A _____ is often described as a snapshot of a company's financial condition.

a. Financial statements
b. Statement of retained earnings
c. 3M Company
d. Balance sheet

32. _____, in accrual accounting, is any account where the asset or liability is not realized until a future date (accounting period), e.g. annuities, charges, taxes, income, etc. The _____ item may be carried, dependent on type of deferral, as either an asset or liability.

a. Pro forma
b. Cash basis accounting
c. Payroll
d. Deferred

33. _____ is an accounting concept, meaning a future tax liability or asset, resulting from temporary differences between book (accounting) value of assets and liabilities and their tax value, or timing differences between the recognition of gains and losses in financial statements and their recognition in a tax computation.

Temporary differences are differences between the carrying amount of an asset or liability recognised in the balance sheet and the amount attributed to that asset or liability for tax purposes (the tax base.)

a. Tax refund
b. Federal tax revenue by state
c. Deficit
d. Deferred tax

34. In financial accounting, a _____ is defined as an obligation of an entity arising from past transactions or events, the settlement of which may result in the transfer or use of assets, provision of services or other yielding of economic benefits in the future.

a. Corporate governance
b. Liability
c. Vested
d. False Claims Act

35. The term _____ describes a reduction in recognized value. In accounting terminology, it refers to recognition of the reduced or zero value of an asset. In income tax statements, it refers to a reduction of taxable income as recognition of certain expenses required to produce the income.

    a. Salvage value
    c. Payroll
    b. Current asset
    d. Write-off

36. In accounting, a _____ is an asset on the balance sheet which is expected to be sold or otherwise used up in the near future, usually within one year, or one business cycle - whichever is longer. Typical _____s include cash, cash equivalents, accounts receivable, inventory, the portion of prepaid accounts which will be used within a year, and short-term investments.

On the balance sheet, assets will typically be classified into _____s and long-term assets.

    a. General ledger
    c. Deferred
    b. Pro forma
    d. Current asset

37. In accounting, _____ are considered liabilities of the business that are to be settled in cash within the fiscal year or the operating cycle, whichever period is longer.

For example accounts payable for goods, services or supplies that were purchased for use in the operation of the business and payable within a normal period of time would be _____.

Bonds, mortgages and loans that are payable over a term exceeding one year would be fixed liabilities.

    a. Current liabilities
    c. Payroll
    b. Treasury stock
    d. Closing entries

38. _____ is the calculated approximation of a result which is usable even if input data may be incomplete or uncertain.

In statistics, see _____ theory, estimator.

In mathematics, approximation or _____ typically means finding upper or lower bounds of a quantity that cannot readily be computed precisely and is also an educated guess.

    a. ABC Television Network
    c. AIG
    b. AMEX
    d. Estimation

39. In economics, the concept of the _____ refers to the decision-making time frame of a firm in which at least one factor of production is fixed. Costs which are fixed in the _____ have no impact on a firms decisions. For example a firm can raise output by increasing the amount of labour through overtime.

    a. 3M Company
    c. BMC Software, Inc.
    b. Long-run
    d. Short-run

40. _____ is a fee paid on borrowed assets. It is the price paid for the use of borrowed money, or, money earned by deposited funds. Assets that are sometimes lent with _____ include money, shares, consumer goods through hire purchase, major assets such as aircraft, and even entire factories in finance lease arrangements. The _____ is calculated upon the value of the assets in the same manner as upon money.

a. AIG
b. Insolvency
c. Interest
d. ABC Television Network

41. An _____ is the price a borrower pays for the use of money they do not own, for instance a small company might borrow from a bank to kick start their business, and the return a lender receives for deferring the use of funds, by lending it to the borrower. _____s are normally expressed as a percentage rate over the period of one year.

_____s targets are also a vital tool of monetary policy and are used to control variables like investment, inflation, and unemployment.

a. AMEX
b. Interest rate
c. ABC Television Network
d. AIG

42. _____ is the process of increasing, or accounting for, an amount over a period of time. Particular instances of the term include:

- _____, the allocation of a lump sum amount to different time periods, particularly for loans and other forms of finance, including related interest or other finance charges.
  - _____ schedule, a table detailing each periodic payment on a loan (typically a mortgage), as generated by an _____ calculator.
  - Negative _____, an _____ schedule where the loan amount actually increases through not paying the full interest
- Amortized analysis, analyzing the execution cost of algorithms over a sequence of operations.
- _____ of capital expenditures of certain assets under accounting rules, particularly intangible assets, in a manner analogous to depreciation.
- _____

a. EBIT
b. Annuity
c. Intangible
d. Amortization

43. In economic models, the _____ time frame assumes no fixed factors of production. Firms can enter or leave the marketplace, and the cost (and availability) of land, labor, raw materials, and capital goods can be assumed to vary. In contrast, in the short-run time frame, certain factors are assumed to be fixed, because there is not sufficient time for them to change.

a. 3M Company
b. Short-run
c. Long-run
d. BMC Software, Inc.

44. A _____ is a type of debt Like all debt instruments, a _____ entails the redistribution of financial assets over time, between the lender and the borrower.

a. Loan
b. Loan to value
c. Lender
d. Debenture

Chapter 7. Cash and Receivables

45. _____ is a process by which a firm can obtain the use of a certain fixed assets for which it must pay a series of contractual, periodic, tax deductable payments. The lessee is the receiver of the services or the assets under the lease contract and the lessor is the owner of the assets. The relationship between the tenant and the landlord is called a tenancy, and can be for a fixed or an indefinite period of time (called the term of the lease.)
   a. Federal Sentencing Guidelines
   b. Resource Conservation and Recovery Act
   c. Property
   d. Leasing

46. In law, _____ refers to the process by which a company (or part of a company) is brought to an end, and the assets and property of the company redistributed. _____ can also be referred to as winding-up or dissolution, although dissolution technically refers to the last stage of _____. The process of _____ also arises when customs, an authority or agency in a country responsible for collecting and safeguarding customs duties, determines the final computation or ascertainment of the duties or drawback accruing on an entry.
   a. BMC Software, Inc.
   b. Bankruptcy protection
   c. 3M Company
   d. Liquidation

47. In economics, _____ or _____ goods or real _____ refers to factors of production used to create goods or services that are not themselves significantly consumed (though they may depreciate) in the production process. _____ goods may be acquired with money or financial _____. In finance and accounting, _____ generally refers to financial wealth, especially that used to start or maintain a business.
   a. Screening
   b. Disclosure
   c. Vyborg Appeal
   d. Capital

48. In mathematics _____ s are numbers or other things that get multiplied. In particular, see:

   - Factorization, the decomposition of an object into a product of other objects
   - Integer factorization, the process of breaking down a composite number into smaller non-trivial divisors
   - A coefficient
   - A divisor of a particular number, or of an element of a monoid
   - A von Neumann algebra with a trivial center

In statistics

   - _____ analysis is the study of how _____ s or certain variables affect variables.

In technology:

   - Human _____ s, a profession that focuses on how people interact with products, tools, or procedures
   - 'Functionality, Application domain, Conditions, Technology, Objects and Responsibility;', In object-oriented programming

In computer science and information technology:

   - Authentication _____, a piece of information used to verify a person's identity for security purposes
   - _____, a Unix command for numbers factorization
   - _____ (programming language), an experimental Forth-like programming language

Chapter 7. Cash and Receivables

In television:

- The O'Reilly _____, an American talk show hosted by Bill O'Reilly on Fox News.
- The Krypton _____, a British game show hosted by Gordon Burns, formally on ITV. Also had an American version.

a. The Goodyear Tire ' Rubber Company
b. Merck ' Co., Inc.
c. Factor
d. Valuation

49. _____ is a structured finance process, which involves pooling and repackaging of cash flow producing financial assets into securities that are then sold to investors. The name '_____' is derived from the fact that the form of financial instruments used to obtain funds from the investors are securities.

As a portfolio risk backed by amortizing cash flows - and unlike general corporate debt - the credit quality of securitized debt is non-stationary due to changes in volatility that are time- and structure-dependent.

a. Market value
b. Cross-border leasing
c. Debtor
d. Securitization

50. _____ is a financial mechanism in which a debtor obtains the right to delay payments to a creditor, for a defined period of time, in exchange for a charge or fee. Essentially, the party that owes money in the present purchases the right to delay the payment until some future date. The discount, or charge, is simply the difference between the original amount owed in the present and the amount that has to be paid in the future to settle the debt.

a. Discount factor
b. Risk aversion
c. Risk adjusted return on capital
d. Discounting

51. _____ is a specific term used in companies' financial reporting from the company-whole point of view. Because that use excludes the effects of changing ownership interest, an economic measure of _____ is necessary for financial analysis from the shareholders' point of view

_____ is defined by the Financial Accounting Standards Board, or FASB, as 'the change in equity [net assets] of a business enterprise during a period from transactions and other events and circumstances from nonowner sources. It includes all changes in equity during a period except those resulting from investments by owners and distributions to owners.'

_____ is the sum of net income and other items that must bypass the income statement because they have not been realized, including items like an unrealized holding gain or loss from available for sale securities and foreign currency translation gains or losses

a. Comprehensive income
b. BMC Software, Inc.
c. BNSF Railway
d. 3M Company

Chapter 7. Cash and Receivables

52. The term _____ is a term applied to practices that are perfunctory, or seek to satisfy the minimum requirements or to conform to a convention or doctrine. It has different meanings in different fields.

In accounting, _____ earnings are those earnings of companies in addition to actual earnings calculated under the Generally Accepted Accounting Principles (GAAP) in their quarterly and yearly financial reports.

- a. Treasury stock
- b. Payroll
- c. Pro forma
- d. Bottom line

53. _____ is a form of corporation equity ownership represented in the securities. It is a stock whose dividends are based on market fluctuations. It is dangerous in comparison to preferred shares and some other investment options, in that in the event of bankruptcy, _____ investors receive their funds after preferred stock holders, bondholders, creditors, etc. On the other hand, common shares on average perform better than preferred shares or bonds over time.

- a. Stock split
- b. Growth investing
- c. 3M Company
- d. Common stock

54. _____ is one of the accounting liquidity ratios, a financial ratio. This ratio measures the number of times, on average, receivables (e.g. Accounts Receivable) are collected during the period. A popular variant of the _____ is to convert it into an Average Collection Period in terms of days.

- a. Capital
- b. Shrinkage
- c. Price-to-sales ratio
- d. Receivable turnover ratio

55. _____ of something is, in finance, the adding together of interest or different investments over a period of time such as atoms (1 - the act or process of accruing; 2 - the amount that accrues.) It holds specific meanings in accounting and payroll.

_____, in accounting, describes the accounting method known as _____ basis, whereby revenues and expenses are recognized when they are accrued, i.e. accumulated (earned or incurred), regardless when the actual cash is received or paid out.

- a. Accounts receivable
- b. Assets
- c. Accrual
- d. Earnings before interest, taxes, depreciation and amortization

56. _____ are standards and interpretations adopted by the International Accounting Standards Board (IASB.)

Many of the standards forming part of _____ are known by the older name of International Accounting Standards (IAS.) IAS were issued between 1973 and 2001 by the board of the International Accounting Standards Committee (IASC.)

- a. ABC Television Network
- b. International Financial Reporting Standards
- c. Out-of-pocket
- d. AIG

Chapter 7. Cash and Receivables

57. The U.S. _____ is an independent agency of the United States government which holds primary responsibility for enforcing the federal securities laws and regulating the securities industry, the nation's stock and options exchanges, and other electronic securities markets. The SEC was created by section 4 of the Securities Exchange Act of 1934 (now codified as 15 U.S.C. §Â§ 78d and commonly referred to as the 1934 Act.)
   a. BNSF Railway
   b. BMC Software, Inc.
   c. 3M Company
   d. Securities and Exchange Commission

58. _____ is the process of matching and comparing figures from accounting records against those presented on a bank statement. Less any items which have no relation to the bank statement, the balance of the accounting ledger should reconcile (match) to the balance of the bank statement.

_____ allows companies or individuals to compare their account records to the bank's records of their account balance in order to uncover any possible discrepancies.

   a. Credit memo
   b. Lower of Cost or Market
   c. Bankruptcy prediction
   d. Bank reconciliation

59. _____ is equal to the income that a firm has after subtracting costs and expenses from the total revenue. _____ can be distributed among holders of common stock as a dividend or held by the firm as retained earnings.

The items deducted will typically include tax expense, financing expense (interest expense), and minority interest. Likewise, preferred stock dividends will be subtracted too, though they are not an expense.

   a. Matching principle
   b. Generally accepted accounting principles
   c. Long-term liabilities
   d. Net income

60. In finance, an _____ is a contract between a buyer and a seller that gives the buyer the right--but not the obligation-- to buy or to sell a particular asset (the underlying asset) at a later time at an agreed price. In return for granting the _____, the seller collects a payment (the premium) from the buyer. A call _____ gives the buyer the right to buy the underlying asset; a put _____ gives the buyer of the _____ the right to sell the underlying asset.
   a. AIG
   b. AMEX
   c. ABC Television Network
   d. Option

61. A _____ has several related meanings:

   - a daily record of events or business; a private _____ is usually referred to as a diary.
   - a newspaper or other periodical, in the literal sense of one published each day;
   - many publications issued at stated intervals, such as magazines, or scholarly academic _____s, or the record of the transactions of a society, are often called _____s. Although _____ is sometimes used, erroneously, as a synonym for 'magazine,' in academic use, a _____ refers to a serious, scholarly publication, most often peer-reviewed. A non-scholarly magazine written for an educated audience about an industry or an area of professional activity is usually called a professional magazine.

The word 'journalist' for one whose business is writing for the public press has been in use since the end of the 17th century.

Open access _____s are scholarly _____s that are available to the reader without financial or other barrier other than access to the internet itself. Some are subsidized, and some require payment on behalf of the author. Subsidized _____s are financed by an academic institution or a government information center.

a. 3M Company
c. BMC Software, Inc.
b. BNSF Railway
d. Journal

62. _____ is often a small amount of discretionary funds in the form of cash used for expenditures where it is not sensible to make the disbursement by check, because of the inconvenience and costs of writing, signing and then cashing the check.

The most common way of accounting expenditures is to use the imprest system. The initial fund would be created by issuing a check for the desired amount.

a. Fixed asset
c. Remittance advice
b. Minority interest
d. Petty cash

Chapter 8. Inventories: Measurement

1. An _____ allows a company to provide a monetary value for items that make up their inventory. Inventories are usually the largest current asset of a business, and proper measurement of them is necessary to assure accurate financial statements. If inventory is not properly measured, expenses and revenues cannot be properly matched and a company could make poor business decisions.
    a. ABC Television Network
    b. AIG
    c. AMEX
    d. Inventory valuation

2. _____ is an approach to valuing and reporting inventory. Normally ending inventory is stated at historical cost (what was paid to obtain it) but there are times when the original cost of the ending inventory is greater than the cost of replacement thus the inventory has lost value. If the inventory has decreased in value below historical cost then its carrying value is reduced and reported on the balance sheet.
    a. Remittance advice
    b. Lower of cost or market
    c. Bankruptcy prediction
    d. Certified Practising Accountant

3. In economics, business, retail, and accounting, a _____ is the value of money that has been used up to produce something, and hence is not available for use anymore. In economics, a _____ is an alternative that is given up as a result of a decision. In business, the _____ may be one of acquisition, in which case the amount of money expended to acquire it is counted as _____.
    a. Cost of quality
    b. Prime cost
    c. Cost allocation
    d. Cost

4. A _____ is any one of a variety of different systems, institutions, procedures, social relations and infrastructures whereby persons trade, and goods and services are exchanged, forming part of the economy. It is an arrangement that allows buyers and sellers to exchange things. _____s vary in size, range, geographic scale, location, types and variety of human communities, as well as the types of goods and services traded.
    a. Perfect competition
    b. Market Failure
    c. Recession
    d. Market

5. In finance, _____ is the process of estimating the potential market value of a financial asset or liability. They can be done on assets (for example, investments in marketable securities such as stocks, options, business enterprises, or intangible assets such as patents and trademarks) or on liabilities (e.g., Bonds issued by a company.) A _____ is required in many contexts including investment analysis, capital budgeting, merger and acquisition transactions, financial reporting, taxable events to determine the proper tax liability, and in litigation.
    a. Vyborg Appeal
    b. Disclosure
    c. Daybook
    d. Valuation

6. In financial accounting, _____ or cost of sales includes the direct costs attributable to the production of the goods sold by a company. This amount includes the materials cost used in creating the goods along with the direct labor costs used to produce the good. It excludes indirect expenses such as distribution costs and sales force costs.
    a. Cost of goods sold
    b. FIFO and LIFO accounting
    c. 3M Company
    d. Reorder point

7. _____s are goods that have completed the manufacturing process but have not yet been sold or distributed to the end user.

Chapter 8. Inventories: Measurement

Manufacturing has three classes of inventory:

1. Raw material
2. Work in process
3. _____s

A good purchased as a 'raw material' goes into the manufacture of a product. A good only partially completed during the manufacturing process is called 'work in process'. When the good is completed as to manufacturing but not yet sold or distributed to the end-user is called a '_____'.

a. 3M Company
c. Reorder point
b. Finished good
d. FIFO and LIFO accounting

8. _____ refers to the methods, practices and operations conducted to promote and sustain certain categories of commercial activity. The term is understood to have different specific meanings depending on the context. Merchandise is a sale goods at a store

In marketing, one of the definitions of _____ is the practice in which the brand or image from one product or service is used to sell another.

a. 3M Company
c. Merchandise
b. Merchandising
d. BMC Software, Inc.

9. _____ consists of the sale of goods or merchandise from a fixed location, such as a department store, boutique or kiosk in small or individual lots for direct consumption by the purchaser. _____ may include subordinated services, such as delivery. Purchasers may be individuals or businesses.

a. BNSF Railway
c. 3M Company
b. Retailing
d. BMC Software, Inc.

10. In business, _____, Overhead cost or _____ expense refers to an ongoing expense of operating a business. The term _____ is usually used to group expenses that are necessary to the continued functioning of the business, but do not directly generate profits.

_____ expenses are all costs on the income statement except for direct labor and direct materials.

a. ABC Television Network
c. AIG
b. Intangible assets
d. Overhead

Chapter 8. Inventories: Measurement

11. _____ means the giving out of information, either voluntarily or to be in compliance with legal regulations or workplace rules.

- In Computer security, full _____ means disclosing full information about vulnerabilities.
- In computing, _____ widget
- Journalism, full _____ refers to disclosing the interests of the writer which may bear on the subject being written about, for example, if the writer has worked with an interview subject in the past.

- In law:
    - The law of England and Wales, _____ refers to a process that may form part of legal proceedings, whereby parties inform to other parties the existence of any relevant documents that are, or have been, in their control. This compares with the process known as discovery in the course of legal proceedings in the United States.
    - In U.S. civil procedure (litigation rules for civil cases), _____ is a stage prior to trial. In civil cases, each party must disclose to the opposing party the following: names of witnesses which it may use to support its side, copies of documents (or mere description of these documents) in its control which it may use to support its side, computation of damages claimed, and certain insurance information. _____ is related to, but technically prior to, the discovery stage.
    - In Company law (known as 'corporate law' in the United States), _____ refers to giving out information about public or limited companies or their officers, which might be kept secret if the company was a private company or a partnership.

- In real property transactions, _____ refers to providing to a buyer information known to the seller or broker/agent concerning the condition or other aspects of real property that would affect the property's value or desirability. These rules regarding what information must be disclosed, and whether the information must be disclosed even if a buyer does not ask, vary from one jurisdiction to the next.

a. Disclosure
c. Tax harmonisation

b. Controlled Foreign Corporations
d. Trailing

12. A _____ is the pinnacle activity involved in selling products or services in return for money or other compensation. It is an act of completion of a commercial activity.

A _____ is completed by the seller, the owner of the goods.

a. Maturity
c. Tertiary sector of economy

b. Sale
d. High yield stock

13. _____ methods are means of managing inventory and financial matters involving the money a company ties up within inventory of produced goods, raw materials, parts, components, or feed stocks. FIFO stands for first-in, first-out, meaning that the oldest inventory items are recorded as sold first. LIFO stands for last-in, first-out, meaning that the most recently purchased items are recorded as sold first.

a. Reorder point
c. Finished good

b. 3M Company
d. FIFO and LIFO accounting

Chapter 8. Inventories: Measurement

14. _____ refers to a business or organization attempting to acquire goods or services to accomplish the goals of the enterprise. Though there are several organizations that attempt to set standards in the _____ process, processes can vary greatly between organizations. Typically the word e;_____e; is not used interchangeably with the word e;procuremente;, since procurement typically includes Expediting, Supplier Quality, and Traffic and Logistics (T'L) in addition to _____.
   a. Supply chain
   b. Purchasing
   c. Consignor
   d. Free port

15. In business and accounting, _____ are everything of value that is owned by a person or company. It is a claim on the property your income of a borrower. The balance sheet of a firm records the monetary value of the _____ owned by the firm.
   a. Accounts receivable
   b. Accrual basis accounting
   c. Earnings before interest, taxes, depreciation and amortization
   d. Assets

16. Discounting is a financial mechanism in which a debtor obtains the right to delay payments to a creditor, for a defined period of time, in exchange for a charge or fee. Essentially, the party that owes money in the present purchases the right to delay the payment until some future date. The _____, or charge, is simply the difference between the original amount owed in the present and the amount that has to be paid in the future to settle the debt.
   a. Discount factor
   b. Discount
   c. Discounting
   d. Risk aversion

17. _____ is a fee paid on borrowed assets. It is the price paid for the use of borrowed money, or, money earned by deposited funds .Assets that are sometimes lent with _____ include money, shares, consumer goods through hire purchase, major assets such as aircraft, and even entire factories in finance lease arrangements. The _____ is calculated upon the value of the assets in the same manner as upon money.
   a. AIG
   b. Insolvency
   c. Interest
   d. ABC Television Network

18. _____ relates to the cost of borrowing money. It is the price that a lender charges a borrower for the use of the lender's money. _____ is different from OPEX and CAPEX, for it relates to the capital structure of a company.
   a. ABC Television Network
   b. Interest
   c. Interest expense
   d. AIG

19. In accounting, _____ has a very specific meaning. It is an outflow of cash or other valuable assets from a person or company to another person or company. This outflow of cash is generally one side of a trade for products or services that have equal or better current or future value to the buyer than to the seller.
   a. AMEX
   b. ABC Television Network
   c. Expense
   d. AIG

20. _____ is an acronym for First In, First Out, an abstraction in ways of organizing and manipulation of data relative to time and prioritization. This expression describes the principle of a queue processing technique or servicing conflicting demands by ordering process by first-come, first-served (FCFS) behaviour: what comes in first is handled first, what comes in next waits until the first is finished, etc.

Chapter 8. Inventories: Measurement

Thus it is analogous to the behaviour of persons queueing (or 'standing in line', in common American parlance), where the persons leave the queue in the order they arrive, or waiting one's turn at a traffic control signal.

a. Trademark
b. Kanban
c. FIFO
d. Risk management

21. Under the average-cost method, it is assumed that the cost of inventory is based on the _____ of the goods available for sale during the period. _____ is computed by dividing the total cost of goods available for sale by the total units available for sale. This gives a weighted-average unit cost that is applied to the units in the ending inventory.

a. Average cost
b. ABC Television Network
c. AIG
d. Ending inventory

22. Under the _____, it is assumed that the cost of inventory is based on the average cost of the goods available for sale during the period. Average cost is computed by dividing the total cost of goods available for sale by the total units available for sale. This gives a weighted-average unit cost that is applied to the units in the ending inventory.

a. AMEX
b. AIG
c. ABC Television Network
d. Average-cost method

23. In accounting, _____ are considered liabilities of the business that are to be settled in cash within the fiscal year or the operating cycle, whichever period is longer.

For example accounts payable for goods, services or supplies that were purchased for use in the operation of the business and payable within a normal period of time would be _____.

Bonds, mortgages and loans that are payable over a term exceeding one year would be fixed liabilities.

a. Treasury stock
b. Current liabilities
c. Closing entries
d. Payroll

24. In financial accounting, a _____ is defined as an obligation of an entity arising from past transactions or events, the settlement of which may result in the transfer or use of assets, provision of services or other yielding of economic benefits in the future.

a. Vested
b. False Claims Act
c. Corporate governance
d. Liability

25. An _____ is a term used in behavioral economics to describe those types of behaviors that impose costs on a person in the long-run that are not taken into account when making decisions in the present. Classical Economics discourages government from creating legislation that targets internalities, because it is assumed that the consumer takes these personal costs into account when paying for the good that causes the _____. For example, cigarettes should be taxed because of the negative consumption externalities that they impose, such as second-hand smoke, not because the smoker harms him or herself by smoking.

a. Internality
b. Authorised capital
c. Operating budget
d. Inventory turnover ratio

Chapter 8. Inventories: Measurement

26. The _____ is the United States federal government agency that collects taxes and enforces the internal revenue laws. It is an agency within the U.S. Dept of the treasury responsible for interpretation and application of Federal tax law. The official U.S. Treasury regulations provide (in part):

The _____ is a bureau of the Department of the Treasury under the immediate direction of the Commissioner of Internal Revenue.

   a. Use tax   b. Income tax
   c. Internal Revenue Service   d. Indirect tax

27. An _____ is a tax levied on the financial income of people, corporations, or other legal entities. Various _____ systems exist, with varying degrees of tax incidence. Income taxation can be progressive, proportional, or regressive.

   a. Income tax   b. Individual Retirement Arrangement
   c. Ordinary income   d. Implied level of government service

28. _____ is equal to the income that a firm has after subtracting costs and expenses from the total revenue. _____ can be distributed among holders of common stock as a dividend or held by the firm as retained earnings.

The items deducted will typically include tax expense, financing expense (interest expense), and minority interest. Likewise, preferred stock dividends will be subtracted too, though they are not an expense.

   a. Matching principle   b. Generally accepted accounting principles
   c. Long-term liabilities   d. Net income

29. In law, _____ refers to the process by which a company (or part of a company) is brought to an end, and the assets and property of the company redistributed. _____ can also be referred to as winding-up or dissolution, although dissolution technically refers to the last stage of _____. The process of _____ also arises when customs, an authority or agency in a country responsible for collecting and safeguarding customs duties, determines the final computation or ascertainment of the duties or drawback accruing on an entry.

   a. BMC Software, Inc.   b. 3M Company
   c. Bankruptcy protection   d. Liquidation

30. The _____ is the national, professional association of CPAs in the United States, with more than 330,000 members, including CPAs in business and industry, public practice, government, and education; student affiliates; and international associates. It sets ethical standards for the profession and U.S. auditing standards for audits of private companies; federal, state and local governments; and non-profit organizations.

Approximately 40% of its members are engaged in the practice of public accounting, in areas such as auditing, accounting, taxation, general business consulting, business valuation, personal financial planning and business technology.

Chapter 8. Inventories: Measurement

a. American Institute of Certified Public Accountants
b. ABC Television Network
c. AIG
d. Other postemployment benefits

31. In accounting/accountancy, _____ are journal entries usually made at the end of an accounting period to allocate income and expenditure to the period in which they actually occurred. The revenue recognition principle is the basis of making _____ that pertain to unearned and accrued revenues under accrual-basis accounting. They are sometimes called Balance Day adjustments because they are made on balance day.

a. Earnings before interest, taxes, depreciation and amortization
b. Accrued expense
c. Accrual
d. Adjusting entries

32. Just in Time could refer to the following:

- _____, an inventory strategy that reduces in-process inventory
- _____ compilation, a technique for improving the performance of bytecode-compiled programming systems

a. Comparable
b. Fiscal
c. Help desk and incident reporting auditing
d. Just-in-time

33. A _____ is the transfer of wealth from one party (such as a person or company) to another. A _____ is usually made in exchange for the provision of goods, services or both, or to fulfill a legal obligation.

The simplest and oldest form of _____ is barter, the exchange of one good or service for another.

a. Payee
b. 3M Company
c. BMC Software, Inc.
d. Payment

34. _____, Gross profit margin or Gross Profit Rate can be defined as the amount of contribution to the business enterprise, after paying for direct-fixed and direct-variable unit costs, required to cover overheads (fixed commitments) and provide a buffer for unknown items. It expresses the relationship between gross profit and sales revenue.

It can be expressed in absolute terms:

Gross Profit = Revenue − Cost of Goods Sold

or as the ratio of gross profit to sales revenue, usually in the form of a percentage:

_____ Percentage = (Revenue-Cost of Goods Sold)/Revenue

Cost of goods sold includes variable costs and fixed costs directly linked to the product, such as material and labor.

a. 3M Company
b. Gross margin
c. BNSF Railway
d. BMC Software, Inc.

Chapter 8. Inventories: Measurement

35. In accounting, _____ or sales profit is the difference between revenue and the cost of making a product or providing a service, before deducting overhead, payroll, taxation, and interest payments. Note that this is different from operating profit (earnings before interest and taxes.)

Net sales are calculated:

   Net sales = Sales - Sales returns and allowances.

a. Participating preferred stock
b. Commercial paper
c. Capital structure
d. Gross profit

36. The _____ is an equation that equals the cost of goods sold divided by the average inventory. Average inventory equals beginning inventory plus ending inventory divided by 2.

The formula for _____:

$$\text{Inventory Turnover} = \frac{\text{Cost of Goods Sold}}{\text{Average Inventory}}$$

The formula for average inventory:

$$\text{Average Inventory} = \frac{\text{Beginning inventory} + \text{Ending inventory}}{2}$$

A low turnover rate may point to overstocking, obsolescence, or deficiencies in the product line or marketing effort.

a. Earnings per share
b. Upside potential ratio
c. Enterprise Value/Sales
d. Inventory turnover

37. _____ is one of the Accounting Liquidity ratios, a financial ratio. This ratio measures the number of times, on average, the inventory is sold during the period. Its purpose is to measure the liquidity of the inventory.

a. Inventory turnover ratio
b. ABC Television Network
c. AIG
d. Ending inventory

38. _____ is the calculated approximation of a result which is usable even if input data may be incomplete or uncertain.

In statistics, see _____ theory, estimator.

In mathematics, approximation or _____ typically means finding upper or lower bounds of a quantity that cannot readily be computed precisely and is also an educated guess.

Chapter 8. Inventories: Measurement

109

a. AMEX
b. AIG
c. ABC Television Network
d. Estimation

39. _____ is a specific term used in companies' financial reporting from the company-whole point of view. Because that use excludes the effects of changing ownership interest, an economic measure of _____ is necessary for financial analysis from the shareholders' point of view

_____ is defined by the Financial Accounting Standards Board, or FASB, as 'the change in equity [net assets] of a business enterprise during a period from transactions and other events and circumstances from nonowner sources. It includes all changes in equity during a period except those resulting from investments by owners and distributions to owners.'

_____ is the sum of net income and other items that must bypass the income statement because they have not been realized, including items like an unrealized holding gain or loss from available for sale securities and foreign currency translation gains or losses.

a. BNSF Railway
b. BMC Software, Inc.
c. 3M Company
d. Comprehensive income

40. _____ in economics and business is the result of an exchange and from that trade we assign a numerical monetary value to a good, service or asset. If Alice trades Bob 4 apples for an orange, the _____ of an orange is 4 apples. Inversely, the _____ of an apple is 1/4 oranges.

a. Transactional Net Margin Method
b. Discounts and allowances
c. Price discrimination
d. Price

Chapter 9. Inventories: Additional Issues

1. _____ is an approach to valuing and reporting inventory. Normally ending inventory is stated at historical cost (what was paid to obtain it) but there are times when the original cost of the ending inventory is greater than the cost of replacement thus the inventory has lost value. If the inventory has decreased in value below historical cost then its carrying value is reduced and reported on the balance sheet.

   a. Remittance advice
   b. Certified Practising Accountant
   c. Bankruptcy prediction
   d. Lower of cost or market

2. In economics, business, retail, and accounting, a _____ is the value of money that has been used up to produce something, and hence is not available for use anymore. In economics, a _____ is an alternative that is given up as a result of a decision. In business, the _____ may be one of acquisition, in which case the amount of money expended to acquire it is counted as _____.

   a. Cost
   b. Prime cost
   c. Cost of quality
   d. Cost allocation

3. A _____ is any one of a variety of different systems, institutions, procedures, social relations and infrastructures whereby persons trade, and goods and services are exchanged, forming part of the economy. It is an arrangement that allows buyers and sellers to exchange things. _____s vary in size, range, geographic scale, location, types and variety of human communities, as well as the types of goods and services traded.

   a. Market
   b. Recession
   c. Market Failure
   d. Perfect competition

4. _____ means the giving out of information, either voluntarily or to be in compliance with legal regulations or workplace rules.

   - In Computer security, full _____ means disclosing full information about vulnerabilities.
   - In computing, _____ widget
   - Journalism, full _____ refers to disclosing the interests of the writer which may bear on the subject being written about, for example, if the writer has worked with an interview subject in the past.

   - In law:
     - The law of England and Wales, _____ refers to a process that may form part of legal proceedings, whereby parties inform to other parties the existence of any relevant documents that are, or have been, in their control. This compares with the process known as discovery in the course of legal proceedings in the United States.
     - In U.S. civil procedure (litigation rules for civil cases), _____ is a stage prior to trial. In civil cases, each party must disclose to the opposing party the following: names of witnesses which it may use to support its side, copies of documents (or mere description of these documents) in its control which it may use to support its side, computation of damages claimed, and certain insurance information. _____ is related to, but technically prior to, the discovery stage.
     - In Company law (known as 'corporate law' in the United States), _____ refers to giving out information about public or limited companies or their officers, which might be kept secret if the company was a private company or a partnership.

   - In real property transactions, _____ refers to providing to a buyer information known to the seller or broker/agent concerning the condition or other aspects of real property that would affect the property's value or desirability. These rules regarding what information must be disclosed, and whether the information must be disclosed even if a buyer does not ask, vary from one jurisdiction to the next.

Chapter 9. Inventories: Additional Issues

111

a. Trailing
c. Tax harmonisation
b. Disclosure
d. Controlled Foreign Corporations

5. The _____ founded on April 1, 2001 is the successor of the International Accounting Standards Committee (IASC) founded in June 1973 in London. It is responsible for developing the International Financial Reporting Standards (new name for the International Accounting Standards issued after 2001), and promoting the use and application of these standards.

The _____ is an independent, privately-funded accounting standard-setter based in London, UK.

a. Emerging technologies
c. International Accounting Standards Board
b. Institute of Management Accountants
d. Information Systems Audit and Control Association

6. _____ is the price at which an asset would trade in a competitive Walrasian auction setting. _____ is often used interchangeably with open _____, fair value or fair _____, although these terms have distinct definitions in different standards, and may differ in some circumstances.

International Valuation Standards defines _____ as 'the estimated amount for which a property should exchange on the date of valuation between a willing buyer and a willing seller in an arme;s-length transaction after proper marketing wherein the parties had each acted knowledgeably, prudently, and without compulsion.'

_____ is a concept distinct from market price, which is e;the price at which one can transacte;, while _____ is e;the true underlying valuee; according to theoretical standards.

a. Debtor
c. Sinking fund
b. Market value
d. Segregated portfolio company

7. _____ is a method of evaluating an asset's worth when held in inventory, in the field of accounting. _____ is part of the Generally Accepted Accounting Principles that apply to valuing inventory, so as to not overstate or understate the value of inventory goods. Net realisable value is generally equal to the selling price of the inventory goods less the selling costs (completion and disposal).

a. 3M Company
c. Revenue recognition
b. Net realizable value
d. BMC Software, Inc.

8. _____ is a demonstration of a process -- such as a variable, term, or object -- relative in terms of the specific process or set of validation tests used to determine its presence and quantity. Properties described in this manner must be sufficiently accessible, so that persons other than the definer may independently measure or test for them at will. An _____ is generally designed to model a conceptual definition.

a. AIG
c. AMEX
b. ABC Television Network
d. Operational definition

9. The term _____ or replacement value refers to the amount that an entity would have to pay, at the present time, to replace any one of its assets.

In the insurance industry, '_____' is a method of computing the value of an item insured. _____ is not market value, but is instead the cost to replace an item or structure at its pre-loss condition.

112 Chapter 9. Inventories: Additional Issues

a. Time and motion study
c. Channel stuffing
b. Consolidated financial statements
d. Replacement cost

10. The phrase _____, according to the Organization for Economic Co-operation and Development, refers to 'creative work undertaken on a systematic basis in order to increase the stock of knowledge, including knowledge of man, culture and society, and the use of this stock of knowledge to devise new applications [sic]'

New product design and development is more than often a crucial factor in the survival of a company. In an industry that is fast changing, firms must continually revise their design and range of products. This is necessary due to continuous technology change and development as well as other competitors and the changing preference of customers.

a. BNSF Railway
c. 3M Company
b. Research and development
d. BMC Software, Inc.

11. In business and accounting, _____ are everything of value that is owned by a person or company. It is a claim on the property your income of a borrower. The balance sheet of a firm records the monetary value of the _____ owned by the firm.

a. Accrual basis accounting
c. Accounts receivable
b. Earnings before interest, taxes, depreciation and amortization
d. Assets

12. In finance, a _____ is a debt security, in which the authorized issuer owes the holders a debt and, depending on the terms of the _____, is obliged to pay interest (the coupon) and/or to repay the principal at a later date, termed maturity. It is a formal contract to repay borrowed money with interest at fixed intervals.

Thus a _____ is like a loan: the issuer is the borrower, the _____ holder is the lender, and the coupon is the interest.

a. Revenue bonds
c. Bond
b. Coupon rate
d. Zero-coupon bond

13. In accounting, _____ are considered liabilities of the business that are to be settled in cash within the fiscal year or the operating cycle, whichever period is longer.

For example accounts payable for goods, services or supplies that were purchased for use in the operation of the business and payable within a normal period of time would be _____.

Bonds, mortgages and loans that are payable over a term exceeding one year would be fixed liabilities.

a. Closing entries
c. Payroll
b. Treasury stock
d. Current liabilities

14. In financial accounting, a _____ is defined as an obligation of an entity arising from past transactions or events, the settlement of which may result in the transfer or use of assets, provision of services or other yielding of economic benefits in the future.

Chapter 9. Inventories: Additional Issues

a. Corporate governance
b. False Claims Act
c. Vested
d. Liability

15. _____, net margin, net _____ or net profit ratio all refer to a measure of profitability. It is calculated by finding the net profit as a percentage of the revenue.

$$\text{Net profit margin} = \frac{\text{Net profit (after taxes)}}{\text{Revenue}} \times 100$$

The _____ is mostly used for internal comparison.

a. BMC Software, Inc.
b. 3M Company
c. Profit margin
d. BNSF Railway

16. An _____ allows a company to provide a monetary value for items that make up their inventory. Inventories are usually the largest current asset of a business, and proper measurement of them is necessary to assure accurate financial statements. If inventory is not properly measured, expenses and revenues cannot be properly matched and a company could make poor business decisions.

a. AMEX
b. AIG
c. Inventory valuation
d. ABC Television Network

17. In finance, _____ is the process of estimating the potential market value of a financial asset or liability. They can be done on assets (for example, investments in marketable securities such as stocks, options, business enterprises, or intangible assets such as patents and trademarks) or on liabilities (e.g., Bonds issued by a company.) A _____ is required in many contexts including investment analysis, capital budgeting, merger and acquisition transactions, financial reporting, taxable events to determine the proper tax liability, and in litigation.

a. Vyborg Appeal
b. Disclosure
c. Daybook
d. Valuation

18. In accounting, _____ or sales profit is the difference between revenue and the cost of making a product or providing a service, before deducting overhead, payroll, taxation, and interest payments. Note that this is different from operating profit (earnings before interest and taxes.)

Net sales are calculated:

Net sales = Sales - Sales returns and allowances.

a. Gross profit
b. Capital structure
c. Commercial paper
d. Participating preferred stock

19. _____ principle is a cornerstone of accrual accounting together with matching principle. They both determine the accounting period, in which revenues and expenses are recognized. According to the principle, revenues are recognized when they are (1) realized or realizable, and are (2) earned (usually when goods are transferred or services rendered), no matter when cash is received.

a. Revenue recognition
b. BMC Software, Inc.
c. Net realizable value
d. 3M Company

20. _____ is the calculated approximation of a result which is usable even if input data may be incomplete or uncertain.

In statistics, see _____ theory, estimator.

In mathematics, approximation or _____ typically means finding upper or lower bounds of a quantity that cannot readily be computed precisely and is also an educated guess .

a. AMEX
b. ABC Television Network
c. AIG
d. Estimation

21. In financial accounting, _____ or cost of sales includes the direct costs attributable to the production of the goods sold by a company. This amount includes the materials cost used in creating the goods along with the direct labor costs used to produce the good. It excludes indirect expenses such as distribution costs and sales force costs.

a. Reorder point
b. Cost of goods sold
c. 3M Company
d. FIFO and LIFO accounting

22. _____, Gross profit margin or Gross Profit Rate can be defined as the amount of contribution to the business enterprise, after paying for direct-fixed and direct-variable unit costs, required to cover overheads (fixed commitments) and provide a buffer for unknown items. It expresses the relationship between gross profit and sales revenue.

It can be expressed in absolute terms:

Gross Profit = Revenue − Cost of Goods Sold

or as the ratio of gross profit to sales revenue, usually in the form of a percentage:

_____ Percentage = (Revenue-Cost of Goods Sold)/Revenue

Cost of goods sold includes variable costs and fixed costs directly linked to the product, such as material and labor.

a. BMC Software, Inc.
b. Gross margin
c. BNSF Railway
d. 3M Company

23. _____ is the amount of inventory a company have in stock at the end of this fiscal year. It is closely related with _____ Cost, which is the amount of money spent to get these goods in stock. It should be calculated at the Lower of Cost or Market.

a. Inventory turnover ratio
b. ABC Television Network
c. AIG
d. Ending inventory

Chapter 9. Inventories: Additional Issues

24. _____ is the difference between the cost of a good or service and its selling price. A _____ is added on to the total cost incurred by the producer of a good or service in order to create a profit. The total cost reflects the total amount of both fixed and variable expenses to produce and distribute a product.

    a. Corporate Bond

    b. Statements of Financial Accounting Standards No. 133, Accounting for Derivative Instruments and Hedging Activities

    c. Merck ' Co., Inc.

    d. Markup

25. _____ consists of the sale of goods or merchandise from a fixed location, such as a department store, boutique or kiosk in small or individual lots for direct consumption by the purchaser. _____ may include subordinated services, such as delivery. Purchasers may be individuals or businesses.

    a. BNSF Railway

    b. 3M Company

    c. BMC Software, Inc.

    d. Retailing

26. Under the average-cost method, it is assumed that the cost of inventory is based on the _____ of the goods available for sale during the period. _____ is computed by dividing the total cost of goods available for sale by the total units available for sale. This gives a weighted-average unit cost that is applied to the units in the ending inventory.

    a. Ending inventory

    b. AIG

    c. ABC Television Network

    d. Average cost

27. Under the _____, it is assumed that the cost of inventory is based on the average cost of the goods available for sale during the period. Average cost is computed by dividing the total cost of goods available for sale by the total units available for sale. This gives a weighted-average unit cost that is applied to the units in the ending inventory.

    a. Average-cost method

    b. AMEX

    c. ABC Television Network

    d. AIG

28. An _____ is a term used in behavioral economics to describe those types of behaviors that impose costs on a person in the long-run that are not taken into account when making decisions in the present. Classical Economics discourages government from creating legislation that targets internalities, because it is assumed that the consumer takes these personal costs into account when paying for the good that causes the _____. For example, cigarettes should be taxed because of the negative consumption externalities that they impose, such as second-hand smoke, not because the smoker harms him or herself by smoking.

    a. Authorised capital

    b. Operating budget

    c. Internality

    d. Inventory turnover ratio

29. The _____ is the United States federal government agency that collects taxes and enforces the internal revenue laws. It is an agency within the U.S. Dept of the treasury responsible for interpretation and application of Federal tax law. The official U.S. Treasury regulations provide (in part):

The _____ is a bureau of the Department of the Treasury under the immediate direction of the Commissioner of Internal Revenue.

a. Use tax
b. Indirect tax
c. Income tax
d. Internal Revenue Service

30. _____ methods are means of managing inventory and financial matters involving the money a company ties up within inventory of produced goods, raw materials, parts, components, or feed stocks. FIFO stands for first-in, first-out, meaning that the oldest inventory items are recorded as sold first. LIFO stands for last-in, first-out, meaning that the most recently purchased items are recorded as sold first.
   a. Finished good
   b. Reorder point
   c. 3M Company
   d. FIFO and LIFO accounting

31. The _____ is the current method of accelerated asset depreciation required by the United States income tax code. Under _____, all assets are divided into classes which dictate the number of years over which an asset's cost will be recovered.

Prior to the Accelerated Cost Recovery System (ACRS), most capital purchases were depreciated using a straight line technique, that allowed for the depreciation of the asset over its useful life.

   a. Categorical grants
   b. 3M Company
   c. BMC Software, Inc.
   d. Modified Accelerated Cost Recovery System

32. An _____ is a tax levied on the financial income of people, corporations, or other legal entities. Various _____ systems exist, with varying degrees of tax incidence. Income taxation can be progressive, proportional, or regressive.
   a. Ordinary income
   b. Income tax
   c. Implied level of government service
   d. Individual Retirement Arrangement

33. _____ is a lightweight markup language, originally created by John Gruber and Aaron Swartz to help maximum readability and 'publishability' of both its input and output forms. The language takes many cues from existing conventions for marking up plain text in email. _____ converts its marked-up text input to valid, well-formed XHTML and replaces left-pointing angle brackets ('<') and ampersands with their corresponding character entity references.
   a. BNSF Railway
   b. BMC Software, Inc.
   c. 3M Company
   d. Markdown

34. Discounting is a financial mechanism in which a debtor obtains the right to delay payments to a creditor, for a defined period of time, in exchange for a charge or fee. Essentially, the party that owes money in the present purchases the right to delay the payment until some future date. The _____, or charge, is simply the difference between the original amount owed in the present and the amount that has to be paid in the future to settle the debt.
   a. Discount factor
   b. Discount
   c. Discounting
   d. Risk aversion

35. Employment is a contract between two parties, one being the employer and the other being the _____. An _____ may be defined as: 'A person in the service of another under any contract of hire, express or implied, oral or written, where the employer has the power or right to control and direct the _____ in the material details of how the work is to be performed.' Black's Law Dictionary page 471 (5th ed. 1979.)

Chapter 9. Inventories: Additional Issues 117

a. Employee
c. AMEX

b. ABC Television Network
d. AIG

36. In bookkeeping, accounting, and finance, _____ are operating revenues earned by a company when it sells its products. Revenue (_____) are reported directly on the income statement as Sales or _____.

In financial ratios that use income statement sales values, 'sales' refers to _____, not gross sales.

a. Historical cost
c. Matching principle

b. Deferred
d. Net sales

37. _____ refers to a business or organization attempting to acquire goods or services to accomplish the goals of the enterprise. Though there are several organizations that attempt to set standards in the _____ process, processes can vary greatly between organizations. Typically the word e;_____e; is not used interchangeably with the word e;procuremente;, since procurement typically includes Expediting, Supplier Quality, and Traffic and Logistics (T'L) in addition to _____.

a. Consignor
c. Free port

b. Supply chain
d. Purchasing

38. A _____ is the pinnacle activity involved in selling products or services in return for money or other compensation. It is an act of completion of a commercial activity.

A _____ is completed by the seller, the owner of the goods.

a. High yield stock
c. Maturity

b. Sale
d. Tertiary sector of economy

39. In finance, an _____ is a contract between a buyer and a seller that gives the buyer the right--but not the obligation--to buy or to sell a particular asset (the underlying asset) at a later time at an agreed price. In return for granting the _____, the seller collects a payment (the premium) from the buyer. A call _____ gives the buyer the right to buy the underlying asset; a put _____ gives the buyer of the _____ the right to sell the underlying asset.

a. ABC Television Network
c. Option

b. AMEX
d. AIG

40. A _____ has several related meanings:

- a daily record of events or business; a private _____ is usually referred to as a diary.
- a newspaper or other periodical, in the literal sense of one published each day;
- many publications issued at stated intervals, such as magazines, or scholarly academic _____s, or the record of the transactions of a society, are often called _____s. Although _____ is sometimes used, erroneously, as a synonym for 'magazine,' in academic use, a _____ refers to a serious, scholarly publication, most often peer-reviewed. A non-scholarly magazine written for an educated audience about an industry or an area of professional activity is usually called a professional magazine.

The word 'journalist' for one whose business is writing for the public press has been in use since the end of the 17th century.

Open access _____s are scholarly _____s that are available to the reader without financial or other barrier other than access to the internet itself. Some are subsidized, and some require payment on behalf of the author. Subsidized _____s are financed by an academic institution or a government information center.

    a. Journal   b. BNSF Railway
    c. 3M Company   d. BMC Software, Inc.

41. _____ is an acronym for First In, First Out, an abstraction in ways of organizing and manipulation of data relative to time and prioritization. This expression describes the principle of a queue processing technique or servicing conflicting demands by ordering process by first-come, first-served (FCFS) behaviour: what comes in first is handled first, what comes in next waits until the first is finished, etc.

Thus it is analogous to the behaviour of persons queueing (or 'standing in line', in common American parlance), where the persons leave the queue in the order they arrive, or waiting one's turn at a traffic control signal.

    a. Trademark   b. Risk management
    c. Kanban   d. FIFO

42. _____ is a specific term used in companies' financial reporting from the company-whole point of view. Because that use excludes the effects of changing ownership interest, an economic measure of _____ is necessary for financial analysis from the shareholders' point of view

_____ is defined by the Financial Accounting Standards Board, or FASB, as 'the change in equity [net assets] of a business enterprise during a period from transactions and other events and circumstances from nonowner sources. It includes all changes in equity during a period except those resulting from investments by owners and distributions to owners.'

_____ is the sum of net income and other items that must bypass the income statement because they have not been realized, including items like an unrealized holding gain or loss from available for sale securities and foreign currency translation gains or losses.

    a. Comprehensive income   b. 3M Company
    c. BNSF Railway   d. BMC Software, Inc.

43. _____ are the earnings returned on the initial investment amount.

In the US, the Financial Accounting Standards Board (FASB) requires companies' income statements to report _____ for each of the major categories of the income statement: continuing operations, discontinued operations, extraordinary items, and net income.

The _____ formula does not include preferred dividends for categories outside of continued operations and net income.

Chapter 9. Inventories: Additional Issues

a. Invested capital
c. Average accounting return
b. Earnings yield
d. Earnings per share

44. The _____ is the main body of domestic statutory tax law of the United States organized topically, including laws covering the income tax, payroll taxes, gift taxes, estate taxes and statutory excise taxes. The _____ is published as Title 26 of the United States Code (USC), and is also known as the internal revenue title.

a. Ordinary income
c. Income tax
b. Equity of condition
d. Internal Revenue Code

45. _____ is a company's earnings per share (EPS) calculated using fully diluted shares outstanding. _____ indicates a 'worst case' scenario, one in which everyone who could have received stock without purchasing it directly for the full market value did so.

To find _____, basic EPS is calculated for each of the categories on the income statement first. Then each of the dilutive securities are ranked based on their effects, from most dilutive to least dilutive and antidilutive. Then the basic EPS number is diluted one by one by applying each one, skipping any instruments that have an antidilutive effect.

a. Return on assets Du Pont
c. Financial ratio
b. Cash conversion cycle
d. Diluted Earnings Per Share

46. Under U.S. Federal income tax law, a _____ occurs when certain tax-deductible expenses exceed taxable revenues for a taxable year. If a taxpayer is taxed during profitable periods without receiving any tax relief (e.g. a refund) during periods of _____s, an unbalanced tax burden results. Consequently, in some situations, Congress allows taxpayers to use the losses in one year to offset the profits of other years.

a. SUTA dumping
c. Revenue Procedures
b. Half-year convention
d. Net operating loss

47. The term _____ refers to government debt, expenditures and revenues, or to finance (particularly financial revenue) in general.

- _____ deficit is the budget deficit of federal or local government
- _____ policy is the discretionary spending of governments. Contrasts with monetary policy.
- _____ year and _____ quarter are reporting periods for firms and other agencies.

See also

- Procurator _____ and Crown Office and Procurator _____ Service

a. Scientific Research and Experimental Development Tax Incentive Program
c. Comparable
b. Swap
d. Fiscal

48. A _____ is a period used for calculating annual financial statements in businesses and other organizations. In many jurisdictions, regulatory laws regarding accounting and taxation require such reports once per twelve months, but do not require that the period reported on constitutes a calendar year (i.e., January through December.) _____s vary between businesses and countries.

   a. BMC Software, Inc.
   b. BNSF Railway
   c. 3M Company
   d. Fiscal year

Chapter 10. Operational Assets: Acquisition and Disposition

1. _____ is a demonstration of a process -- such as a variable, term, or object -- relative in terms of the specific process or set of validation tests used to determine its presence and quantity. Properties described in this manner must be sufficiently accessible, so that persons other than the definer may independently measure or test for them at will. An _____ is generally designed to model a conceptual definition.
    a. Operational definition
    b. ABC Television Network
    c. AMEX
    d. AIG

2. In business and accounting, _____ are everything of value that is owned by a person or company. It is a claim on the property your income of a borrower. The balance sheet of a firm records the monetary value of the _____ owned by the firm.
    a. Accrual basis accounting
    b. Earnings before interest, taxes, depreciation and amortization
    c. Accounts receivable
    d. Assets

3. _____ are defined as identifiable non-monetary assets that cannot be seen, touched or physically measured, which are created through time and/or effort and that are identifiable as a separate asset. There are two primary forms of intangibles - legal intangibles (such as trade secrets (e.g., customer lists), copyrights, patents, trademarks, and goodwill) and competitive intangibles (such as knowledge activities (know-how, knowledge), collaboration activities, leverage activities, and structural activities.) Legal intangibles are known under the generic term intellectual property and generate legal property rights defensible in a court of law.
    a. AIG
    b. Overhead
    c. Intangible assets
    d. ABC Television Network

4. _____ is a fee paid on borrowed assets. It is the price paid for the use of borrowed money , or, money earned by deposited funds .Assets that are sometimes lent with _____ include money, shares, consumer goods through hire purchase, major assets such as aircraft, and even entire factories in finance lease arrangements. The _____ is calculated upon the value of the assets in the same manner as upon money.
    a. Insolvency
    b. ABC Television Network
    c. AIG
    d. Interest

5. In physics, and more specifically kinematics, _____ is the change in velocity over time. Because velocity is a vector, it can change in two ways: a change in magnitude and/or a change in direction. In one dimension, _____ is the rate at which something speeds up or slows down.
    a. AMEX
    b. ABC Television Network
    c. Acceleration
    d. AIG

6. _____ refers to any one of several methods by which a company, for 'financial accounting' and/or tax purposes, depreciates a fixed asset in such a way that the amount of depreciation taken each year is higher during the earlier years of an assete;s life. For financial accounting purposes, _____ is generally used when an asset is expected to be much more productive during its early years, so that depreciation expense will more accurately represent how much of an assete;s usefulness is being used up each year. For tax purposes, _____ provides a way of deferring corporate income taxes by reducing taxable income in current years, in exchange for increased taxable income in future years.
    a. Indirect tax
    b. Effective marginal tax rates
    c. User charge
    d. Accelerated depreciation

Chapter 10. Operational Assets: Acquisition and Disposition

7. _____ is the process of increasing, or accounting for, an amount over a period of time. Particular instances of the term include:

- _____, the allocation of a lump sum amount to different time periods, particularly for loans and other forms of finance, including related interest or other finance charges.
    - _____ schedule, a table detailing each periodic payment on a loan (typically a mortgage), as generated by an _____ calculator.
    - Negative _____, an _____ schedule where the loan amount actually increases through not paying the full interest
- Amortized analysis, analyzing the execution cost of algorithms over a sequence of operations.
- _____ of capital expenditures of certain assets under accounting rules, particularly intangible assets, in a manner analogous to depreciation.
- _____

a. Annuity
c. Intangible
b. EBIT
d. Amortization

8. _____ is any physical or virtual entity that is owned by an individual or jointly by a group of individuals. An owner of _____ has the right to consume, sell, rent, mortgage, transfer and exchange his or her _____. Important widely-recognized types of _____ include real _____, personal _____ (other physical possessions), and intellectual _____ (rights over artistic creations, inventions, etc.), although the latter is not always as widely recognized or enforced.

a. Disclosure requirement
c. Primary authority
b. Fiduciary
d. Property

9. _____, also known as property, plant, and equipment (PP&E), is a term used in accountancy for assets and property which cannot easily be converted into cash. This can be compared with current assets such as cash or bank accounts, which are described as liquid assets. In most cases, only tangible assets are referred to as fixed.

a. Fixed asset
c. Minority interest
b. Subledger
d. Bankruptcy prediction

10. An _____ is the buying of one company by another. An _____ may be friendly or hostile. In the former case, the companies cooperate in negotiations; in the latter case, the takeover target is unwilling to be bought or the target's board has no prior knowledge of the offer. _____ usually refers to a purchase of a smaller firm by a larger one. Sometimes, however, a smaller firm will acquire management control of a larger or longer established company and keep its name for the combined entity. This is known as a reverse takeover.

a. AMEX
c. ABC Television Network
b. Acquisition
d. AIG

11. In economics, business, retail, and accounting, a _____ is the value of money that has been used up to produce something, and hence is not available for use anymore. In economics, a _____ is an alternative that is given up as a result of a decision. In business, the _____ may be one of acquisition, in which case the amount of money expended to acquire it is counted as _____.

a. Prime cost
c. Cost allocation
b. Cost of quality
d. Cost

12. _____ is a term used in accounting, economics and finance to spread the cost of an asset over the span of several years.

In simple words we can say that _____ is the reduction in the value of an asset due to usage, passage of time, wear and tear, technological outdating or obsolescence, depletion, inadequacy, rot, rust, decay or other such factors.

In accounting, _____ is a term used to describe any method of attributing the historical or purchase cost of an asset across its useful life, roughly corresponding to normal wear and tear.

 a. Net profit
 c. Depreciation
 b. Current asset
 d. General ledger

13. In finance, _____ is the process of estimating the potential market value of a financial asset or liability. They can be done on assets (for example, investments in marketable securities such as stocks, options, business enterprises, or intangible assets such as patents and trademarks) or on liabilities (e.g., Bonds issued by a company.) A _____ is required in many contexts including investment analysis, capital budgeting, merger and acquisition transactions, financial reporting, taxable events to determine the proper tax liability, and in litigation.

 a. Daybook
 c. Vyborg Appeal
 b. Disclosure
 d. Valuation

14. _____ is a process of attributing cost to particular cost centres. For example the wage of the driver of the purchasing department can be allocated to the purchasing department cost centre. It is not necessary to share the wage cost over several different cost centers.

 a. Cost of quality
 c. Cost accounting
 b. Variable cost
 d. Cost allocation

Chapter 10. Operational Assets: Acquisition and Disposition

15. _____ means the giving out of information, either voluntarily or to be in compliance with legal regulations or workplace rules.

- In Computer security, full _____ means disclosing full information about vulnerabilities.
- In computing, _____ widget
- Journalism, full _____ refers to disclosing the interests of the writer which may bear on the subject being written about, for example, if the writer has worked with an interview subject in the past.

- In law:
    - The law of England and Wales, _____ refers to a process that may form part of legal proceedings, whereby parties inform to other parties the existence of any relevant documents that are, or have been, in their control. This compares with the process known as discovery in the course of legal proceedings in the United States.
    - In U.S. civil procedure (litigation rules for civil cases), _____ is a stage prior to trial. In civil cases, each party must disclose to the opposing party the following: names of witnesses which it may use to support its side, copies of documents (or mere description of these documents) in its control which it may use to support its side, computation of damages claimed, and certain insurance information. _____ is related to, but technically prior to, the discovery stage.
    - In Company law (known as 'corporate law' in the United States), _____ refers to giving out information about public or limited companies or their officers, which might be kept secret if the company was a private company or a partnership.

- In real property transactions, _____ refers to providing to a buyer information known to the seller or broker/agent concerning the condition or other aspects of real property that would affect the property's value or desirability. These rules regarding what information must be disclosed, and whether the information must be disclosed even if a buyer does not ask, vary from one jurisdiction to the next.

a. Trailing
b. Controlled Foreign Corporations
c. Tax harmonisation
d. Disclosure

16. A _____ is any one of a variety of different systems, institutions, procedures, social relations and infrastructures whereby persons trade, and goods and services are exchanged, forming part of the economy. It is an arrangement that allows buyers and sellers to exchange things. _____s vary in size, range, geographic scale, location, types and variety of human communities, as well as the types of goods and services traded.
a. Perfect competition
b. Market Failure
c. Recession
d. Market

17. _____ or land amelioration refers to investments making land more usable by humans. In terms of accounting, _____s refer to any variety of projects that increase the value of the property. Most are depreciable, but some _____s are not able to be depreciated because a useful life cannot be determined.
a. BNSF Railway
b. Land improvement
c. BMC Software, Inc.
d. 3M Company

18. A _____ is a set of exclusive rights granted by a state to an inventor or his assignee for a limited period of time in exchange for a disclosure of an invention.

Chapter 10. Operational Assets: Acquisition and Disposition

The procedure for granting _____s, the requirements placed on the _____ee and the extent of the exclusive rights vary widely between countries according to national laws and international agreements. Typically, however, a _____ application must include one or more claims defining the invention which must be new, inventive, and useful or industrially applicable.

- a. Trust indenture
- b. Patent
- c. Negligence
- d. FLSA

19. A _____ or trade mark, identified by the symbols â„¢ (not yet registered) and Â® (registered), is a distinctive sign or indicator used by an individual, business organization or other legal entity to identify that the products and/or services to consumers with which the _____ appears originate from a unique source, and to distinguish its products or services from those of other entities. A _____ is a type of intellectual property, and typically a name, word, phrase, logo, symbol, design, image, or a combination of these elements. There is also a range of non-conventional _____s comprising marks which do not fall into these standard categories.

- a. Risk management
- b. Kanban
- c. FIFO
- d. Trademark

20. _____ provide for future disposal of assets as required by SFAS 143.

Firms must recognize the _____ liability in the period it was acquired, generally acquisition. The liability equals the market value, and if that is not available the present value of cash flows that will be required to extinguish the liability. An asset equal to the initial liability is added to the Balance Sheet, and depreciated over the life of the asset. The result is an increase in both assets and liabilities.

- a. ABC Television Network
- b. Asset retirement obligations
- c. AMEX
- d. AIG

21. _____ is the value on a given date of a future payment or series of future payments, discounted to reflect the time value of money and other factors such as investment risk. _____ calculations are widely used in business and economics to provide a means to compare cash flows at different times on a meaningful 'like to like' basis.

The most commonly applied model of the time value of money is compound interest.

- a. Future value
- b. Present value
- c. 3M Company
- d. Net present value

Chapter 10. Operational Assets: Acquisition and Disposition

22. _____ is the balance of the amounts of cash being received and paid by a business during a defined period of time, sometimes tied to a specific project. Measurement of _____ can be used

- to evaluate the state or performance of a business or project.
- to determine problems with liquidity. Being profitable does not necessarily mean being liquid. A company can fail because of a shortage of cash, even while profitable.
- to project rate of returns. The time of _____s into and out of projects are used as inputs to financial models such as internal rate of return, and net present value.
- to examine income or growth of a business when it is believed that accrual accounting concepts do not represent economic realities. Alternately, _____ can be used to 'validate' the net income generated by accrual accounting.

_____ as a generic term may be used differently depending on context, and certain _____ definitions may be adapted by analysts and users for their own uses. Common terms include operating _____ and free _____.

  a. Cash flow
  b. Flow-through entity
  c. Controlling interest
  d. Commercial paper

23. _____ is a concept that denotes the precise probability of specific eventualities. Technically, the notion of _____ is independent from the notion of value and, as such, eventualities may have both beneficial and adverse consequences. However, in general usage the convention is to focus only on potential negative impact to some characteristic of value that may arise from a future event.
  a. Discount factor
  b. Risk
  c. Discounting
  d. Risk adjusted return on capital

24. _____ refers to a business or organization attempting to acquire goods or services to accomplish the goals of the enterprise. Though there are several organizations that attempt to set standards in the _____ process, processes can vary greatly between organizations. Typically the word e;_____e; is not used interchangeably with the word e;procuremente;, since procurement typically includes Expediting, Supplier Quality, and Traffic and Logistics (T'L) in addition to _____.
  a. Consignor
  b. Purchasing
  c. Free port
  d. Supply chain

25. A _____ is the name which a business trades under for commercial purposes, although its registered, legal name, used for contracts and other formal situations, may be another. Pharmaceuticals also have _____s, often dissimilar to their chemical names

Trading names are sometimes registered as trademarks or are regarded as brands.

  a. Consumer-to-business
  b. Trade name
  c. Fund accounting
  d. Price variance

26. _____ is one of a series of accounting transactions dealing with the billing of customers who owe money to a person, company or organization for goods and services that have been provided to the customer. In most business entities this is typically done by generating an invoice and mailing or electronically delivering it to the customer, who in turn must pay it within an established timeframe called credit or payment terms.

Chapter 10. Operational Assets: Acquisition and Disposition

An example of a common payment term is Net 30, meaning payment is due in the amount of the invoice 30 days from the date of invoice.

a. Accrual
b. Accrued revenue
c. Adjusting entries
d. Accounts receivable

27. _____, also called fair price (in a commonplace conflation of the two distinct concepts), is a concept used in finance and economics, defined as a rational and unbiased estimate of the potential market price of a good, service, or asset, taking into account such objective factors as:

- acquisition/production/distribution costs, replacement costs, or costs of close substitutes
- actual utility at a given level of development of social productive capability
- supply vs. demand

and subjective factors such as

- risk characteristics
- cost of capital
- individually perceived utility

In accounting, _____ is used as an estimate of the market value of an asset (or liability) for which a market price cannot be determined (usually because there is no established market for the asset.) Under GAAP (FAS 157), _____ is the amount at which the asset could be bought or sold in a current transaction between willing parties, or transferred to an equivalent party, other than in a liquidation sale. This is used for assets whose carrying value is based on mark-to-market valuations; for assets carried at historical cost, the _____ of the asset is not used. One example of where _____ is an issue is a College kitchen with a cost of $2 million which was built 5 years ago.

a. BMC Software, Inc.
b. 3M Company
c. BNSF Railway
d. Fair value

28. A _____ is a habit, a preparation, a state of readiness, or a tendency to act in a specified way.

The terms dispositional belief and occurrent belief refer, in the former case, to a belief that is held in the mind but not currently being considered, and in the latter case, to a belief that is currently being considered by the mind.

In Bourdieu's theory of fields _____s are the natural tendencies of each individual to take on a certain position in any field.

a. BMC Software, Inc.
b. 3M Company
c. BNSF Railway
d. Disposition

29. A _____ is a one-time payment of money, as opposed to a series of payments made over time.

Chapter 10. Operational Assets: Acquisition and Disposition

a. Trade name
b. Lump sum
c. Manufacturing operations
d. Redemption value

30. In accounting, _____ are considered liabilities of the business that are to be settled in cash within the fiscal year or the operating cycle, whichever period is longer.

For example accounts payable for goods, services or supplies that were purchased for use in the operation of the business and payable within a normal period of time would be _____.

Bonds, mortgages and loans that are payable over a term exceeding one year would be fixed liabilities.

a. Treasury stock
b. Payroll
c. Current liabilities
d. Closing entries

31. In financial accounting, a _____ is defined as an obligation of an entity arising from past transactions or events, the settlement of which may result in the transfer or use of assets, provision of services or other yielding of economic benefits in the future.
a. False Claims Act
b. Vested
c. Corporate governance
d. Liability

32. _____, in accrual accounting, is any account where the asset or liability is not realized until a future date (accounting period), e.g. annuities, charges, taxes, income, etc. The _____ item may be carried, dependent on type of deferral, as either an asset or liability.
a. Payroll
b. Cash basis accounting
c. Pro forma
d. Deferred

33. Discounting is a financial mechanism in which a debtor obtains the right to delay payments to a creditor, for a defined period of time, in exchange for a charge or fee. Essentially, the party that owes money in the present purchases the right to delay the payment until some future date. The _____, or charge, is simply the difference between the original amount owed in the present and the amount that has to be paid in the future to settle the debt.
a. Discounting
b. Risk aversion
c. Discount
d. Discount factor

34. A _____, also referred to as a note payable in accounting, is a contract where one party (the maker or issuer) makes an unconditional promise in writing to pay a sum of money to the other (the payee), either at a fixed or determinable future time or on demand of the payee, under specific terms. They differ from IOUs in that they contain a specific promise to pay, rather than simply acknowledging that a debt exists.

The terms of a note typically include the principal amount, the interest rate if any, and the maturity date.

a. BNSF Railway
b. BMC Software, Inc.
c. 3M Company
d. Promissory note

35. A _____ is the transfer of wealth from one party (such as a person or company) to another. A _____ is usually made in exchange for the provision of goods, services or both, or to fulfill a legal obligation.

Chapter 10. Operational Assets: Acquisition and Disposition

The simplest and oldest form of _____ is barter, the exchange of one good or service for another.

a. BMC Software, Inc.
c. 3M Company
b. Payee
d. Payment

36. Simply put, _____ is the value of money figuring in a given amount of interest for a given amount of time. For example 100 dollars of todays money held for a year at 5 percent interest is worth 105 dollars, therefore 100 dollars paid now or 105 dollars paid exactly one year from now is the same amount of payment of money with that given intersest at that given amount of time. This notion dates at least to Martín de Azpilcueta of the School of Salamanca.

a. Merck ' Co., Inc.
c. Collusion
b. Competition law
d. Time value of money

37. In economic models, the _____ time frame assumes no fixed factors of production. Firms can enter or leave the marketplace, and the cost (and availability) of land, labor, raw materials, and capital goods can be assumed to vary. In contrast, in the short-run time frame, certain factors are assumed to be fixed, because there is not sufficient time for them to change.

a. 3M Company
c. Short-run
b. BMC Software, Inc.
d. Long-run

38. An _____ is the price a borrower pays for the use of money they do not own, for instance a small company might borrow from a bank to kick start their business, and the return a lender receives for deferring the use of funds, by lending it to the borrower. _____s are normally expressed as a percentage rate over the period of one year.

_____s targets are also a vital tool of monetary policy and are used to control variables like investment, inflation, and unemployment.

a. Interest rate
c. ABC Television Network
b. AMEX
d. AIG

39. An _____ is a derivative in which one party exchanges a stream of interest payments for another party's stream of cash flows. They can be used by hedgers to manage their fixed or floating assets and liabilities. They can also be used by speculators to replicate unfunded bond exposures to profit from changes in interest rates.

a. AMEX
c. Interest rate swap
b. ABC Television Network
d. AIG

40. A _____ is a fungible, negotiable instrument representing financial value. they are broadly categorized into debt securities (such as banknotes, bonds and debentures), and equity securities; e.g., common stocks. The company or other entity issuing the _____ is called the issuer,

a. 3M Company
c. Security
b. BMC Software, Inc.
d. Tracking stock

41. In finance, a _____ is a derivative in which two counterparties agree to exchange one stream of cash flow against another stream. These streams are called the legs of the _____.

The cash flows are calculated over a notional principal amount, which is usually not exchanged between counterparties.

a. Controlled Foreign Corporations
b. Swap
c. Department of the Treasury
d. Total-factor productivity

42. In economics, _____ or _____ goods or real _____ refers to factors of production used to create goods or services that are not themselves significantly consumed (though they may depreciate) in the production process. _____ goods may be acquired with money or financial _____. In finance and accounting, _____ generally refers to financial wealth, especially that used to start or maintain a business.

a. Vyborg Appeal
b. Screening
c. Disclosure
d. Capital

43. _____ is the planning process used to determine whether a firm's long term investments such as new machinery, replacement machinery, new plants, new products, and research development projects are worth pursuing. It is budget for major capital, or investment, expenditures.

Many formal methods are used in _____, including the techniques such as

- Net present value
- Profitability index
- Internal rate of return
- Modified Internal Rate of Return
- Equivalent annuity

These methods use the incremental cash flows from each potential investment, or project. Techniques based on accounting earnings and accounting rules are sometimes used - though economists consider this to be improper - such as the accounting rate of return, and 'return on investment.' Simplified and hybrid methods are used as well, such as payback period and discounted payback period.

a. Preferred stock
b. Gross profit
c. Cash flow
d. Capital budgeting

44. A _____ is the pinnacle activity involved in selling products or services in return for money or other compensation. It is an act of completion of a commercial activity.

A _____ is completed by the seller, the owner of the goods.

a. Sale
b. High yield stock
c. Tertiary sector of economy
d. Maturity

Chapter 10. Operational Assets: Acquisition and Disposition

45. _____, in law and economics, is a form of risk management primarily used to hedge against the risk of a contingent loss. _____ is defined as the equitable transfer of the risk of a loss, from one entity to another, in exchange for a premium, and can be thought of as a guaranteed small loss to prevent a large, possibly devastating loss. An insurer is a company selling the _____; an insured is the person or entity buying the _____.
   a. AMEX
   b. AIG
   c. ABC Television Network
   d. Insurance

46. In accounting, _____ or carrying value is the value of an asset according to its balance sheet account balance. For assets, the value is based on the original cost of the asset less any depreciation, amortization or impairment costs made against the asset. Traditionally, a company's _____ is its total assets minus intangible assets and liabilities.
   a. Generally accepted accounting principles
   b. Depreciation
   c. Matching principle
   d. Book value

47. In accounting, _____ is the original monetary value of an economic item. In some circumstances, assets and liabilities may be shown at their _____, as if there had been no change in value since the date of acquisition. The balance sheet value of the item may therefore differ from the 'true' value.
   a. Cost of goods sold
   b. Matching principle
   c. Bottom line
   d. Historical cost

48. In business, _____, Overhead cost or _____ expense refers to an ongoing expense of operating a business. The term _____ is usually used to group expenses that are necessary to the continued functioning of the business, but do not directly generate profits.

_____ expenses are all costs on the income statement except for direct labor and direct materials.

   a. ABC Television Network
   b. Overhead
   c. AIG
   d. Intangible assets

49. _____ was a maxim coined by Josiah Warren, indicating a (prescriptive) version of the labor theory of value. Warren maintained that the just compensation for labor (or for its product) could only be an equivalent amount of labor (or a product embodying an equivalent amount.) Thus, profit, rent, and interest were considered unjust economic arrangements.
   a. Cost the limit of price
   b. BMC Software, Inc.
   c. Politicized issue
   d. 3M Company

50. In finance, _____ is the interest that has accumulated since the principal investment, or since the previous interest payment if there has been one already. For a financial instrument such as a bond, interest is calculated and paid in set intervals.

The primary formula for calculating the interest accrued in a given period is:

$$I_A = T \times P \times R$$

where I_A is the _____, T is the fraction of the year, P is the principal, and R is the annualized interest rate.

Chapter 10. Operational Assets: Acquisition and Disposition

a. ABC Television Network
b. AIG
c. Interest
d. Accrued interest

51. The phrase _____, according to the Organization for Economic Co-operation and Development, refers to 'creative work undertaken on a systematic basis in order to increase the stock of knowledge, including knowledge of man, culture and society, and the use of this stock of knowledge to devise new applications [sic]'

New product design and development is more than often a crucial factor in the survival of a company. In an industry that is fast changing, firms must continually revise their design and range of products. This is necessary due to continuous technology change and development as well as other competitors and the changing preference of customers.

a. 3M Company
b. BNSF Railway
c. BMC Software, Inc.
d. Research and development

52. _____ is a specific term used in companies' financial reporting from the company-whole point of view. Because that use excludes the effects of changing ownership interest, an economic measure of _____ is necessary for financial analysis from the shareholders' point of view

_____ is defined by the Financial Accounting Standards Board, or FASB, as 'the change in equity [net assets] of a business enterprise during a period from transactions and other events and circumstances from nonowner sources. It includes all changes in equity during a period except those resulting from investments by owners and distributions to owners.'

_____ is the sum of net income and other items that must bypass the income statement because they have not been realized, including items like an unrealized holding gain or loss from available for sale securities and foreign currency translation gains or losses.

a. 3M Company
b. Comprehensive income
c. BNSF Railway
d. BMC Software, Inc.

53. The term _____ describes a reduction in recognized value. In accounting terminology, it refers to recognition of the reduced or zero value of an asset. In income tax statements, it refers to a reduction of taxable income as recognition of certain expenses required to produce the income.

a. Current asset
b. Write-off
c. Payroll
d. Salvage value

54. _____ methods are means of managing inventory and financial matters involving the money a company ties up within inventory of produced goods, raw materials, parts, components, or feed stocks. FIFO stands for first-in, first-out, meaning that the oldest inventory items are recorded as sold first. LIFO stands for last-in, first-out, meaning that the most recently purchased items are recorded as sold first.

a. Finished good
b. 3M Company
c. Reorder point
d. FIFO and LIFO accounting

55. In law, _____ refers to the process by which a company (or part of a company) is brought to an end, and the assets and property of the company redistributed. _____ can also be referred to as winding-up or dissolution, although dissolution technically refers to the last stage of _____. The process of _____ also arises when customs, an authority or agency in a country responsible for collecting and safeguarding customs duties, determines the final computation or ascertainment of the duties or drawback accruing on an entry.

    a. Bankruptcy protection   b. 3M Company

    c. BMC Software, Inc.   d. Liquidation

Chapter 11. Operational Assets: Utilization and Impairment

1. _____ is a demonstration of a process -- such as a variable, term, or object -- relative in terms of the specific process or set of validation tests used to determine its presence and quantity. Properties described in this manner must be sufficiently accessible, so that persons other than the definer may independently measure or test for them at will. An _____ is generally designed to model a conceptual definition.

    a. AMEX
    b. AIG
    c. ABC Television Network
    d. Operational definition

2. In business and accounting, _____ are everything of value that is owned by a person or company. It is a claim on the property your income of a borrower. The balance sheet of a firm records the monetary value of the _____ owned by the firm.

    a. Earnings before interest, taxes, depreciation and amortization
    b. Accounts receivable
    c. Accrual basis accounting
    d. Assets

3. _____ means the giving out of information, either voluntarily or to be in compliance with legal regulations or workplace rules.

    - In Computer security, full _____ means disclosing full information about vulnerabilities.
    - In computing, _____ widget
    - Journalism, full _____ refers to disclosing the interests of the writer which may bear on the subject being written about, for example, if the writer has worked with an interview subject in the past.

    - In law:
        - The law of England and Wales, _____ refers to a process that may form part of legal proceedings, whereby parties inform to other parties the existence of any relevant documents that are, or have been, in their control. This compares with the process known as discovery in the course of legal proceedings in the United States.
        - In U.S. civil procedure (litigation rules for civil cases), _____ is a stage prior to trial. In civil cases, each party must disclose to the opposing party the following: names of witnesses which it may use to support its side, copies of documents (or mere description of these documents) in its control which it may use to support its side, computation of damages claimed, and certain insurance information. _____ is related to, but technically prior to, the discovery stage.
        - In Company law (known as 'corporate law' in the United States), _____ refers to giving out information about public or limited companies or their officers, which might be kept secret if the company was a private company or a partnership.

    - In real property transactions, _____ refers to providing to a buyer information known to the seller or broker/agent concerning the condition or other aspects of real property that would affect the property's value or desirability. These rules regarding what information must be disclosed, and whether the information must be disclosed even if a buyer does not ask, vary from one jurisdiction to the next.

    a. Controlled Foreign Corporations
    b. Trailing
    c. Tax harmonisation
    d. Disclosure

Chapter 11. Operational Assets: Utilization and Impairment

4. _____ methods are means of managing inventory and financial matters involving the money a company ties up within inventory of produced goods, raw materials, parts, components, or feed stocks. FIFO stands for first-in, first-out, meaning that the oldest inventory items are recorded as sold first. LIFO stands for last-in, first-out, meaning that the most recently purchased items are recorded as sold first.
   a. FIFO and LIFO accounting
   b. 3M Company
   c. Finished good
   d. Reorder point

5. In law, _____ refers to the process by which a company (or part of a company) is brought to an end, and the assets and property of the company redistributed. _____ can also be referred to as winding-up or dissolution, although dissolution technically refers to the last stage of _____. The process of _____ also arises when customs, an authority or agency in a country responsible for collecting and safeguarding customs duties, determines the final computation or ascertainment of the duties or drawback accruing on an entry.
   a. 3M Company
   b. Liquidation
   c. BMC Software, Inc.
   d. Bankruptcy protection

6. _____ is the process of increasing, or accounting for, an amount over a period of time. Particular instances of the term include:

   - _____, the allocation of a lump sum amount to different time periods, particularly for loans and other forms of finance, including related interest or other finance charges.
     - _____ schedule, a table detailing each periodic payment on a loan (typically a mortgage), as generated by an _____ calculator.
     - Negative _____, an _____ schedule where the loan amount actually increases through not paying the full interest
   - Amortized analysis, analyzing the execution cost of algorithms over a sequence of operations.
   - _____ of capital expenditures of certain assets under accounting rules, particularly intangible assets, in a manner analogous to depreciation.
   - _____

   a. EBIT
   b. Annuity
   c. Intangible
   d. Amortization

7. In economics, business, retail, and accounting, a _____ is the value of money that has been used up to produce something, and hence is not available for use anymore. In economics, a _____ is an alternative that is given up as a result of a decision. In business, the _____ may be one of acquisition, in which case the amount of money expended to acquire it is counted as _____.
   a. Prime cost
   b. Cost allocation
   c. Cost of quality
   d. Cost

8. _____ is a process of attributing cost to particular cost centres. For example the wage of the driver of the purchasing department can be allocated to the purchasing department cost centre. It is not necessary to share the wage cost over several different cost centers.
   a. Cost accounting
   b. Cost of quality
   c. Variable cost
   d. Cost allocation

Chapter 11. Operational Assets: Utilization and Impairment

9. _____ is a term used in accounting, economics and finance to spread the cost of an asset over the span of several years.

In simple words we can say that _____ is the reduction in the value of an asset due to usage, passage of time, wear and tear, technological outdating or obsolescence, depletion, inadequacy, rot, rust, decay or other such factors.

In accounting, _____ is a term used to describe any method of attributing the historical or purchase cost of an asset across its useful life, roughly corresponding to normal wear and tear.

   a. Net profit   b. General ledger
   c. Depreciation   d. Current asset

10. _____ is a fee paid on borrowed assets. It is the price paid for the use of borrowed money , or, money earned by deposited funds .Assets that are sometimes lent with _____ include money, shares, consumer goods through hire purchase, major assets such as aircraft, and even entire factories in finance lease arrangements. The _____ is calculated upon the value of the assets in the same manner as upon money.
   a. ABC Television Network   b. Interest
   c. Insolvency   d. AIG

11. _____ is a cornerstone of accrual accounting together with the revenue recognition principle. They both determine the accounting period, in which revenues and expenses are recognized. According to the principle, expenses are recognized when obligations are (1) incurred (usually when goods are transferred or services rendered, e.g. sold), and (2) offset against recognized revenues, which were generated from those expenses (related on the cause-and-effect basis), no matter when cash is paid out.
   a. Payroll   b. Matching principle
   c. Net sales   d. Current liabilities

12. _____ is one of the constituents of a leasing calculus or operation. It describes the future value of a good in terms of percentage of depreciation of its initial value.
   a. Residual value   b. Round-tripping
   c. 3M Company   d. Net pay

13. Straight-line depreciation is the simplest and most often used technique, in which the company estimates the _____ of the asset at the end of the period during which it will be used to generate revenues (useful life), and will expense a portion of original cost in equal increments over that period. The _____ is an estimate of the value of the asset at the time it will be sold or disposed of; it may be zero. _____ is scrap value, by another name.
   a. Salvage value   b. Net profit
   c. Closing entries   d. Generally accepted accounting principles

14. In physics, and more specifically kinematics, _____ is the change in velocity over time. Because velocity is a vector, it can change in two ways: a change in magnitude and/or a change in direction. In one dimension, _____ is the rate at which something speeds up or slows down.
   a. ABC Television Network   b. AIG
   c. AMEX   d. Acceleration

Chapter 11. Operational Assets: Utilization and Impairment

15. _____ refers to any one of several methods by which a company, for 'financial accounting' and/or tax purposes, depreciates a fixed asset in such a way that the amount of depreciation taken each year is higher during the earlier years of an assete;s life. For financial accounting purposes, _____ is generally used when an asset is expected to be much more productive during its early years, so that depreciation expense will more accurately represent how much of an assete;s usefulness is being used up each year. For tax purposes, _____ provides a way of deferring corporate income taxes by reducing taxable income in current years, in exchange for increased taxable income in future years.
    a. Indirect tax
    b. Effective marginal tax rates
    c. User charge
    d. Accelerated depreciation

16. There are several methods for calculating depreciation, generally based on either the passage of time or the level of activity (or use) of the asset.

    _____ is the simplest and most often used technique, in which the company estimates the salvage value of the asset at the end of the period during which it will be used to generate revenues (useful life), and will expense a portion of original cost in equal increments over that period.

    a. Pro forma
    b. Straight-line depreciation
    c. Current asset
    d. Closing entries

17. _____ are defined as identifiable non-monetary assets that cannot be seen, touched or physically measured, which are created through time and/or effort and that are identifiable as a separate asset. There are two primary forms of intangibles - legal intangibles (such as trade secrets (e.g., customer lists), copyrights, patents, trademarks, and goodwill) and competitive intangibles (such as knowledge activities (know-how, knowledge), collaboration activities, leverage activities, and structural activities.) Legal intangibles are known under the generic term intellectual property and generate legal property rights defensible in a court of law.
    a. AIG
    b. Overhead
    c. ABC Television Network
    d. Intangible assets

18. The _____ is the current method of accelerated asset depreciation required by the United States income tax code. Under _____, all assets are divided into classes which dictate the number of years over which an asset's cost will be recovered.

    Prior to the Accelerated Cost Recovery System (ACRS), most capital purchases were depreciated using a straight line technique, that allowed for the depreciation of the asset over its useful life.

    a. 3M Company
    b. Categorical grants
    c. BMC Software, Inc.
    d. Modified Accelerated Cost Recovery System

19. _____, also known as Merck Sharp ' Dohme or MSD outside the USA and Canada, is one of the largest pharmaceutical companies in the world. The headquarters of the company is located in Whitehouse Station, New Jersey, an unincorporated area in Readington Township.
    a. Merck ' Co., Inc.
    b. Pension System
    c. Procter ' Gamble
    d. Social Security

20. In accounting, _____ are considered liabilities of the business that are to be settled in cash within the fiscal year or the operating cycle, whichever period is longer.

Chapter 11. Operational Assets: Utilization and Impairment

For example accounts payable for goods, services or supplies that were purchased for use in the operation of the business and payable within a normal period of time would be _____.

Bonds, mortgages and loans that are payable over a term exceeding one year would be fixed liabilities.

a. Treasury stock
b. Current liabilities
c. Closing entries
d. Payroll

21. In financial accounting, a _____ is defined as an obligation of an entity arising from past transactions or events, the settlement of which may result in the transfer or use of assets, provision of services or other yielding of economic benefits in the future.

a. Vested
b. False Claims Act
c. Corporate governance
d. Liability

22. In tax accounting the _____ is the default applicable convention used for federal income tax purposes. Like other conventions, the _____ affects the depreciation deduction computation in the year in which the property is placed into service. Using the _____, a taxpayer claims a half of a year's depreciation for the first taxable year, regardless of when the property was actually put into service.

a. Half-year convention
b. Taxable income
c. Reverse Morris trust
d. Revenue Procedures

23. In finance, _____ is the interest that has accumulated since the principal investment, or since the previous interest payment if there has been one already. For a financial instrument such as a bond, interest is calculated and paid in set intervals.

The primary formula for calculating the interest accrued in a given period is:

$$I_A = T \times P \times R$$

where I_A is the _____, T is the fraction of the year, P is the principal, and R is the annualized interest rate.

a. Interest
b. Accrued interest
c. ABC Television Network
d. AIG

24. _____ is a specific term used in companies' financial reporting from the company-whole point of view. Because that use excludes the effects of changing ownership interest, an economic measure of _____ is necessary for financial analysis from the shareholders' point of view

_____ is defined by the Financial Accounting Standards Board, or FASB, as 'the change in equity [net assets] of a business enterprise during a period from transactions and other events and circumstances from nonowner sources. It includes all changes in equity during a period except those resulting from investments by owners and distributions to owners.'

_____ is the sum of net income and other items that must bypass the income statement because they have not been realized, including items like an unrealized holding gain or loss from available for sale securities and foreign currency translation gains or losses.

   a. BNSF Railway
   b. 3M Company
   c. Comprehensive income
   d. BMC Software, Inc.

25. The _____ is a 'voluntary organization of persons interested in accounting education and research'. It was formed in 1916. Its main publication, the The Accounting Review, was first published in 1926.
   a. Australian Accounting Standards Board
   b. American Accounting Association
   c. International Accounting Standards Board
   d. Institute of Management Accountants

26. _____ is any physical or virtual entity that is owned by an individual or jointly by a group of individuals. An owner of _____ has the right to consume, sell, rent, mortgage, transfer and exchange his or her _____. Important widely-recognized types of _____ include real _____, personal _____ (other physical possessions), and intellectual _____ (rights over artistic creations, inventions, etc.), although the latter is not always as widely recognized or enforced.
   a. Property
   b. Disclosure requirement
   c. Primary authority
   d. Fiduciary

27. _____, also known as property, plant, and equipment (PP&E), is a term used in accountancy for assets and property which cannot easily be converted into cash. This can be compared with current assets such as cash or bank accounts, which are described as liquid assets. In most cases, only tangible assets are referred to as fixed.
   a. Subledger
   b. Fixed asset
   c. Bankruptcy prediction
   d. Minority interest

28. A _____ is any one of a variety of different systems, institutions, procedures, social relations and infrastructures whereby persons trade, and goods and services are exchanged, forming part of the economy. It is an arrangement that allows buyers and sellers to exchange things. _____s vary in size, range, geographic scale, location, types and variety of human communities, as well as the types of goods and services traded.
   a. Perfect competition
   b. Market Failure
   c. Recession
   d. Market

29. In law, tangibility is the attribute of being detectable with the senses.

In criminal law, one of the elements of an offense of larceny is that the stolen property must be _____.

In the context of intellectual property, expression in _____ form is one of the requirements for copyright protection.

   a. Contingent liabilities
   b. Headnote
   c. Nonacquiescence
   d. Tangible

140   Chapter 11. Operational Assets: Utilization and Impairment

30. _____ is one of a series of accounting transactions dealing with the billing of customers who owe money to a person, company or organization for goods and services that have been provided to the customer. In most business entities this is typically done by generating an invoice and mailing or electronically delivering it to the customer, who in turn must pay it within an established timeframe called credit or payment terms.

An example of a common payment term is Net 30, meaning payment is due in the amount of the invoice 30 days from the date of invoice.

a. Accrued revenue
b. Accounts receivable
c. Accrual
d. Adjusting entries

31. _____, also called fair price (in a commonplace conflation of the two distinct concepts), is a concept used in finance and economics, defined as a rational and unbiased estimate of the potential market price of a good, service, or asset, taking into account such objective factors as:

- acquisition/production/distribution costs, replacement costs, or costs of close substitutes
- actual utility at a given level of development of social productive capability
- supply vs. demand

and subjective factors such as

- risk characteristics
- cost of capital
- individually perceived utility

In accounting, _____ is used as an estimate of the market value of an asset (or liability) for which a market price cannot be determined (usually because there is no established market for the asset.) Under GAAP (FAS 157), _____ is the amount at which the asset could be bought or sold in a current transaction between willing parties, or transferred to an equivalent party, other than in a liquidation sale. This is used for assets whose carrying value is based on mark-to-market valuations; for assets carried at historical cost, the _____ of the asset is not used. One example of where _____ is an issue is a College kitchen with a cost of $2 million which was built 5 years ago.

a. BNSF Railway
b. Fair value
c. 3M Company
d. BMC Software, Inc.

32. A _____ is a habit, a preparation, a state of readiness, or a tendency to act in a specified way.

The terms dispositional belief and occurrent belief refer, in the former case, to a belief that is held in the mind but not currently being considered, and in the latter case, to a belief that is currently being considered by the mind.

In Bourdieu's theory of fields _____s are the natural tendencies of each individual to take on a certain position in any field.

Chapter 11. Operational Assets: Utilization and Impairment

a. BNSF Railway
b. BMC Software, Inc.
c. 3M Company
d. Disposition

33. A _____ is the pinnacle activity involved in selling products or services in return for money or other compensation. It is an act of completion of a commercial activity.

A _____ is completed by the seller, the owner of the goods.

a. High yield stock
b. Tertiary sector of economy
c. Maturity
d. Sale

34. _____ is fixing any sort of mechanical or electrical device should it become out of order or broken (known as repair or unscheduled maintenance) as well as performing the routine actions which keep the device in working order (known as scheduled maintenance) or prevent trouble from arising (preventive maintenance.) The MRO business is seeing a major boom with the emergence of international carriers and private aviation in Asia. The MRO business in India alone is expected to grow to $45Bn from the current $0.5Bn in the next decade.

a. Maintenance, repair and operations
b. BNSF Railway
c. BMC Software, Inc.
d. 3M Company

35. The phrase _____, according to the Organization for Economic Co-operation and Development, refers to 'creative work undertaken on a systematic basis in order to increase the stock of knowledge, including knowledge of man, culture and society, and the use of this stock of knowledge to devise new applications [sic]'

New product design and development is more than often a crucial factor in the survival of a company. In an industry that is fast changing, firms must continually revise their design and range of products. This is necessary due to continuous technology change and development as well as other competitors and the changing preference of customers.

a. BNSF Railway
b. 3M Company
c. BMC Software, Inc.
d. Research and development

36. Book Value = Original Cost - _____

Book value at the end of year becomes book value at the beginning of next year. The asset is depreciated until the book value equals scrap value.

If the vehicle were to be sold and the sales price exceeded the depreciated value (net book value) then the excess would be considered a gain and subject to depreciation recapture.

a. AMEX
b. ABC Television Network
c. AIG
d. Accumulated depreciation

Chapter 12. Investments

1. _____ means the giving out of information, either voluntarily or to be in compliance with legal regulations or workplace rules.

- In Computer security, full _____ means disclosing full information about vulnerabilities.
- In computing, _____ widget
- Journalism, full _____ refers to disclosing the interests of the writer which may bear on the subject being written about, for example, if the writer has worked with an interview subject in the past.

- In law:
    - The law of England and Wales, _____ refers to a process that may form part of legal proceedings, whereby parties inform to other parties the existence of any relevant documents that are, or have been, in their control. This compares with the process known as discovery in the course of legal proceedings in the United States.
    - In U.S. civil procedure (litigation rules for civil cases), _____ is a stage prior to trial. In civil cases, each party must disclose to the opposing party the following: names of witnesses which it may use to support its side, copies of documents (or mere description of these documents) in its control which it may use to support its side, computation of damages claimed, and certain insurance information. _____ is related to, but technically prior to, the discovery stage.
    - In Company law (known as 'corporate law' in the United States), _____ refers to giving out information about public or limited companies or their officers, which might be kept secret if the company was a private company or a partnership.

- In real property transactions, _____ refers to providing to a buyer information known to the seller or broker/agent concerning the condition or other aspects of real property that would affect the property's value or desirability. These rules regarding what information must be disclosed, and whether the information must be disclosed even if a buyer does not ask, vary from one jurisdiction to the next.

a. Trailing
b. Disclosure
c. Controlled Foreign Corporations
d. Tax harmonisation

2. A _____ is a fungible, negotiable instrument representing financial value. they are broadly categorized into debt securities (such as banknotes, bonds and debentures), and equity securities; e.g., common stocks. The company or other entity issuing the _____ is called the issuer.

a. BMC Software, Inc.
b. Tracking stock
c. Security
d. 3M Company

3. In economics, business, retail, and accounting, a _____ is the value of money that has been used up to produce something, and hence is not available for use anymore. In economics, a _____ is an alternative that is given up as a result of a decision. In business, the _____ may be one of acquisition, in which case the amount of money expended to acquire it is counted as _____.

a. Prime cost
b. Cost allocation
c. Cost of quality
d. Cost

4. _____ is that which is owed; usually referencing assets owed, but the term can also cover moral obligations and other interactions not requiring money. In the case of assets, _____ is a means of using future purchasing power in the present before a summation has been earned. Some companies and corporations use _____ as a part of their overall corporate finance strategy.

Chapter 12. Investments

a. Lender
b. Loan
c. Debenture
d. Debt

5. _____ in accounting is the process of treating equity investments, usually 20-50%, in associate companies. The investor keeps such equities as an asset. Proportional share of associate company's net income increases the investment, and proportional payment of dividends decreases it.
   a. ABC Television Network
   b. AIG
   c. Out-of-pocket
   d. Equity method

6. _____ is a fee paid on borrowed assets. It is the price paid for the use of borrowed money, or, money earned by deposited funds. Assets that are sometimes lent with _____ include money, shares, consumer goods through hire purchase, major assets such as aircraft, and even entire factories in finance lease arrangements. The _____ is calculated upon the value of the assets in the same manner as upon money.
   a. AIG
   b. Insolvency
   c. Interest
   d. ABC Television Network

7. An _____ is the price a borrower pays for the use of money they do not own, for instance a small company might borrow from a bank to kick start their business, and the return a lender receives for deferring the use of funds, by lending it to the borrower. _____s are normally expressed as a percentage rate over the period of one year.

_____s targets are also a vital tool of monetary policy and are used to control variables like investment, inflation, and unemployment.

   a. ABC Television Network
   b. Interest rate
   c. AMEX
   d. AIG

8. An _____ is a derivative in which one party exchanges a stream of interest payments for another party's stream of cash flows. They can be used by hedgers to manage their fixed or floating assets and liabilities. They can also be used by speculators to replicate unfunded bond exposures to profit from changes in interest rates.
   a. Interest rate swap
   b. ABC Television Network
   c. AMEX
   d. AIG

9. A _____ is any one of a variety of different systems, institutions, procedures, social relations and infrastructures whereby persons trade, and goods and services are exchanged, forming part of the economy. It is an arrangement that allows buyers and sellers to exchange things. _____s vary in size, range, geographic scale, location, types and variety of human communities, as well as the types of goods and services traded.
   a. Perfect competition
   b. Market Failure
   c. Recession
   d. Market

10. _____ is a life of security. It may also refer to the final payment date of a loan or other financial instrument, at which point all remaining interest and principal is due to be paid.

1, 3, 6 months _____ band can be calculated by using 30-day per month periods. For _____ bands over a year it is acceptable to use 365 day per year. For example with a Treasury Bond, its _____ is the date on which the principal is paid.

Chapter 12. Investments

a. Factor

c. Maturity

b. Statements of Financial Accounting Standards No. 133, Accounting for Derivative Instruments and Hedging Activities

d. The Goodyear Tire ' Rubber Company

11. In finance, a _____ is a derivative in which two counterparties agree to exchange one stream of cash flow against another stream. These streams are called the legs of the _____.

The cash flows are calculated over a notional principal amount, which is usually not exchanged between counterparties.

a. Department of the Treasury

c. Controlled Foreign Corporations

b. Total-factor productivity

d. Swap

12. _____ of something is, in finance, the adding together of interest or different investments over a period of time such as atoms (1 - the act or process of accruing; 2 - the amount that accrues.) It holds specific meanings in accounting and payroll.

_____, in accounting, describes the accounting method known as _____ basis, whereby revenues and expenses are recognized when they are accrued, i.e. accumulated (earned or incurred), regardless when the actual cash is received or paid out.

a. Assets

c. Accrual

b. Earnings before interest, taxes, depreciation and amortization

d. Accounts receivable

13. _____ is a method of accounting whereby economic activities (rather than cash flow) of financial events are considered, because of two complementary principles, which (together) determine the point, at which expenses and revenues are recognized. According to revenue recognition principle, revenues are realized when earned, whether or not they are received in cash.

a. Accrual

c. Earnings before interest, taxes, depreciation and amortization

b. Accrued revenue

d. Accrual basis accounting

14. _____ or fair value accounting refers to the accounting standards of assigning a value to a position held in a financial instrument based on the current fair market price for the instrument or similar instruments. Fair value accounting has been a part of US Generally Accepted Accounting Principles (GAAP) since the early 1990s. The use of fair value measurements has increased steadily over the past decade, primarily in response to investor demand for relevant and timely financial statements that will aid in making better informed decisions.

a. Mark-to-market

c. Market liquidity

b. Financial instruments

d. Transfer agent

Chapter 12. Investments

15. _____, also called fair price (in a commonplace conflation of the two distinct concepts), is a concept used in finance and economics, defined as a rational and unbiased estimate of the potential market price of a good, service, or asset, taking into account such objective factors as:

- acquisition/production/distribution costs, replacement costs, or costs of close substitutes
- actual utility at a given level of development of social productive capability
- supply vs. demand

and subjective factors such as

- risk characteristics
- cost of capital
- individually perceived utility

In accounting, _____ is used as an estimate of the market value of an asset (or liability) for which a market price cannot be determined (usually because there is no established market for the asset.) Under GAAP (FAS 157), _____ is the amount at which the asset could be bought or sold in a current transaction between willing parties, or transferred to an equivalent party, other than in a liquidation sale. This is used for assets whose carrying value is based on mark-to-market valuations; for assets carried at historical cost, the _____ of the asset is not used. One example of where _____ is an issue is a College kitchen with a cost of $2 million which was built 5 years ago.

a. BMC Software, Inc.
c. BNSF Railway
b. 3M Company
d. Fair value

16. _____ are generally defined as increases (decreases) in the replacement costs of the assets held during a given period. _____ and losses accrue to the owners of assets and liabilities purely as a result of holding the assets or liabilities over time, without transforming them in any way.

For example, if a company holds bottles of wine in its inventory and that specific wine becomes more expensive on the market, the replacement cost of the wine in the inventory increases as it has become more expensive for the company to replace its current stock of wine.

a. Holding gains
c. Net worth
b. Fair market value
d. Par value

17. _____ is generally understood in financial circles as the point at which revenue is recognized, typically through a transaction which involves the exchange of an asset, product, or service for cash or its equivalents.

This approach gives the accounting division a strictly objective basis for changing the books. For example, a homeowner may believe that his house has grown in value during a strong market, or fallen in value during a weak market, but until the house is actually sold for a specific price to a specific buyer, the change in value can only be estimated and is considered unrealized.

a. Merck ' Co., Inc.
b. Realization
c. Valuation
d. Total-factor productivity

18. _____ is a subsection in equity where 'other comprehensive income' is accumulated (summed or 'aggregated'.)

The balance of _____ is presented in the Equity section of the Balance Sheet as is the Retained Earnings balance, which aggregates past and current Earnings, and past and current Dividends.

Other comprehensive income is the difference between net income and comprehensive income and represents the certain gains and losses of the enterprise.

a. Inventory turnover ratio
b. Accumulated other comprehensive income
c. Operating budget
d. Authorised capital

19. In business and accounting, _____ are everything of value that is owned by a person or company. It is a claim on the property your income of a borrower. The balance sheet of a firm records the monetary value of the _____ owned by the firm.

a. Earnings before interest, taxes, depreciation and amortization
b. Accrual basis accounting
c. Accounts receivable
d. Assets

20. _____ is a specific term used in companies' financial reporting from the company-whole point of view. Because that use excludes the effects of changing ownership interest, an economic measure of _____ is necessary for financial analysis from the shareholders' point of view

_____ is defined by the Financial Accounting Standards Board, or FASB, as 'the change in equity [net assets] of a business enterprise during a period from transactions and other events and circumstances from nonowner sources. It includes all changes in equity during a period except those resulting from investments by owners and distributions to owners.'

_____ is the sum of net income and other items that must bypass the income statement because they have not been realized, including items like an unrealized holding gain or loss from available for sale securities and foreign currency translation gains or losses.

a. BNSF Railway
b. BMC Software, Inc.
c. 3M Company
d. Comprehensive income

21. In financial accounting, a _____ or statement of financial position is a summary of a person's or organization's balances. Assets, liabilities and ownership equity are listed as of a specific date, such as the end of its financial year. A _____ is often described as a snapshot of a company's financial condition.

a. 3M Company
b. Balance sheet
c. Financial statements
d. Statement of retained earnings

22. In financial accounting, a _____ is defined as an obligation of an entity arising from past transactions or events, the settlement of which may result in the transfer or use of assets, provision of services or other yielding of economic benefits in the future.

Chapter 12. Investments

a. Vested
b. Liability
c. False Claims Act
d. Corporate governance

23. An _____ is a tax levied on the financial income of people, corporations, or other legal entities. Various _____ systems exist, with varying degrees of tax incidence. Income taxation can be progressive, proportional, or regressive.

a. Implied level of government service
b. Income tax
c. Ordinary income
d. Individual Retirement Arrangement

24. _____ are the earnings returned on the initial investment amount.

In the US, the Financial Accounting Standards Board (FASB) requires companies' income statements to report _____ for each of the major categories of the income statement: continuing operations, discontinued operations, extraordinary items, and net income.

The _____ formula does not include preferred dividends for categories outside of continued operations and net income.

a. Earnings yield
b. Earnings per share
c. Average accounting return
d. Invested capital

25. _____ are financial statements that factor the holding company's subsidiaries into its aggregated accounting figure. It is a representation of how the holding company is doing as a group. The consolidated accounts should provide a true and fair view of the financial and operating conditions of the group.

a. Redemption value
b. Consolidated financial statements
c. Committee on Accounting Procedure
d. Replacement cost

26. _____ are formal records of a business' financial activities.

In British English, including United Kingdom company law, _____ are often referred to as accounts, although the term _____ is also used, particularly by accountants.

_____ provide an overview of a business' financial condition in both short and long term.

a. Notes to the financial statements
b. Financial statements
c. Statement of retained earnings
d. 3M Company

27. A _____, in business matters, is an entity that is controlled by a bigger and more powerful entity. The controlled entity is called a company, corporation, or limited liability company, and the controlling entity is called its parent (or the parent company.) The reason for this distinction is that a lone company cannot be a _____ of any organization; only an entity representing a legal fiction as a separate entity can be a _____.

a. Parent company
b. BMC Software, Inc.
c. Subsidiary
d. 3M Company

28. In finance, an _____ is a contract between a buyer and a seller that gives the buyer the right--but not the obligation--to buy or to sell a particular asset (the underlying asset) at a later time at an agreed price. In return for granting the _____, the seller collects a payment (the premium) from the buyer. A call _____ gives the buyer the right to buy the underlying asset; a put _____ gives the buyer of the _____ the right to sell the underlying asset.
   a. ABC Television Network
   b. AIG
   c. AMEX
   d. Option

29. In accounting, _____ or carrying value is the value of an asset according to its balance sheet account balance. For assets, the value is based on the original cost of the asset less any depreciation, amortization or impairment costs made against the asset. Traditionally, a company's _____ is its total assets minus intangible assets and liabilities.
   a. Matching principle
   b. Generally accepted accounting principles
   c. Book value
   d. Depreciation

30. In physics, and more specifically kinematics, _____ is the change in velocity over time. Because velocity is a vector, it can change in two ways: a change in magnitude and/or a change in direction. In one dimension, _____ is the rate at which something speeds up or slows down.
   a. AMEX
   b. ABC Television Network
   c. AIG
   d. Acceleration

31. _____ refers to any one of several methods by which a company, for 'financial accounting' and/or tax purposes, depreciates a fixed asset in such a way that the amount of depreciation taken each year is higher during the earlier years of an assete;s life. For financial accounting purposes, _____ is generally used when an asset is expected to be much more productive during its early years, so that depreciation expense will more accurately represent how much of an assete;s usefulness Is being used up each year. For tax purposes, _____ provides a way of deferring corporate income taxes by reducing taxable income in current years, in exchange for increased taxable income In future years.
   a. Effective marginal tax rates
   b. Indirect tax
   c. User charge
   d. Accelerated depreciation

32. _____ is the process of increasing, or accounting for, an amount over a period of time. Particular instances of the term include:

   - _____, the allocation of a lump sum amount to different time periods, particularly for loans and other forms of finance, including related interest or other finance charges.
     - _____ schedule, a table detailing each periodic payment on a loan (typically a mortgage), as generated by an _____ calculator.
     - Negative _____, an _____ schedule where the loan amount actually increases through not paying the full interest
   - Amortized analysis, analyzing the execution cost of algorithms over a sequence of operations.
   - _____ of capital expenditures of certain assets under accounting rules, particularly intangible assets, in a manner analogous to depreciation.
   - _____

   a. EBIT
   b. Intangible
   c. Annuity
   d. Amortization

Chapter 12. Investments

33. An _____ is the buying of one company by another. An _____ may be friendly or hostile. In the former case, the companies cooperate in negotiations; in the latter case, the takeover target is unwilling to be bought or the target's board has no prior knowledge of the offer. _____ usually refers to a purchase of a smaller firm by a larger one. Sometimes, however, a smaller firm will acquire management control of a larger or longer established company and keep its name for the combined entity. This is known as a reverse takeover.

   a. AIG
   b. AMEX
   c. ABC Television Network
   d. Acquisition

34. _____ is a term used in accounting, economics and finance to spread the cost of an asset over the span of several years.

   In simple words we can say that _____ is the reduction in the value of an asset due to usage, passage of time, wear and tear, technological outdating or obsolescence, depletion, inadequacy, rot, rust, decay or other such factors.

   In accounting, _____ is a term used to describe any method of attributing the historical or purchase cost of an asset across its useful life, roughly corresponding to normal wear and tear.

   a. General ledger
   b. Net profit
   c. Current asset
   d. Depreciation

35. In financial accounting, a _____ or Statement of cash flows is a financial statement that shows a company's flow of cash. The money coming into the business is called cash inflow, and money going out from the business is called cash outflow. The statement shows how changes in balance sheet and income accounts affect cash and cash equivalents, and breaks the analysis down to operating, investing, and financing activities.

   a. 3M Company
   b. BNSF Railway
   c. Cash flow statement
   d. BMC Software, Inc.

36. _____ is the balance of the amounts of cash being received and paid by a business during a defined period of time, sometimes tied to a specific project. Measurement of _____ can be used

   - to evaluate the state or performance of a business or project.
   - to determine problems with liquidity. Being profitable does not necessarily mean being liquid. A company can fail because of a shortage of cash, even while profitable.
   - to project rate of returns. The time of _____s into and out of projects are used as inputs to financial models such as internal rate of return, and net present value.
   - to examine income or growth of a business when it is believed that accrual accounting concepts do not represent economic realities. Alternately, _____ can be used to 'validate' the net income generated by accrual accounting.

   _____ as a generic term may be used differently depending on context, and certain _____ definitions may be adapted by analysts and users for their own uses. Common terms include operating _____ and free _____.

   a. Flow-through entity
   b. Controlling interest
   c. Commercial paper
   d. Cash flow

Chapter 12. Investments

37. A _____ is the pinnacle activity involved in selling products or services in return for money or other compensation. It is an act of completion of a commercial activity.

A _____ is completed by the seller, the owner of the goods.

   a. Sale
   c. Tertiary sector of economy
   b. High yield stock
   d. Maturity

38. In economic models, the _____ time frame assumes no fixed factors of production. Firms can enter or leave the marketplace, and the cost (and availability) of land, labor, raw materials, and capital goods can be assumed to vary. In contrast, in the short-run time frame, certain factors are assumed to be fixed, because there is not sufficient time for them to change.

   a. Short-run
   c. BMC Software, Inc.
   b. 3M Company
   d. Long-run

39. In economics, the concept of the _____ refers to the decision-making time frame of a firm in which at least one factor of production is fixed. Costs which are fixed in the _____ have no impact on a firms decisions. For example a firm can raise output by increasing the amount of labour through overtime.

   a. Long-run
   c. BMC Software, Inc.
   b. 3M Company
   d. Short-run

40. _____s are cash, evidence of an ownership interest in an entity or deliver, cash or another _____.

_____s can be categorized by form depending on whether they are cash instruments or derivative instruments:

- Cash instruments are _____s whose value is determined directly by markets. They can be divided into securities, which are readily transferable, and other cash instruments such as loans and deposits, where both borrower and lender have to agree on a transfer.
- Derivative instruments are _____s which derive their value from the value and characteristics of one or more underlying assets. They can be divided into exchange-traded derivatives and over-the-counter (OTC) derivatives.

Alternatively, _____s can be categorized by 'asset class' depending on whether they are equity based (reflecting ownership of the issuing entity) or debt based (reflecting a loan the investor has made to the issuing entity.) If it is debt, it can be further categorised into short term (less than one year) or long term.

Foreign Exchange instruments and transactions are neither debt nor equity based and belong in their own category.

   a. Financial instrument
   c. Mark-to-market
   b. Market price
   d. Financial instruments

41. _____ are cash, evidence of an ownership interest in an entity, or a contractual right to receive, or deliver, cash or another financial instrument.

Chapter 12. Investments

_____ can be categorized by form depending on whether they are cash instruments or derivative instruments:

- Cash instruments are _____ whose value is determined directly by markets. They can be divided into securities, which are readily transferable, and other cash instruments such as loans and deposits, where both borrower and lender have to agree on a transfer.
- Derivative instruments are _____ which derive their value from the value and characteristics of one or more underlying assets. They can be divided into exchange-traded derivatives and over-the-counter (OTC) derivatives.

Alternatively, _____ can be categorized by 'asset class' depending on whether they are equity based (reflecting ownership of the issuing entity) or debt based (reflecting a loan the investor has made to the issuing entity.) If it is debt, it can be further categorised into short term (less than one year) or long term.

Foreign Exchange instruments and transactions are neither debt nor equity based and belong in their own category.

a. Market liquidity
b. Spot rate
c. Financial instruments
d. Transfer agent

42. Procter is a surname, and may also refer to:

- Bryan Waller Procter (pseud. Barry Cornwall), English poet
- Goodwin Procter, American law firm
- _____, consumer products multinational

a. Screening
b. Markup
c. Welfare
d. Procter ' Gamble

43. A _____ is a time deposit, a financial product commonly offered to consumers by banks, thrift institutions, and credit unions.

They are similar to savings accounts in that they are insured and thus virtually risk-free; they are 'money in the bank' (_____s are insured by the FDIC for banks or by the NCUA for credit unions.) They are different from savings accounts in that the _____ has a specific, fixed term (often three months, six months, or one to five years), and, usually, a fixed interest rate.

a. Certificate of deposit
b. Prime rate
c. Reserve requirement
d. Transactional account

44. In accounting, _____ are considered liabilities of the business that are to be settled in cash within the fiscal year or the operating cycle, whichever period is longer.

For example accounts payable for goods, services or supplies that were purchased for use in the operation of the business and payable within a normal period of time would be _____.

Bonds, mortgages and loans that are payable over a term exceeding one year would be fixed liabilities.

a. Payroll
b. Closing entries
c. Treasury stock
d. Current liabilities

45. _____ is the state or fact of exclusive rights and control over property, which may be an object, land/real estate or intellectual property. An _____ right is also referred to as title.

_____ is the key building block in the development of the capitalist socio-economic system.

a. ABC Television Network
b. Administrative proceeding
c. Ownership
d. Encumbrance

46. _____ is often a small amount of discretionary funds in the form of cash used for expenditures where it is not sensible to make the disbursement by check, because of the inconvenience and costs of writing, signing and then cashing the check.

The most common way of accounting expenditures is to use the imprest system. The initial fund would be created by issuing a check for the desired amount.

a. Remittance advice
b. Fixed asset
c. Petty cash
d. Minority interest

47. _____, in law and economics, is a form of risk management primarily used to hedge against the risk of a contingent loss. _____ is defined as the equitable transfer of the risk of a loss, from one entity to another, in exchange for a premium, and can be thought of as a guaranteed small loss to prevent a large, possibly devastating loss. An insurer is a company selling the _____; an insured is the person or entity buying the _____.

a. AMEX
b. Insurance
c. ABC Television Network
d. AIG

48. _____ represents claims for which formal instruments of credit are issued as evidence of debt, such as a promissory note. The credit instrument normally requires the debtor to pay interest and extends for time periods of 60-90 days or longer.

a. Moving average
b. Notes receivable
c. Public offering
d. Restricted stock

49. _____ is the corporate management term for the act of partially dismantling or otherwise reorganizing a company for the purpose of making it more profitable. Also known as corporate _____, debt _____ and financial _____.

_____ is often done as part of a bankruptcy or of a strategic takeover by another firm, such as a leveraged buyout by a private equity firm.

a. Fair market value
b. Net worth
c. Payback period
d. Restructuring

Chapter 13. Current Liabilities and Contingencies

1. In accounting, _____ are considered liabilities of the business that are to be settled in cash within the fiscal year or the operating cycle, whichever period is longer.

For example accounts payable for goods, services or supplies that were purchased for use in the operation of the business and payable within a normal period of time would be _____.

Bonds, mortgages and loans that are payable over a term exceeding one year would be fixed liabilities.

   a. Treasury stock
   c. Payroll
   b. Current liabilities
   d. Closing entries

2. In financial accounting, a _____ is defined as an obligation of an entity arising from past transactions or events, the settlement of which may result in the transfer or use of assets, provision of services or other yielding of economic benefits in the future.

   a. Corporate governance
   c. Vested
   b. False Claims Act
   d. Liability

3. The basic _____ is the foundation for the double-entry bookkeeping system. It shows how assets were financed: either by borrowing money from someone (liability) or by paying your own money (shareholders' equity.)

   Assets = Liabilities + (Shareholders or Owners equity)

For example: A student buys a computer for $945.

   a. AMEX
   c. AIG
   b. ABC Television Network
   d. Accounting equation

4. A _____ is a party (e.g. person, organization, company, or government) that has a claim to the services of a second party. It is a person or institution to whom money is owed. The first party, in general, has provided some property or service to the second party under the assumption (usually enforced by contract) that the second party will return an equivalent property or service.

   a. Payback period
   c. Treasury company
   b. Par value
   d. Creditor

5. In accounting, a _____ is an asset on the balance sheet which is expected to be sold or otherwise used up in the near future, usually within one year, or one business cycle - whichever is longer. Typical _____s include cash, cash equivalents, accounts receivable, inventory, the portion of prepaid accounts which will be used within a year, and short-term investments.

On the balance sheet, assets will typically be classified into _____s and long-term assets.

   a. Deferred
   c. General ledger
   b. Pro forma
   d. Current asset

Chapter 13. Current Liabilities and Contingencies

6. _____ is a concept that denotes the precise probability of specific eventualities. Technically, the notion of _____ is independent from the notion of value and, as such, eventualities may have both beneficial and adverse consequences. However, in general usage the convention is to focus only on potential negative impact to some characteristic of value that may arise from a future event.
   a. Risk
   b. Discount factor
   c. Risk adjusted return on capital
   d. Discounting

7. Simply put, _____ is the value of money figuring in a given amount of interest for a given amount of time. For example 100 dollars of todays money held for a year at 5 percent interest is worth 105 dollars, therefore 100 dollars paid now or 105 dollars paid exactly one year from now is the same amount of payment of money with that given intersest at that given amount of time. This notion dates at least to Martín de Azpilcueta of the School of Salamanca.
   a. Competition law
   b. Merck ' Co., Inc.
   c. Time value of money
   d. Collusion

8. In business and accounting, _____ are everything of value that is owned by a person or company. It is a claim on the property your income of a borrower. The balance sheet of a firm records the monetary value of the _____ owned by the firm.
   a. Accrual basis accounting
   b. Assets
   c. Accounts receivable
   d. Earnings before interest, taxes, depreciation and amortization

9. _____ is a file or account that contains money that a person or company owes to suppliers, but has not paid yet (a form of debt.) When you receive an invoice you add it to the file, and then you remove it when you pay. Thus, the A/P is a form of credit that suppliers offer to their purchasers by allowing them to pay for a product or service after it has already been received.
   a. Earnings before interest, taxes, depreciation and amortization
   b. Accounts receivable
   c. Accrual
   d. Accounts payable

10. In economic models, the _____ time frame assumes no fixed factors of production. Firms can enter or leave the marketplace, and the cost (and availability) of land, labor, raw materials, and capital goods can be assumed to vary. In contrast, in the short-run time frame, certain factors are assumed to be fixed, because there is not sufficient time for them to change.
    a. Short-run
    b. BMC Software, Inc.
    c. 3M Company
    d. Long-run

Chapter 13. Current Liabilities and Contingencies

11. _____ means the giving out of information, either voluntarily or to be in compliance with legal regulations or workplace rules.

- In Computer security, full _____ means disclosing full information about vulnerabilities.
- In computing, _____ widget
- Journalism, full _____ refers to disclosing the interests of the writer which may bear on the subject being written about, for example, if the writer has worked with an interview subject in the past.

- In law:
    - The law of England and Wales, _____ refers to a process that may form part of legal proceedings, whereby parties inform to other parties the existence of any relevant documents that are, or have been, in their control. This compares with the process known as discovery in the course of legal proceedings in the United States.
    - In U.S. civil procedure (litigation rules for civil cases), _____ is a stage prior to trial. In civil cases, each party must disclose to the opposing party the following: names of witnesses which it may use to support its side, copies of documents (or mere description of these documents) in its control which it may use to support its side, computation of damages claimed, and certain insurance information. _____ is related to, but technically prior to, the discovery stage.
    - In Company law (known as 'corporate law' in the United States), _____ refers to giving out information about public or limited companies or their officers, which might be kept secret if the company was a private company or a partnership.

- In real property transactions, _____ refers to providing to a buyer information known to the seller or broker/agent concerning the condition or other aspects of real property that would affect the property's value or desirability. These rules regarding what information must be disclosed, and whether the information must be disclosed even if a buyer does not ask, vary from one jurisdiction to the next.

a. Controlled Foreign Corporations
c. Trailing
b. Tax harmonisation
d. Disclosure

12. A _____, also referred to as a note payable in accounting, is a contract where one party (the maker or issuer) makes an unconditional promise in writing to pay a sum of money to the other (the payee), either at a fixed or determinable future time or on demand of the payee, under specific terms. They differ from IOUs in that they contain a specific promise to pay, rather than simply acknowledging that a debt exists.

The terms of a note typically include the principal amount, the interest rate if any, and the maturity date.

a. BNSF Railway
c. 3M Company
b. BMC Software, Inc.
d. Promissory note

13. In economics, the concept of the _____ refers to the decision-making time frame of a firm in which at least one factor of production is fixed. Costs which are fixed in the _____ have no impact on a firms decisions. For example a firm can raise output by increasing the amount of labour through overtime.

a. Short-run
c. BMC Software, Inc.
b. 3M Company
d. Long-run

Chapter 13. Current Liabilities and Contingencies

14. A _____ is any credit facility extended to a business by a bank or financial institution. A _____ may take several forms such as cash credit, overdraft, demand loan, export packing credit, term loan, discounting or purchase of commercial bills etc. It is like an account that can readily be tapped into if the need arises or not touched at all and saved for emergencies.
    a. Line of credit
    b. BMC Software, Inc.
    c. Simple interest
    d. 3M Company

15. _____ are securities that can be easily converted into cash. Such securities will generally have highly liquid markets allowing the security to be sold at a reasonable price very quickly. This is a usual feature in real estate .
    a. 3M Company
    b. Tracking stock
    c. BMC Software, Inc.
    d. Marketable

16. A _____ is a fungible, negotiable instrument representing financial value. they are broadly categorized into debt securities (such as banknotes, bonds and debentures), and equity securities; e.g., common stocks. The company or other entity issuing the _____ is called the issuer.
    a. 3M Company
    b. Tracking stock
    c. BMC Software, Inc.
    d. Security

17. Discounting is a financial mechanism in which a debtor obtains the right to delay payments to a creditor, for a defined period of time, in exchange for a charge or fee. Essentially, the party that owes money in the present purchases the right to delay the payment until some future date. The _____, or charge, is simply the difference between the original amount owed in the present and the amount that has to be paid in the future to settle the debt.
    a. Discount factor
    b. Risk aversion
    c. Discount
    d. Discounting

18. _____ is a fee paid on borrowed assets. It is the price paid for the use of borrowed money , or, money earned by deposited funds .Assets that are sometimes lent with _____ include money, shares, consumer goods through hire purchase, major assets such as aircraft, and even entire factories in finance lease arrangements. The _____ is calculated upon the value of the assets in the same manner as upon money.
    a. Interest
    b. Insolvency
    c. AIG
    d. ABC Television Network

19. An _____ is the price a borrower pays for the use of money they do not own, for instance a small company might borrow from a bank to kick start their business, and the return a lender receives for deferring the use of funds, by lending it to the borrower. _____s are normally expressed as a percentage rate over the period of one year.

    _____s targets are also a vital tool of monetary policy and are used to control variables like investment, inflation, and unemployment.

    a. ABC Television Network
    b. AMEX
    c. AIG
    d. Interest rate

20. A _____ is the pinnacle activity involved in selling products or services in return for money or other compensation. It is an act of completion of a commercial activity.

    A _____ is completed by the seller, the owner of the goods.

Chapter 13. Current Liabilities and Contingencies

a. Maturity
b. Tertiary sector of economy
c. High yield stock
d. Sale

21. In the global money market, _____ is an unsecured promissory note with a fixed maturity of one to 270 days. _____ is a money-market security issued (sold) by large banks and corporations to get money to meet short term debt obligations (for example, payroll), and is only backed by an issuing bank or corporation's promise to pay the face amount on the maturity date specified on the note. Since it is not backed by collateral, only firms with excellent credit ratings from a recognized rating agency will be able to sell their _____ at a reasonable price.
    a. Flow-through entity
    b. Gross profit margin
    c. Controlling interest
    d. Commercial paper

22. _____s are cash, evidence of an ownership interest in an entity or deliver, cash or another _____.

    _____s can be categorized by form depending on whether they are cash instruments or derivative instruments:

    - Cash instruments are _____s whose value is determined directly by markets. They can be divided into securities, which are readily transferable, and other cash instruments such as loans and deposits, where both borrower and lender have to agree on a transfer.
    - Derivative instruments are _____s which derive their value from the value and characteristics of one or more underlying assets. They can be divided into exchange-traded derivatives and over-the-counter (OTC) derivatives.

    Alternatively, _____s can be categorized by 'asset class' depending on whether they are equity based (reflecting ownership of the issuing entity) or debt based (reflecting a loan the investor has made to the issuing entity.) If it is debt, it can be further categorised into short term (less than one year) or long term.

    Foreign Exchange instruments and transactions are neither debt nor equity based and belong in their own category.

    a. Market price
    b. Financial instruments
    c. Mark-to-market
    d. Financial instrument

23. _____ are cash, evidence of an ownership interest in an entity, or a contractual right to receive, or deliver, cash or another financial instrument.

Chapter 13. Current Liabilities and Contingencies

_____ can be categorized by form depending on whether they are cash instruments or derivative instruments:

- Cash instruments are _____ whose value is determined directly by markets. They can be divided into securities, which are readily transferable, and other cash instruments such as loans and deposits, where both borrower and lender have to agree on a transfer.
- Derivative instruments are _____ which derive their value from the value and characteristics of one or more underlying assets. They can be divided into exchange-traded derivatives and over-the-counter (OTC) derivatives.

Alternatively, _____ can be categorized by 'asset class' depending on whether they are equity based (reflecting ownership of the issuing entity) or debt based (reflecting a loan the investor has made to the issuing entity.) If it is debt, it can be further categorised into short term (less than one year) or long term.

Foreign Exchange instruments and transactions are neither debt nor equity based and belong in their own category.

a. Market liquidity
b. Spot rate
c. Transfer agent
d. Financial instruments

24. A _____ is a type of debt Like all debt instruments, a _____ entails the redistribution of financial assets over time, between the lender and the borrower.
a. Loan to value
b. Debenture
c. Lender
d. Loan

25. A _____ is a time deposit, a financial product commonly offered to consumers by banks, thrift institutions, and credit unions.

They are similar to savings accounts in that they are insured and thus virtually risk-free; they are 'money in the bank' (_____s are insured by the FDIC for banks or by the NCUA for credit unions.) They are different from savings accounts in that the _____ has a specific, fixed term (often three months, six months, or one to five years), and, usually, a fixed interest rate.

a. Prime rate
b. Transactional account
c. Reserve requirement
d. Certificate of deposit

26. In finance, _____ is the interest that has accumulated since the principal investment, or since the previous interest payment if there has been one already. For a financial instrument such as a bond, interest is calculated and paid in set intervals.

The primary formula for calculating the interest accrued in a given period is:

$$I_A = T \times P \times R$$

where I_A is the _____, T is the fraction of the year, P is the principal, and R is the annualized interest rate.

a. ABC Television Network
b. Accrued interest
c. AIG
d. Interest

27. _____ are liabilities which have occurred, but have not been paid or logged under accounts payable during an accounting period; in other words, obligations for goods and services provided to a company for which invoices have not yet been received. Examples would include accrued wages payable, accrued sales tax payable, and accrued rent payable.

There are two general types of _____:

- Routine and recurring
- Infrequent or non-routine

Most companies pay their employees on a predetermined schedule. Let's say that the 'Imaginary company Ltd.' pays its employees each Friday for the hours worked that week.

a. AIG
b. AMEX
c. ABC Television Network
d. Accrued liabilities

28. Employment is a contract between two parties, one being the employer and the other being the _____. An _____ may be defined as: 'A person in the service of another under any contract of hire, express or implied, oral or written, where the employer has the power or right to control and direct the _____ in the material details of how the work is to be performed.' Black's Law Dictionary page 471 (5th ed. 1979.)

a. AIG
b. AMEX
c. ABC Television Network
d. Employee

29. A _____ is a compensation, usually financial, received by a worker in exchange for their labor.

Compensation in terms of _____s is given to worker and compensation in terms of salary is given to employees. Compensation is a monetary benefits given to employees in returns of the services provided by them.

a. BMC Software, Inc.
b. 3M Company
c. Retirement plan
d. Wage

30. _____ is the state or fact of exclusive rights and control over property, which may be an object, land/real estate or intellectual property. An _____ right is also referred to as title.

_____ is the key building block in the development of the capitalist socio-economic system.

a. Administrative proceeding
b. ABC Television Network
c. Encumbrance
d. Ownership

Chapter 13. Current Liabilities and Contingencies

31. In finance, a _____ is a debt security, in which the authorized issuer owes the holders a debt and, depending on the terms of the _____, is obliged to pay interest (the coupon) and/or to repay the principal at a later date, termed maturity. It is a formal contract to repay borrowed money with interest at fixed intervals.

Thus a _____ is like a loan: the issuer is the borrower, the _____ holder is the lender, and the coupon is the interest.

   a. Coupon rate
   c. Revenue bonds
   b. Zero-coupon bond
   d. Bond

32. A _____ is a rest from work, a hiatus, typically lasting two or more months. The concept of a _____ has a source in several places in the Bible, where there is a commandment to desist from working the fields in the seventh year. In the strict sense therefore, a _____ lasts a year.

   a. BNSF Railway
   c. 3M Company
   b. BMC Software, Inc.
   d. Sabbatical

33. A _____, also client, buyer or purchaser is the buyer or user of the paid products of an individual or organization, mostly called the supplier or seller. This is typically through purchasing or renting goods or services.

   a. 3M Company
   c. BNSF Railway
   b. Customer
   d. BMC Software, Inc.

34. A _____ is a type of bond that allows the issuer of the bond to retain the privilege of redeeming the bond at some point before the bond reaches the date of maturity. In other words, on the call dates, the issuer has the right, but not the obligation, to buy back the bonds from the bond holders at the call price. Technically speaking, the bonds are not really bought and held by the issuer but cancelled immediately.

   a. Callable bond
   c. Coupon rate
   b. Catastrophe bonds
   d. Zero-coupon

35. _____ is that which is owed; usually referencing assets owed, but the term can also cover moral obligations and other interactions not requiring money. In the case of assets, _____ is a means of using future purchasing power in the present before a summation has been earned. Some companies and corporations use _____ as a part of their overall corporate finance strategy.

   a. Debt
   c. Lender
   b. Debenture
   d. Loan

36. _____ refers to the replacement of an existing debt obligation with a debt obligation bearing different terms. The most common consumer _____ is for a home mortgage.

_____ may be undertaken to reduce interest rate/interest costs (by _____ at a lower rate), to extend the repayment time, to pay off other debt(s), to reduce one's periodic payment obligations (sometimes by taking a longer-term loan), to reduce or alter risk (such as by _____ from a variable-rate to a fixed-rate loan), and/or to raise cash for investment, consumption, or the payment of a dividend.

   a. 3M Company
   c. BMC Software, Inc.
   b. BNSF Railway
   d. Refinancing

Chapter 13. Current Liabilities and Contingencies

37. An _____ is a tax levied on the financial income of people, corporations, or other legal entities. Various _____ systems exist, with varying degrees of tax incidence. Income taxation can be progressive, proportional, or regressive.
   a. Individual Retirement Arrangement
   b. Implied level of government service
   c. Ordinary income
   d. Income tax

38. _____ methods are means of managing inventory and financial matters involving the money a company ties up within inventory of produced goods, raw materials, parts, components, or feed stocks. FIFO stands for first-in, first-out, meaning that the oldest inventory items are recorded as sold first. LIFO stands for last-in, first-out, meaning that the most recently purchased items are recorded as sold first.
   a. Reorder point
   b. 3M Company
   c. FIFO and LIFO accounting
   d. Finished good

39. In law, _____ refers to the process by which a company (or part of a company) is brought to an end, and the assets and property of the company redistributed. _____ can also be referred to as winding-up or dissolution, although dissolution technically refers to the last stage of _____. The process of _____ also arises when customs, an authority or agency in a country responsible for collecting and safeguarding customs duties, determines the final computation or ascertainment of the duties or drawback accruing on an entry.
   a. 3M Company
   b. Bankruptcy protection
   c. Liquidation
   d. BMC Software, Inc.

40. An _____ is quite usually a standard guarantee from the seller of a product that specifies the extent to which the quality or performance of the product is assured and states the conditions under which the product can be returned, replaced, or repaired. It is often given in the form of a specific, written 'Warranty' document. However, a warranty may also arise by operation of law based upon the seller's description of the goods, and perhaps their source and quality, and any material deviation from that specification would violate the guarantee.
   a. Exclusive right
   b. Escheat
   c. Operating Lease
   d. Express warranty

41. _____ is the balance of the amounts of cash being received and paid by a business during a defined period of time, sometimes tied to a specific project. Measurement of _____ can be used

   - to evaluate the state or performance of a business or project.
   - to determine problems with liquidity. Being profitable does not necessarily mean being liquid. A company can fail because of a shortage of cash, even while profitable.
   - to project rate of returns. The time of _____s into and out of projects are used as inputs to financial models such as internal rate of return, and net present value.
   - to examine income or growth of a business when it is believed that accrual accounting concepts do not represent economic realities. Alternately, _____ can be used to 'validate' the net income generated by accrual accounting.

   _____ as a generic term may be used differently depending on context, and certain _____ definitions may be adapted by analysts and users for their own uses. Common terms include operating _____ and free _____.

Chapter 13. Current Liabilities and Contingencies

a. Commercial paper
c. Controlling interest
b. Flow-through entity
d. Cash flow

42. _____ of something is, in finance, the adding together of interest or different investments over a period of time such as atoms (1 - the act or process of accruing; 2 - the amount that accrues.) It holds specific meanings in accounting and payroll.

_____, in accounting, describes the accounting method known as _____ basis, whereby revenues and expenses are recognized when they are accrued, i.e. accumulated (earned or incurred), regardless when the actual cash is received or paid out.

a. Assets
c. Earnings before interest, taxes, depreciation and amortization
b. Accounts receivable
d. Accrual

43. In marketing a _____ is a ticket or document that can be exchanged for a financial discount or rebate when purchasing a product. Customarily, _____s are issued by manufacturers of consumer packaged goods or by retailers, to be used in retail stores as a part of sales promotions. They are often widely distributed through mail, magazines, newspapers, the Internet, and mobile devices such as cell phones.

a. Merchandising
c. 3M Company
b. BMC Software, Inc.
d. Coupon

44. The Exxon Mobil Corporation is an American oil and gas corporation. It is a direct descendant of John D. Rockefeller's Standard Oil company, formed on November 30, 1999, by the merger of Exxon and Mobil.

_____ is the world's largest publicly traded company when measured by either revenue or market capitalization.

a. Abby Joseph Cohen
c. ExxonMobil
b. Arthur Betz Laffer
d. Alan Greenspan

45. _____ is the term used to refer to the standard framework of guidelines for financial accounting used in any given jurisdiction. _____ includes the standards, conventions, and rules accountants follow in recording and summarizing transactions, and in the preparation of financial statements.

Financial accounting information must be assembled and reported objectively.

a. General ledger
c. Generally accepted accounting principles
b. Current asset
d. Long-term liabilities

46. In finance, the _____ or quick ratio or liquid ratio measures the ability of a company to use its near cash or quick assets to immediately extinguish or retire its current liabilities. Quick assets include those current assets that presumably can be quickly converted to cash at close to their book values.

Chapter 13. Current Liabilities and Contingencies

$$\text{Quick (Acid Test) Ratio} = \frac{\text{Cash} + \text{Marketable Securities} + \text{Accounts Receivables}}{\text{Current Liabilities}}$$

Generally, the acid test ratio should be 1:1 or better, however this varies widely by industry.

a. Invested capital
c. Acid-test
b. Earnings per share
d. Inventory turnover

47. The _____ is a financial ratio that measures whether or not a firm has enough resources to pay its debts over the next 12 months. It compares a firm's current assets to its current liabilities. It is expressed as follows:

$$\text{Current ratio} = \frac{\text{Current Assets}}{\text{Current Liabilities}}$$

For example, if WXY Company's current assets are $50,000,000 and its current liabilities are $40,000,000, then its _____ would be $50,000,000 divided by $40,000,000, which equals 1.25.

a. Net Interest Income
c. Return on capital
b. Times interest earned
d. Current ratio

48. _____ is a business, economics or investment term that refers to an asset's ability to be easily converted through an act of buying or selling without causing a significant movement in the price and with minimum loss of value. Money, or cash on hand, is the most liquid asset. An act of exchange of a less liquid asset with a more liquid asset is called liquidation.

a. Transfer agent
c. Spot rate
b. Market liquidity
d. Financial instruments

49. _____, in accrual accounting, is any account where the asset or liability is not realized until a future date (accounting period), e.g. annuities, charges, taxes, income, etc. The _____ item may be carried, dependent on type of deferral, as either an asset or liability.

a. Payroll
c. Cash basis accounting
b. Pro forma
d. Deferred

50. _____ is an accounting concept, meaning a future tax liability or asset, resulting from temporary differences between book (accounting) value of assets and liabilities and their tax value, or timing differences between the recognition of gains and losses in financial statements and their recognition in a tax computation.

Temporary differences are differences between the carrying amount of an asset or liability recognised in the balance sheet and the amount attributed to that asset or liability for tax purposes (the tax base.)

a. Federal tax revenue by state
c. Deferred tax
b. Tax refund
d. Deficit

Chapter 13. Current Liabilities and Contingencies

51. The _____ (or _____, 26 U.S.C. ch.23) is a United States federal law that imposes a federal employer tax used to fund state workforce agencies. Employers report this tax by filing an annual Form 940 with the Internal Revenue Service.
   a. Fuel tax
   b. Form 1099
   c. Carbon tax
   d. FUTA

52. The _____ tax is a United States payroll tax imposed by the federal government on both employees and employers to fund Social Security and Medicare --federal programs that provide benefits for retirees, the disabled, and children of deceased workers. Social Security benefits include old-age, survivors, and disability insurance (OASDI); Medicare provides hospital insurance benefits. The amount that one pays in payroll taxes throughout one's working career is indirectly tied to the social security benefits annuity that one receives as a retiree.
   a. Windfall profits tax
   b. Deficit
   c. Tax protester Sixteenth Amendment arguments
   d. Federal Insurance Contributions Act

53. The _____ is a United States federal law that imposes a federal employer tax used to fund state workforce agencies. Employers report this tax by filing an annual Form 940 with the Internal Revenue Service.
   a. Tax evasion
   b. Transfer tax
   c. Council Tax
   d. Federal Unemployment Tax Act

54. _____ and benefits in kind are various non-wage compensations provided to employees in addition to their normal wages or salaries. Where an employee exchanges (cash) wages for some other form of benefit, this is generally referred to as a 'salary sacrifice' arrangement. In most countries, most kinds of _____ are taxable to at least some degree.
   a. ABC Television Network
   b. AMEX
   c. Employee benefits
   d. AIG

55. _____, in law and economics, is a form of risk management primarily used to hedge against the risk of a contingent loss. _____ is defined as the equitable transfer of the risk of a loss, from one entity to another, in exchange for a premium, and can be thought of as a guaranteed small loss to prevent a large, possibly devastating loss. An insurer is a company selling the _____; an insured is the person or entity buying the _____.
   a. ABC Television Network
   b. AIG
   c. AMEX
   d. Insurance

56. An _____ is a term used in behavioral economics to describe those types of behaviors that impose costs on a person in the long-run that are not taken into account when making decisions in the present. Classical Economics discourages government from creating legislation that targets internalities, because it is assumed that the consumer takes these personal costs into account when paying for the good that causes the _____. For example, cigarettes should be taxed because of the negative consumption externalities that they impose, such as second-hand smoke, not because the smoker harms him or herself by smoking.
   a. Operating budget
   b. Authorised capital
   c. Inventory turnover ratio
   d. Internality

57. The _____ is the main body of domestic statutory tax law of the United States organized topically, including laws covering the income tax , payroll taxes, gift taxes, estate taxes and statutory excise taxes. The _____ is published as Title 26 of the United States Code (USC), and is also known as the internal revenue title.

Chapter 13. Current Liabilities and Contingencies

a. Internal Revenue Code
c. Equity of condition

b. Income tax
d. Ordinary income

58. _____ in the United States currently refers to the federal Old-Age, Survivors, and Disability Insurance (OASDI) program.

The original _____ Act and the current version of the Act, as amended encompass several social welfare and social insurance programs. The larger and better known programs are:

- Federal Old-Age, Survivors, and Disability Insurance
- Unemployment benefits
- Temporary Assistance for Needy Families
- Health Insurance for Aged and Disabled (Medicare)
- Grants to States for Medical Assistance Programs (Medicaid)
- State Children's Health Insurance Program (SCHIP)
- Supplemental Security Income (Social SecurityI)

U.S. _____ is a social insurance program funded through dedicated payroll taxes called Federal Insurance Contributions Act (FICA.) Tax deposits are formally entrusted to Federal Old-Age and Survivors Insurance Trust Fund, or Federal Disability Insurance Trust Fund, Federal Hospital Insurance Trust Fund or the Federal Supplementary Medical Insurance Trust Fund.

a. Comparable
c. Price-to-sales ratio

b. Sale
d. Social Security

59. _____ is an amount withheld by the party making a payment to another (payee) and paid to the taxation authorities. The amount the payer deducts may vary, depending on the nature of the product or service being paid for. The payee is assessed on the gross amount, and the tax to be withheld (the _____) is computed in that assessment.

a. Tax wedge
c. Tax advantage

b. Salaries tax
d. Withholding tax

60. In a company, _____ is the sum of all financial records of salaries, wages, bonuses and deductions.

A paycheck, is traditionally a paper document issued by an employer to pay an employee for services rendered. While most commonly used in the United States, recently the physical paycheck has been increasingly replaced by electronic direct deposit to bank accounts.

a. 3M Company
c. Tax expense

b. Payroll
d. Total Expense Ratio

61. _____ generally refers to two kinds of taxes: Taxes which employers are required to withhold from employees' pay Pay-As-You-Earn or Pay-As-You-Go tax; and taxes which are paid from the employer's own funds and which are directly related to employing a worker, which may be either fixed charges or proportionally linked to an employee's pay.

In Australia, the _____ is a specific tax which is paid to states and territories by employers, not by employees. The tax is not deducted from the worker's pay.

   a. Nonbusiness Energy Property Tax Credit
   c. Federal Unemployment Tax Act
   b. Passive foreign investment company
   d. Payroll tax

Chapter 14. Bonds and Long-Term Notes

1. In economic models, the _____ time frame assumes no fixed factors of production. Firms can enter or leave the marketplace, and the cost (and availability) of land, labor, raw materials, and capital goods can be assumed to vary. In contrast, in the short-run time frame, certain factors are assumed to be fixed, because there is not sufficient time for them to change.
   a. BMC Software, Inc.
   b. 3M Company
   c. Long-run
   d. Short-run

2. _____ is that which is owed; usually referencing assets owed, but the term can also cover moral obligations and other interactions not requiring money. In the case of assets, _____ is a means of using future purchasing power in the present before a summation has been earned. Some companies and corporations use _____ as a part of their overall corporate finance strategy.
   a. Debt
   b. Loan
   c. Debenture
   d. Lender

3. In finance, a _____ is a debt security, in which the authorized issuer owes the holders a debt and, depending on the terms of the _____, is obliged to pay interest (the coupon) and/or to repay the principal at a later date, termed maturity. It is a formal contract to repay borrowed money with interest at fixed intervals.

   Thus a _____ is like a loan: the issuer is the borrower, the _____ holder is the lender, and the coupon is the interest.

   a. Zero-coupon bond
   b. Revenue bonds
   c. Coupon rate
   d. Bond

4. A _____ is a type of bond that allows the issuer of the bond to retain the privilege of redeeming the bond at some point before the bond reaches the date of maturity. In other words, on the call dates, the issuer has the right, but not the obligation, to buy back the bonds from the bond holders at the call price. Technically speaking, the bonds are not really bought and held by the issuer but cancelled immediately.
   a. Catastrophe bonds
   b. Zero-coupon
   c. Coupon rate
   d. Callable bond

5. In finance, a _____ is a type of bond that can be converted into shares of stock in the issuing company, usually at some pre-announced ratio. It is a hybrid security with debt- and equity-like features. Although it typically has a low coupon rate, the holder is compensated with the ability to convert the bond to common stock, usually at a substantial discount to the stock's market value.
   a. Zero-coupon
   b. Convertible bond
   c. Coupon rate
   d. Zero-coupon bond

Chapter 14. Bonds and Long-Term Notes

6. A _____ has several related meanings:

   - a daily record of events or business; a private _____ is usually referred to as a diary.
   - a newspaper or other periodical, in the literal sense of one published each day;
   - many publications issued at stated intervals, such as magazines, or scholarly academic _____s, or the record of the transactions of a society, are often called _____s. Although _____ is sometimes used, erroneously, as a synonym for 'magazine,' in academic use, a _____ refers to a serious, scholarly publication, most often peer-reviewed. A non-scholarly magazine written for an educated audience about an industry or an area of professional activity is usually called a professional magazine.

The word 'journalist' for one whose business is writing for the public press has been in use since the end of the 17th century.

Open access _____s are scholarly _____s that are available to the reader without financial or other barrier other than access to the internet itself. Some are subsidized, and some require payment on behalf of the author. Subsidized _____s are financed by an academic institution or a government information center.

   a. BMC Software, Inc.
   c. Journal
   b. 3M Company
   d. BNSF Railway

7. A _____ is the transfer of an interest in property (or the equivalent in law - a charge) to a lender as a security for a debt - usually a loan of money. While a _____ in itself is not a debt, it is the lender's security for a debt. It is a transfer of an interest in land (or the equivalent) from the owner to the _____ lender, on the condition that this interest will be returned to the owner when the terms of the _____ have been satisfied or performed.
   a. 3M Company
   c. BMC Software, Inc.
   b. BNSF Railway
   d. Mortgage

8. A _____ Is a fungible, negotiable instrument representing financial value. they are broadly categorized into debt securities (such as banknotes, bonds and debentures), and equity securities; e.g., common stocks. The company or other entity issuing the _____ is called the issuer.
   a. 3M Company
   c. BMC Software, Inc.
   b. Tracking stock
   d. Security

9. In finance, _____ is the interest that has accumulated since the principal investment, or since the previous interest payment if there has been one already. For a financial instrument such as a bond, interest is calculated and paid in set intervals.

The primary formula for calculating the interest accrued in a given period is:

$$I_A = T \times P \times R$$

where I_A is the _____, T is the fraction of the year, P is the principal, and R is the annualized interest rate.

a. ABC Television Network
b. Interest
c. AIG
d. Accrued interest

10. In marketing a _____ is a ticket or document that can be exchanged for a financial discount or rebate when purchasing a product. Customarily, _____s are issued by manufacturers of consumer packaged goods or by retailers, to be used in retail stores as a part of sales promotions. They are often widely distributed through mail, magazines, newspapers, the Internet, and mobile devices such as cell phones.

a. Merchandising
b. BMC Software, Inc.
c. 3M Company
d. Coupon

11. The _____ of a bond is the amount of interest paid per year expressed as a percentage of the face value of the bond. It is the interest rate that a bond issuer will pay to a bondholder.

For example if you hold $10,000 nominal of a bond described as a 4.5% loan stock, you will receive $450 in interest each year (probably in two installments of $225 each.)

a. Coupon rate
b. Convertible bond
c. Callable bond
d. Revenue bonds

12. _____ is a fee paid on borrowed assets. It is the price paid for the use of borrowed money , or, money earned by deposited funds .Assets that are sometimes lent with _____ include money, shares, consumer goods through hire purchase, major assets such as aircraft, and even entire factories in finance lease arrangements. The _____ is calculated upon the value of the assets in the same manner as upon money.

a. Interest
b. ABC Television Network
c. AIG
d. Insolvency

13. An _____ is the price a borrower pays for the use of money they do not own, for instance a small company might borrow from a bank to kick start their business, and the return a lender receives for deferring the use of funds, by lending it to the borrower. _____s are normally expressed as a percentage rate over the period of one year.

_____s targets are also a vital tool of monetary policy and are used to control variables like investment, inflation, and unemployment.

a. AMEX
b. AIG
c. ABC Television Network
d. Interest rate

14. An _____ is a derivative in which one party exchanges a stream of interest payments for another party's stream of cash flows. They can be used by hedgers to manage their fixed or floating assets and liabilities. They can also be used by speculators to replicate unfunded bond exposures to profit from changes in interest rates.

a. AIG
b. Interest rate swap
c. AMEX
d. ABC Television Network

15. _____ is a life of security. It may also refer to the final payment date of a loan or other financial instrument, at which point all remaining interest and principal is due to be paid.

Chapter 14. Bonds and Long-Term Notes

1, 3, 6 months _____ band can be calculated by using 30-day per month periods. For _____ bands over a year it is acceptable to use 365 day per year. For example with a Treasury Bond, its _____ is the date on which the principal is paid.

a. The Goodyear Tire ' Rubber Company
b. Factor
c. Statements of Financial Accounting Standards No. 133, Accounting for Derivative Instruments and Hedging Activities
d. Maturity

16. _____, in finance and accounting, means stated value or face value. From this comes the expressions at par (at the _____), over par (over _____) and under par (under _____).

_____ is a nominal value of a security which is determined by an issuer company at a minimum price. _____ of an equity (a stock) is a somewhat archaic concept. The _____ of a stock was the share price upon initial offering; the issuing company promised not to issue further shares below _____, so investors could be confident that no one else was receiving a more favorable issue price. This was far more important in unregulated equity markets than in the regulated markets that exist today.

a. Net worth
b. Restructuring
c. Creditor
d. Par value

17. In finance, a _____ is a derivative in which two counterparties agree to exchange one stream of cash flow against another stream. These streams are called the legs of the _____.

The cash flows are calculated over a notional principal amount, which is usually not exchanged between counterparties.

a. Department of the Treasury
b. Controlled Foreign Corporations
c. Total-factor productivity
d. Swap

18. A _____ is a debt security issued by a business entity, such as a corporation, or by a government. It differs from the more common types of investment securities in that it is unregistered - no records are kept of the owner, or the transactions involving ownership. Whoever physically holds the paper on which the bond is issued owns the instrument.

a. Coupon rate
b. Bearer bond
c. Revenue bonds
d. Convertible bond

19. _____ is a legal document issued to lenders and describes key terms such as the interest rate, maturity date, convertibility, pledge, promises, representations, covenants, and other terms of the bond offering. When the Offering Memorandum is prepared in advance of marketing a Bond, the indenture will typically be summarised in the 'Description of Notes' section.

a. Bond indenture
b. Consumer protection laws
c. Malpractice
d. Leasing

20. A _____ is defined as a certificate of agreement of loans which is given under the company's stamp and carries an undertaking that the _____ holder will get a fixed return (fixed on the basis of interest rates) and the principal amount whenever the _____ matures.

In finance, a _____ is a long-term debt instrument used by governments and large companies to obtain funds. It is defined as 'any form of borrowing that commits a firm to pay interest and repay capital.

a. Loan to value
b. Loan
c. Debenture
d. Credit rating

21. _____ are financial bonds that mature in installments over a period of time. In effect, a $100,000, 5-year serial bond would mature in a $20,000 annuity over a 5-year interval. Bond issues consisting of a series of blocks of securities maturing in sequence, the coupon rate can be different.

a. Household and Dependent Care Credit
b. Serial bonds
c. Just-in-time
d. Low Income Housing Tax Credit

22. A _____ is a fund established by a government agency or business for the purpose of reducing debt.

The _____ was first used in Great Britain in the 18th century to reduce national debt. While used by Robert Walpole in 1716 and effectively in the 1720s and early 1730s, it originated in the commercial tax syndicates of the Italian peninsula of the 14th century to retire redeemable public debt of those cities.

a. Treasury company
b. Segregated portfolio company
c. Payback period
d. Sinking fund

23. An _____ is a legal contract between two parties, particularly for indentured labour or a term of apprenticeship but also for certain land transactions. The term comes from the medieval English '_____ of retainer' -- a legal contract written in duplicate on the same sheet, with the copies separated by cutting along a jagged line so that the teeth of the two parts could later be refitted to confirm authenticity. Each party to the deed would then retain a part.

a. Operating Lease
b. Impracticability
c. Employee Retirement Income Security Act
d. Indenture

24. In investment, the _____ assesses the credit worthiness of a corporation's debt issues. It is analogous to credit ratings for individuals and countries. The credit rating is a financial indicator to potential investors of debt securities such as bonds.

a. Holding gains
b. Market value
c. Treasury company
d. Bond credit rating

25. A _____ is any one of a variety of different systems, institutions, procedures, social relations and infrastructures whereby persons trade, and goods and services are exchanged, forming part of the economy. It is an arrangement that allows buyers and sellers to exchange things. _____s vary in size, range, geographic scale, location, types and variety of human communities, as well as the types of goods and services traded.

a. Perfect competition
b. Market Failure
c. Recession
d. Market

Chapter 14. Bonds and Long-Term Notes 173

26. _____ in economics and business is the result of an exchange and from that trade we assign a numerical monetary value to a good, service or asset. If Alice trades Bob 4 apples for an orange, the _____ of an orange is 4 apples. Inversely, the _____ of an apple is 1/4 oranges.
   a. Price discrimination
   b. Discounts and allowances
   c. Transactional Net Margin Method
   d. Price

27. _____ are the most liquid assets found within the asset portion of a company's balance sheet. Cash equivalents are assets that are readily convertible into cash, such as money market holdings, short-term government bonds or Treasury bills, marketable securities and commercial paper. _____ are distinguished from other investments through their short-term existence; they mature within 3 months whereas short-term investments are 12 months or less, and long-term investments are any investments that mature in excess of 12 months.
   a. Debtor
   b. Cash and cash equivalents
   c. Par value
   d. Payback period

28. Simply put, _____ is the value of money figuring in a given amount of interest for a given amount of time. For example 100 dollars of todays money held for a year at 5 percent interest is worth 105 dollars, therefore 100 dollars paid now or 105 dollars paid exactly one year from now is the same amount of payment of money with that given intersest at that given amount of time. This notion dates at least to Martín de Azpilcueta of the School of Salamanca.
   a. Competition law
   b. Merck ' Co., Inc.
   c. Collusion
   d. Time value of money

29. The term _____ is used in finance theory to refer to any terminating stream of fixed payments over a specified period of time. This usage is most commonly seen in academic discussions of finance, usually in connection with the valuation of the stream of payments, taking into account time value of money concepts such as interest rate and future value.

Examples of these are regular deposits to a savings account, monthly home mortgage payments and monthly insurance payments.

   a. Improvement
   b. Appropriation
   c. Intangible
   d. Annuity

30. _____ is the balance of the amounts of cash being received and paid by a business during a defined period of time, sometimes tied to a specific project. Measurement of _____ can be used

- to evaluate the state or performance of a business or project.
- to determine problems with liquidity. Being profitable does not necessarily mean being liquid. A company can fail because of a shortage of cash, even while profitable.
- to project rate of returns. The time of _____s into and out of projects are used as inputs to financial models such as internal rate of return, and net present value.
- to examine income or growth of a business when it is believed that accrual accounting concepts do not represent economic realities. Alternately, _____ can be used to 'validate' the net income generated by accrual accounting.

_____ as a generic term may be used differently depending on context, and certain _____ definitions may be adapted by analysts and users for their own uses. Common terms include operating _____ and free _____.

Chapter 14. Bonds and Long-Term Notes

a. Commercial paper
b. Flow-through entity
c. Cash flow
d. Controlling interest

31. _____ of something is, in finance, the adding together of interest or different investments over a period of time such as atoms (1 - the act or process of accruing; 2 - the amount that accrues.) It holds specific meanings in accounting and payroll.

_____, in accounting, describes the accounting method known as _____ basis, whereby revenues and expenses are recognized when they are accrued, i.e. accumulated (earned or incurred), regardless when the actual cash is received or paid out.

a. Accounts receivable
b. Accrual
c. Earnings before interest, taxes, depreciation and amortization
d. Assets

32. _____ is a method of accounting whereby economic activities (rather than cash flow) of financial events are considered, because of two complementary principles, which (together) determine the point, at which expenses and revenues are recognized. According to revenue recognition principle, revenues are realized when earned, whether or not they are received in cash.

a. Earnings before interest, taxes, depreciation and amortization
b. Accrual basis accounting
c. Accrued revenue
d. Accrual

33. _____ is the process of increasing, or accounting for, an amount over a period of time. Particular instances of the term include:

- _____, the allocation of a lump sum amount to different time periods, particularly for loans and other forms of finance, including related interest or other finance charges.
    - _____ schedule, a table detailing each periodic payment on a loan (typically a mortgage), as generated by an _____ calculator.
    - Negative _____, an _____ schedule where the loan amount actually increases through not paying the full interest
- Amortized analysis, analyzing the execution cost of algorithms over a sequence of operations.
- _____ of capital expenditures of certain assets under accounting rules, particularly intangible assets, in a manner analogous to depreciation.
- _____

a. Amortization
b. Annuity
c. EBIT
d. Intangible

34. Discounting is a financial mechanism in which a debtor obtains the right to delay payments to a creditor, for a defined period of time, in exchange for a charge or fee. Essentially, the party that owes money in the present purchases the right to delay the payment until some future date. The _____, or charge, is simply the difference between the original amount owed in the present and the amount that has to be paid in the future to settle the debt.

Chapter 14. Bonds and Long-Term Notes   175

a. Risk aversion
b. Discount factor
c. Discounting
d. Discount

35. A _____ is a bond bought at a price lower than its face value, with the face value repaid at the time of maturity. It does not make periodic interest payments, or so-called 'coupons,' hence the term _____. Investors earn return from the compounded interest all paid at maturity plus the difference between the discounted price of the bond and its par value.

a. Premium bond
b. Callable bond
c. Municipal bond
d. Zero-coupon bond

36. The _____ is a financial market where participants buy and sell debt securities, usually in the form of bonds. As of 2006, the size of the international _____ is an estimated $44.9 trillion, of which the size of the outstanding U.S. _____ debt was $25.2 trillion.

Nearly all of the $923 billion average daily trading volume in the U.S. _____ takes place between broker-dealers and large institutions in a decentralized, over-the-counter market.

a. Demand curve
b. Bond market
c. Convertible bond
d. Variance

37. _____ is the price at which an asset would trade in a competitive Walrasian auction setting. _____ is often used interchangeably with open _____, fair value or fair _____, although these terms have distinct definitions in different standards, and may differ in some circumstances.

International Valuation Standards defines _____ as 'the estimated amount for which a property should exchange on the date of valuation between a willing buyer and a willing seller in an arme;s-length transaction after proper marketing wherein the parties had each acted knowledgeably, prudently, and without compulsion.'

_____ is a concept distinct from market price, which is e;the price at which one can transacte;, while _____ is e;the true underlying valuee; according to theoretical standards.

a. Sinking fund
b. Segregated portfolio company
c. Debtor
d. Market value

38. _____ is the value on a given date of a future payment or series of future payments, discounted to reflect the time value of money and other factors such as investment risk. _____ calculations are widely used in business and economics to provide a means to compare cash flows at different times on a meaningful 'like to like' basis.

The most commonly applied model of the time value of money is compound interest.

a. Net present value
b. Future value
c. 3M Company
d. Present value

39. A _____ is like a lottery bond issued by the United Kingdom government's National Savings and Investments scheme. The government promises to buy back the bond, on request, for its original price.

_____s were introduced by the government in 1956, with the aim of encouraging saving and controlling inflation, with the first bonds going on sale on 1 November of that year.

a. Revenue bonds
b. Zero-coupon bond
c. Callable bond
d. Premium bond

40. A _____ bond is a bond bought at a price lower than its face value, with the face value repaid at the time of maturity. It does not make periodic interest payments, or have so-called 'coupons,' hence the term _____ bond. Investors earn return from the compounded interest all paid at maturity plus the difference between the discounted price of the bond and its par value.

a. Callable bond
b. Zero-coupon
c. Catastrophe bonds
d. Municipal bond

41. In accounting/accountancy, _____ are journal entries usually made at the end of an accounting period to allocate income and expenditure to the period in which they actually occurred. The revenue recognition principle is the basis of making _____ that pertain to unearned and accrued revenues under accrual-basis accounting. They are sometimes called Balance Day adjustments because they are made on balance day.

a. Accrual
b. Earnings before interest, taxes, depreciation and amortization
c. Accrued expense
d. Adjusting entries

42. _____ are formal records of a business' financial activities.

In British English, including United Kingdom company law, _____ are often referred to as accounts, although the term _____ is also used, particularly by accountants.

_____ provide an overview of a business' financial condition in both short and long term.

a. 3M Company
b. Statement of retained earnings
c. Notes to the financial statements
d. Financial statements

43. There are several methods for calculating depreciation, generally based on either the passage of time or the level of activity (or use) of the asset.

_____ is the simplest and most often used technique, in which the company estimates the salvage value of the asset at the end of the period during which it will be used to generate revenues (useful life), and will expense a portion of original cost in equal increments over that period.

a. Current asset
b. Straight-line depreciation
c. Closing entries
d. Pro forma

44. In economics, business, retail, and accounting, a _____ is the value of money that has been used up to produce something, and hence is not available for use anymore. In economics, a _____ is an alternative that is given up as a result of a decision. In business, the _____ may be one of acquisition, in which case the amount of money expended to acquire it is counted as _____.

Chapter 14. Bonds and Long-Term Notes

a. Prime cost
b. Cost
c. Cost of quality
d. Cost allocation

45. In the United States, a _____ is an offering of securities that are not registered with the Securities and Exchange Commission (SEC.) Such offerings exploit an exemption offered by the Securities Act of 1933 that comes with several restrictions, including a prohibition against general solicitation. This exemption allows companies to avoid quarterly reporting requirements and many of the legal liabilities associated with the Sarbanes-Oxley Act.
   a. BMC Software, Inc.
   b. Private placement
   c. 3M Company
   d. BNSF Railway

46. A _____ is a bond issued by a corporation. It is a bond that a corporation issues to raise money in order to expand its business. The term is usually applied to longer-term debt instruments, generally with a maturity date falling at least a year after their issue date.
   a. Corporate bond
   b. Screening
   c. Disclosure
   d. Merck ' Co., Inc.

47. A _____ is a contract conferring a right on one person to possess property belonging to another person (called a landlord or lessor) to the exclusion of the owner landlord. It is a rental agreement between landlord and tenant. The relationship between the tenant and the landlord is called a tenancy, and the right to possession by the tenant is sometimes called a leasehold interest.
   a. Robinson-Patman Act
   b. Model Code of Professional Responsibility
   c. Federal Sentencing Guidelines
   d. Lease

48. A _____, also referred to as a note payable in accounting, is a contract where one party (the maker or issuer) makes an unconditional promise in writing to pay a sum of money to the other (the payee), either at a fixed or determinable future time or on demand of the payee, under specific terms. They differ from IOUs in that they contain a specific promise to pay, rather than simply acknowledging that a debt exists.

The terms of a note typically include the principal amount, the interest rate if any, and the maturity date.

   a. BMC Software, Inc.
   b. 3M Company
   c. BNSF Railway
   d. Promissory note

49. In business and accounting, _____ are everything of value that is owned by a person or company. It is a claim on the property your income of a borrower. The balance sheet of a firm records the monetary value of the _____ owned by the firm.
   a. Earnings before interest, taxes, depreciation and amortization
   b. Accounts receivable
   c. Accrual basis accounting
   d. Assets

50. A _____ is the pinnacle activity involved in selling products or services in return for money or other compensation. It is an act of completion of a commercial activity.

A _____ is completed by the seller, the owner of the goods.

Chapter 14. Bonds and Long-Term Notes

a. Maturity
c. Tertiary sector of economy
b. High yield stock
d. Sale

51. In economics, _____ or _____ goods or real _____ refers to factors of production used to create goods or services that are not themselves significantly consumed (though they may depreciate) in the production process. _____ goods may be acquired with money or financial _____. In finance and accounting, _____ generally refers to financial wealth, especially that used to start or maintain a business.
    a. Vyborg Appeal
    c. Disclosure
    b. Screening
    d. Capital

52. _____ is a type of lease - the other being an operating lease. A _____ effectively allows a firm to finance the purchase of an asset, even if, strictly speaking, the firm never acquires the asset. Typically, a _____ will give the lessee control over an asset for a large proportion of the asset's useful life, providing them the benefits and risks of ownership.
    a. Profitability index
    c. Finance lease
    b. 3M Company
    d. Debt ratio

53. _____ means the giving out of information, either voluntarily or to be in compliance with legal regulations or workplace rules.

- In Computer security, full _____ means disclosing full information about vulnerabilities.
- In computing, _____ widget
- Journalism, full _____ refers to disclosing the interests of the writer which may bear on the subject being written about, for example, if the writer has worked with an interview subject in the past.

- In law:
    - The law of England and Wales, _____ refers to a process that may form part of legal proceedings, whereby parties inform to other parties the existence of any relevant documents that are, or have been, in their control. This compares with the process known as discovery in the course of legal proceedings in the United States.
    - In U.S. civil procedure (litigation rules for civil cases), _____ is a stage prior to trial. In civil cases, each party must disclose to the opposing party the following: names of witnesses which it may use to support its side, copies of documents (or mere description of these documents) in its control which it may use to support its side, computation of damages claimed, and certain insurance information. _____ is related to, but technically prior to, the discovery stage.
    - In Company law (known as 'corporate law' in the United States), _____ refers to giving out information about public or limited companies or their officers, which might be kept secret if the company was a private company or a partnership.

- In real property transactions, _____ refers to providing to a buyer information known to the seller or broker/agent concerning the condition or other aspects of real property that would affect the property's value or desirability. These rules regarding what information must be disclosed, and whether the information must be disclosed even if a buyer does not ask, vary from one jurisdiction to the next.

a. Disclosure
c. Controlled Foreign Corporations
b. Trailing
d. Tax harmonisation

54. _____, also called fair price (in a commonplace conflation of the two distinct concepts), is a concept used in finance and economics, defined as a rational and unbiased estimate of the potential market price of a good, service, or asset, taking into account such objective factors as:

- acquisition/production/distribution costs, replacement costs, or costs of close substitutes
- actual utility at a given level of development of social productive capability
- supply vs. demand

and subjective factors such as

- risk characteristics
- cost of capital
- individually perceived utility

In accounting, _____ is used as an estimate of the market value of an asset (or liability) for which a market price cannot be determined (usually because there is no established market for the asset.) Under GAAP (FAS 157), _____ is the amount at which the asset could be bought or sold in a current transaction between willing parties, or transferred to an equivalent party, other than in a liquidation sale. This is used for assets whose carrying value is based on mark-to-market valuations; for assets carried at historical cost, the _____ of the asset is not used. One example of where _____ is an issue is a College kitchen with a cost of $2 million which was built 5 years ago.

a. Fair value
b. BMC Software, Inc.
c. 3M Company
d. BNSF Railway

55. _____ methods are means of managing inventory and financial matters involving the money a company ties up within inventory of produced goods, raw materials, parts, components, or feed stocks. FIFO stands for first-In, first-out, meaning that the oldest inventory items are recorded as sold first. LIFO stands for last-in, first-out, meaning that the most recently purchased items are recorded as sold first.

a. Finished good
b. Reorder point
c. FIFO and LIFO accounting
d. 3M Company

56. In financial accounting, a _____ is defined as an obligation of an entity arising from past transactions or events, the settlement of which may result in the transfer or use of assets, provision of services or other yielding of economic benefits in the future.

a. False Claims Act
b. Corporate governance
c. Vested
d. Liability

57. Procter is a surname, and may also refer to:

- Bryan Waller Procter (pseud. Barry Cornwall), English poet
- Goodwin Procter, American law firm
- _____, consumer products multinational

Chapter 14. Bonds and Long-Term Notes

a. Markup
b. Screening
c. Welfare
d. Procter ' Gamble

58. _____ refers to a business or organization attempting to acquire goods or services to accomplish the goals of the enterprise. Though there are several organizations that attempt to set standards in the _____ process, processes can vary greatly between organizations. Typically the word e;_____e; is not used interchangeably with the word e;procuremente;, since procurement typically includes Expediting, Supplier Quality, and Traffic and Logistics (T'L) in addition to _____.
   a. Supply chain
   b. Free port
   c. Consignor
   d. Purchasing

59. In law, _____ refers to the process by which a company (or part of a company) is brought to an end, and the assets and property of the company redistributed. _____ can also be referred to as winding-up or dissolution, although dissolution technically refers to the last stage of _____. The process of _____ also arises when customs, an authority or agency in a country responsible for collecting and safeguarding customs duties, determines the final computation or ascertainment of the duties or drawback accruing on an entry.
   a. 3M Company
   b. Bankruptcy protection
   c. BMC Software, Inc.
   d. Liquidation

60. _____ is a concept that denotes the precise probability of specific eventualities. Technically, the notion of _____ is independent from the notion of value and, as such, eventualities may have both beneficial and adverse consequences. However, in general usage the convention is to focus only on potential negative impact to some characteristic of value that may arise from a future event.
   a. Risk adjusted return on capital
   b. Discount factor
   c. Discounting
   d. Risk

61. In financial accounting, a _____ or Statement of cash flows is a financial statement that shows a company's flow of cash. The money coming into the business is called cash inflow, and money going out from the business is called cash outflow. The statement shows how changes in balance sheet and income accounts affect cash and cash equivalents, and breaks the analysis down to operating, investing, and financing activities.
   a. BNSF Railway
   b. BMC Software, Inc.
   c. 3M Company
   d. Cash flow statement

62. _____ or interest coverage ratio is a measure of a company's ability to honor its debt payments. It may be calculated as either EBIT or EBITDA divided by the total interest payable.

   a. Capital recovery factor
   b. Yield Gap
   c. Return of capital
   d. Times interest earned

63. Most patent law systems require that a patent application disclose a claimed invention in sufficient detail for the notional person skilled in the art to carry out that claimed invention. This requirement is often known as sufficiency of disclosure or enablement, depending on the jurisdiction.

The _____ lies at the heart and origin of patent law. A state or government grants an inventor, or the inventor's assignee, a monopoly for a given period of time in exchange for the inventor disclosing to the public how to make or practice his or her invention. If a patent fails to contain such information, then the bargain is violated, and the patent is unenforceable.

a. Pre-emption right
b. False Claims Act
c. Tax patent
d. Disclosure requirement

64. The _____ is a financial ratio indicating the relative proportion of equity to all used to finance a company's assets. The two components are often taken from the firm's balance sheet or statement of financial position (so-called book value), but the ratio may also be calculated using market values for both, if the company's equities are publicly traded.

The _____ is especially in Central Europe a very common financial ratio while in the US the debt to _____ is more often used in financial (research) reports.

a. Earnings yield
b. Average accounting return
c. Efficiency ratio
d. Equity ratio

65. The _____ percentage shows how profitable a company's assets are in generating revenue.

_____ can be computed as:

$$ROA = \frac{\text{Net Income - Interest Expense - Interest Tax savings}}{\text{Average Total Assets}}$$

This number tells you what the company can do with what it has, i.e. how many dollars of earnings they derive from each dollar of assets they control. Its a useful number for comparing competing companies in the same industry.

a. Capital employed
b. Statutory Liquidity Ratio
c. Return on sales
d. Return on assets

66. _____, in accrual accounting, is any account where the asset or liability is not realized until a future date (accounting period), e.g. annuities, charges, taxes, income, etc. The _____ item may be carried, dependent on type of deferral, as either an asset or liability.

a. Payroll
b. Deferred
c. Pro forma
d. Cash basis accounting

67. In financial accounting, a _____ or statement of financial position is a summary of a person's or organization's balances. Assets, liabilities and ownership equity are listed as of a specific date, such as the end of its financial year. A _____ is often described as a snapshot of a company's financial condition.

a. 3M Company
b. Balance sheet
c. Financial statements
d. Statement of retained earnings

Chapter 14. Bonds and Long-Term Notes

68. _____ is a process by which a firm can obtain the use of a certain fixed assets for which it must pay a series of contractual, periodic, tax deductable payments. The lessee is the receiver of the services or the assets under the lease contract and the lessor is the owner of the assets. The relationship between the tenant and the landlord is called a tenancy, and can be for a fixed or an indefinite period of time (called the term of the lease.)
   a. Resource Conservation and Recovery Act
   b. Property
   c. Federal Sentencing Guidelines
   d. Leasing

69. _____ is an economic concept with commonplace familiarity. It is the price that a good or service is offered at, or will fetch, in the marketplace. It is of interest mainly in the study of microeconomics.
   a. Market price
   b. Transfer agent
   c. Spot rate
   d. Financial instruments

70. In accounting, _____ or carrying value is the value of an asset according to its balance sheet account balance. For assets, the value is based on the original cost of the asset less any depreciation, amortization or impairment costs made against the asset. Traditionally, a company's _____ is its total assets minus intangible assets and liabilities.
   a. Depreciation
   b. Matching principle
   c. Generally accepted accounting principles
   d. Book value

71. In finance, an _____ is a contract between a buyer and a seller that gives the buyer the right--but not the obligation--to buy or to sell a particular asset (the underlying asset) at a later time at an agreed price. In return for granting the _____, the seller collects a payment (the premium) from the buyer. A call _____ gives the buyer the right to buy the underlying asset; a put _____ gives the buyer of the _____ the right to sell the underlying asset.
   a. ABC Television Network
   b. AIG
   c. AMEX
   d. Option

72. The _____ is a 'voluntary organization of persons interested in accounting education and research'. It was formed in 1916. Its main publication, the The Accounting Review, was first published in 1926.
   a. International Accounting Standards Board
   b. Institute of Management Accountants
   c. Australian Accounting Standards Board
   d. American Accounting Association

73. A _____ is a party (e.g. person, organization, company, or government) that has a claim to the services of a second party. It is a person or institution to whom money is owed. The first party, in general, has provided some property or service to the second party under the assumption (usually enforced by contract) that the second party will return an equivalent property or service.
   a. Creditor
   b. Par value
   c. Treasury company
   d. Payback period

74. _____ is the corporate management term for the act of partially dismantling or otherwise reorganizing a company for the purpose of making it more profitable. Also known as corporate _____, debt _____ and financial _____.

_____ is often done as part of a bankruptcy or of a strategic takeover by another firm, such as a leveraged buyout by a private equity firm.

   a. Payback period
   b. Net worth
   c. Fair market value
   d. Restructuring

75. A _____ is the transfer of wealth from one party (such as a person or company) to another. A _____ is usually made in exchange for the provision of goods, services or both, or to fulfill a legal obligation.

The simplest and oldest form of _____ is barter, the exchange of one good or service for another.

a. Payee
c. Payment

b. BMC Software, Inc.
d. 3M Company

Chapter 15. Leases

1. A _____ is a contract conferring a right on one person to possess property belonging to another person (called a landlord or lessor) to the exclusion of the owner landlord. It is a rental agreement between landlord and tenant. The relationship between the tenant and the landlord is called a tenancy, and the right to possession by the tenant is sometimes called a leasehold interest.
    a. Federal Sentencing Guidelines
    b. Lease
    c. Robinson-Patman Act
    d. Model Code of Professional Responsibility

2. In economics, _____ or _____ goods or real _____ refers to factors of production used to create goods or services that are not themselves significantly consumed (though they may depreciate) in the production process. _____ goods may be acquired with money or financial _____. In finance and accounting, _____ generally refers to financial wealth, especially that used to start or maintain a business.
    a. Capital
    b. Vyborg Appeal
    c. Screening
    d. Disclosure

3. _____ is a type of lease - the other being an operating lease. A _____ effectively allows a firm to finance the purchase of an asset, even if, strictly speaking, the firm never acquires the asset. Typically, a _____ will give the lessee control over an asset for a large proportion of the asset's useful life, providing them the benefits and risks of ownership.
    a. Finance lease
    b. Profitability index
    c. 3M Company
    d. Debt ratio

4. _____ is a specific term used in companies' financial reporting from the company-whole point of view. Because that use excludes the effects of changing ownership interest, an economic measure of _____ is necessary for financial analysis from the shareholders' point of view

    _____ is defined by the Financial Accounting Standards Board, or FASB, as 'the change in equity [net assets] of a business enterprise during a period from transactions and other events and circumstances from nonowner sources. It includes all changes in equity during a period except those resulting from investments by owners and distributions to owners.'

    _____ is the sum of net income and other items that must bypass the income statement because they have not been realized, including items like an unrealized holding gain or loss from available for sale securities and foreign currency translation gains or losses.

    a. BMC Software, Inc.
    b. Comprehensive income
    c. 3M Company
    d. BNSF Railway

5. _____ are the earnings returned on the initial investment amount.

In the US, the Financial Accounting Standards Board (FASB) requires companies' income statements to report _____ for each of the major categories of the income statement: continuing operations, discontinued operations, extraordinary items, and net income.

The _____ formula does not include preferred dividends for categories outside of continued operations and net income.

a. Earnings per share
b. Earnings yield
c. Average accounting return
d. Invested capital

6. An _____ is a lease whose term is short compared to the useful life of the asset or piece of equipment (an airliner, a ship etc.) being leased. An _____ is commonly used to acquire equipment on a relatively short-term basis.
   a. Employee Retirement Income Security Act
   b. Express warranty
   c. Issued shares
   d. Operating lease

7. _____ refers to a business or organization attempting to acquire goods or services to accomplish the goals of the enterprise. Though there are several organizations that attempt to set standards in the _____ process, processes can vary greatly between organizations. Typically the word e;_____e; is not used interchangeably with the word e;procuremente;, since procurement typically includes Expediting, Supplier Quality, and Traffic and Logistics (T'L) in addition to _____.
   a. Supply chain
   b. Consignor
   c. Free port
   d. Purchasing

8. In business and accounting, _____ are everything of value that is owned by a person or company. It is a claim on the property your income of a borrower. The balance sheet of a firm records the monetary value of the _____ owned by the firm.
   a. Accrual basis accounting
   b. Accounts receivable
   c. Earnings before interest, taxes, depreciation and amortization
   d. Assets

9. _____ is a process by which a firm can obtain the use of a certain fixed assets for which it must pay a series of contractual, periodic, tax deductible payments. The lessee is the receiver of the services or the assets under the lease contract and the lessor is the owner of the assets. The relationship between the tenant and the landlord is called a tenancy, and can be for a fixed or an indefinite period of time (called the term of the lease.)
   a. Federal Sentencing Guidelines
   b. Resource Conservation and Recovery Act
   c. Property
   d. Leasing

10. _____ is the process of increasing, or accounting for, an amount over a period of time. Particular instances of the term include:

    - _____, the allocation of a lump sum amount to different time periods, particularly for loans and other forms of finance, including related interest or other finance charges.
        o _____ schedule, a table detailing each periodic payment on a loan (typically a mortgage), as generated by an _____ calculator.
        o Negative _____, an _____ schedule where the loan amount actually increases through not paying the full interest
    - Amortized analysis, analyzing the execution cost of algorithms over a sequence of operations.
    - _____ of capital expenditures of certain assets under accounting rules, particularly intangible assets, in a manner analogous to depreciation.
    - _____

a. Amortization
b. Annuity
c. EBIT
d. Intangible

11. Discounting is a financial mechanism in which a debtor obtains the right to delay payments to a creditor, for a defined period of time, in exchange for a charge or fee. Essentially, the party that owes money in the present purchases the right to delay the payment until some future date. The _____, or charge, is simply the difference between the original amount owed in the present and the amount that has to be paid in the future to settle the debt.

a. Discount
b. Risk aversion
c. Discounting
d. Discount factor

12. The _____ is an interest rate a central bank charges depository institutions that borrow reserves from it.

The term _____ has two meanings:

- the same as interest rate; the term 'discount' does not refer to the meaning of the word, but to the purpose of using the quantity, such as computations of present value, e.g. net present value or discounted cash flow

- the annual effective _____, which is the annual interest divided by the capital including that interest; this rate is lower than the interest rate; it corresponds to using the value after a year as the nominal value, and seeing the initial value as the nominal value minus a discount; it is used for Treasury Bills and similar financial instruments

The annual effective _____ is the annual interest divided by the capital including that interest, which is the interest rate divided by 100% plus the interest rate. It is the annual discount factor to be applied to the future cash flow, to find the discount, subtracted from a future value to find the value one year earlier.

For example, suppose there is a government bond that sells for $95 and pays $100 in a year's time.

a. Municipal bond
b. Convertible bond
c. Process time
d. Discount rate

13. In financial accounting, a _____ or statement of financial position is a summary of a person's or organization's balances. Assets, liabilities and ownership equity are listed as of a specific date, such as the end of its financial year. A _____ is often described as a snapshot of a company's financial condition.

a. Statement of retained earnings
b. 3M Company
c. Financial statements
d. Balance sheet

14. _____ is a fee paid on borrowed assets. It is the price paid for the use of borrowed money, or, money earned by deposited funds. Assets that are sometimes lent with _____ include money, shares, consumer goods through hire purchase, major assets such as aircraft, and even entire factories in finance lease arrangements. The _____ is calculated upon the value of the assets in the same manner as upon money.

a. Interest
b. Insolvency
c. AIG
d. ABC Television Network

Chapter 15. Leases

15. In finance, an _____ is a contract between a buyer and a seller that gives the buyer the right--but not the obligation-- to buy or to sell a particular asset (the underlying asset) at a later time at an agreed price. In return for granting the _____, the seller collects a payment (the premium) from the buyer. A call _____ gives the buyer the right to buy the underlying asset; a put _____ gives the buyer of the _____ the right to sell the underlying asset.
   a. AIG
   b. ABC Television Network
   c. Option
   d. AMEX

16. A _____ proof is a mathematical proof that a particular theory is consistent. The early development of mathematical proof theory was driven by the desire to provide finitary _____ proofs for all of mathematics as part of Hilbert's program. Hilbert's program was strongly impacted by incompleteness theorems, which showed that sufficiently strong proof theories cannot prove their own _____.
   a. Consumption
   b. Monte Carlo methods
   c. Consistency
   d. Daybook

17. _____ refers to services paid for in advance. Examples include tolls, pay as you go cell phones, and stored-value cards such as gift cards and preloaded credit cards. _____ accounts are assets, and they are increased by debiting the account(s.)
   a. 3M Company
   b. BMC Software, Inc.
   c. Prepaid
   d. BNSF Railway

18. _____ is generally understood in financial circles as the point at which revenue is recognized, typically through a transaction which involves the exchange of an asset, product, or service for cash or its equivalents.

This approach gives the accounting division a strictly objective basis for changing the books. For example, a homeowner may believe that his house has grown in value during a strong market, or fallen in value during a weak market, but until the house is actually sold for a specific price to a specific buyer, the change in value can only be estimated and is considered unrealized.

   a. Total-factor productivity
   b. Valuation
   c. Merck ' Co., Inc.
   d. Realization

19. There are several methods for calculating depreciation, generally based on either the passage of time or the level of activity (or use) of the asset.

_____ is the simplest and most often used technique, in which the company estimates the salvage value of the asset at the end of the period during which it will be used to generate revenues (useful life), and will expense a portion of original cost in equal increments over that period.

   a. Current asset
   b. Closing entries
   c. Pro forma
   d Straight-line depreciation

20. In finance, a _____ is a debt security, in which the authorized issuer owes the holders a debt and, depending on the terms of the _____, is obliged to pay interest (the coupon) and/or to repay the principal at a later date, termed maturity. It is a formal contract to repay borrowed money with interest at fixed intervals.

Chapter 15. Leases

Thus a _____ is like a loan: the issuer is the borrower, the _____ holder is the lender, and the coupon is the interest.

a. Zero-coupon bond
c. Bond

b. Coupon rate
d. Revenue bonds

21. A _____ is the transfer of wealth from one party (such as a person or company) to another. A _____ is usually made in exchange for the provision of goods, services or both, or to fulfill a legal obligation.

The simplest and oldest form of _____ is barter, the exchange of one good or service for another.

a. BMC Software, Inc.
c. Payee

b. 3M Company
d. Payment

22. A _____ estate is an ownership interest in land in which a lessee or a tenant holds real property by some form of title from a lessor or landlord.

_____ is a form of property tenure where one party buys the right to occupy land or a building for a given length of time. As lease is a legal estate, _____ estate can be bought and sold on the open market.

a. 3M Company
c. Real Estate Investment Trust

b. Liquidation value
d. Leasehold

23. _____ is any physical or virtual entity that is owned by an individual or jointly by a group of individuals. An owner of _____ has the right to consume, sell, rent, mortgage, transfer and exchange his or her _____. Important widely-recognized types of _____ include real _____, personal _____ (other physical possessions), and intellectual _____ (rights over artistic creations, inventions, etc.), although the latter is not always as widely recognized or enforced.

a. Fiduciary
c. Primary authority

b. Disclosure requirement
d. Property

24. _____, also known as property, plant, and equipment (PP&E), is a term used in accountancy for assets and property which cannot easily be converted into cash. This can be compared with current assets such as cash or bank accounts, which are described as liquid assets. In most cases, only tangible assets are referred to as fixed.

a. Bankruptcy prediction
c. Minority interest

b. Subledger
d. Fixed asset

25. _____ is the difference between operating revenues and operating expenses, but it is also sometimes used as a synonym for EBIT and operating profit. This is true if the firm has no non-_____.

A professional investor contemplating a change to the capital structure of a firm first evaluates a firm's fundamental earnings potential (reflected by Earnings Before Interest, Taxes, Depreciation and Amortization EBITDA and EBIT), and then determines the optimal use of debt vs. equity.

a. AMEX
b. AIG
c. ABC Television Network
d. Operating income

26. A _____ is the pinnacle activity involved in selling products or services in return for money or other compensation. It is an act of completion of a commercial activity.

A _____ is completed by the seller, the owner of the goods.

a. Sale
b. Maturity
c. Tertiary sector of economy
d. High yield stock

27. In physics, and more specifically kinematics, _____ is the change in velocity over time. Because velocity is a vector, it can change in two ways: a change in magnitude and/or a change in direction. In one dimension, _____ is the rate at which something speeds up or slows down.

a. ABC Television Network
b. AIG
c. AMEX
d. Acceleration

28. _____ refers to any one of several methods by which a company, for 'financial accounting' and/or tax purposes, depreciates a fixed asset in such a way that the amount of depreciation taken each year is higher during the earlier years of an assete;s life. For financial accounting purposes, _____ is generally used when an asset is expected to be much more productive during its early years, so that depreciation expense will more accurately represent how much of an assete;s usefulness is being used up each year. For tax purposes, _____ provides a way of deferring corporate income taxes by reducing taxable income in current years, in exchange for increased taxable income in future years.

a. Effective marginal tax rates
b. Indirect tax
c. User charge
d. Accelerated depreciation

29. _____ means the giving out of information, either voluntarily or to be in compliance with legal regulations or workplace rules.

- In Computer security, full _____ means disclosing full information about vulnerabilities.
- In computing, _____ widget
- Journalism, full _____ refers to disclosing the interests of the writer which may bear on the subject being written about, for example, if the writer has worked with an interview subject in the past.

- In law:
    - The law of England and Wales, _____ refers to a process that may form part of legal proceedings, whereby parties inform to other parties the existence of any relevant documents that are, or have been, in their control. This compares with the process known as discovery in the course of legal proceedings in the United States.
    - In U.S. civil procedure (litigation rules for civil cases), _____ is a stage prior to trial. In civil cases, each party must disclose to the opposing party the following: names of witnesses which it may use to support its side, copies of documents (or mere description of these documents) in its control which it may use to support its side, computation of damages claimed, and certain insurance information. _____ is related to, but technically prior to, the discovery stage.
    - In Company law (known as 'corporate law' in the United States), _____ refers to giving out information about public or limited companies or their officers, which might be kept secret if the company was a private company or a partnership.

- In real property transactions, _____ refers to providing to a buyer information known to the seller or broker/agent concerning the condition or other aspects of real property that would affect the property's value or desirability. These rules regarding what information must be disclosed, and whether the information must be disclosed even if a buyer does not ask, vary from one jurisdiction to the next.

a. Disclosure
b. Trailing
c. Controlled Foreign Corporations
d. Tax harmonisation

30. Most patent law systems require that a patent application disclose a claimed invention in sufficient detail for the notional person skilled in the art to carry out that claimed invention. This requirement is often known as sufficiency of disclosure or enablement, depending on the jurisdiction.

The _____ lies at the heart and origin of patent law. A state or government grants an inventor, or the inventor's assignee, a monopoly for a given period of time in exchange for the inventor disclosing to the public how to make or practice his or her invention. If a patent fails to contain such information, then the bargain is violated, and the patent is unenforceable.

a. False Claims Act
b. Disclosure requirement
c. Tax patent
d. Pre-emption right

31. _____ is a term used in accounting, economics and finance to spread the cost of an asset over the span of several years.

Chapter 15. Leases

In simple words we can say that _____ is the reduction in the value of an asset due to usage, passage of time, wear and tear, technological outdating or obsolescence, depletion, inadequacy, rot, rust, decay or other such factors.

In accounting, _____ is a term used to describe any method of attributing the historical or purchase cost of an asset across its useful life, roughly corresponding to normal wear and tear.

a. General ledger
c. Current asset
b. Depreciation
d. Net profit

32. _____ is a concept that denotes the precise probability of specific eventualities. Technically, the notion of _____ is independent from the notion of value and, as such, eventualities may have both beneficial and adverse consequences. However, in general usage the convention is to focus only on potential negative impact to some characteristic of value that may arise from a future event.

a. Risk
c. Discount factor
b. Risk adjusted return on capital
d. Discounting

33. In finance, _____ is the interest that has accumulated since the principal investment, or since the previous interest payment if there has been one already. For a financial instrument such as a bond, interest is calculated and paid in set intervals.

The primary formula for calculating the interest accrued in a given period is:

$$I_A = T \times P \times R$$

where I_A is the _____, T is the fraction of the year, P is the principal, and R is the annualized interest rate.

a. AIG
c. ABC Television Network
b. Interest
d. Accrued interest

34. _____ is one of a series of accounting transactions dealing with the billing of customers who owe money to a person, company or organization for goods and services that have been provided to the customer. In most business entities this is typically done by generating an invoice and mailing or electronically delivering it to the customer, who in turn must pay it within an established timeframe called credit or payment terms.

An example of a common payment term is Net 30, meaning payment is due in the amount of the invoice 30 days from the date of invoice.

a. Accrued revenue
c. Accrual
b. Accounts receivable
d. Adjusting entries

192 Chapter 15. Leases

35. _____, also called fair price (in a commonplace conflation of the two distinct concepts), is a concept used in finance and economics, defined as a rational and unbiased estimate of the potential market price of a good, service, or asset, taking into account such objective factors as:

- acquisition/production/distribution costs, replacement costs, or costs of close substitutes
- actual utility at a given level of development of social productive capability
- supply vs. demand

and subjective factors such as

- risk characteristics
- cost of capital
- individually perceived utility

In accounting, _____ is used as an estimate of the market value of an asset (or liability) for which a market price cannot be determined (usually because there is no established market for the asset.) Under GAAP (FAS 157), _____ is the amount at which the asset could be bought or sold in a current transaction between willing parties, or transferred to an equivalent party, other than in a liquidation sale. This is used for assets whose carrying value is based on mark-to-market valuations; for assets carried at historical cost, the _____ of the asset is not used. One example of where _____ is an issue is a College kitchen with a cost of $2 million which was built 5 years ago.

a. BMC Software, Inc.
b. 3M Company
c. Fair value
d. BNSF Railway

36. In economics, business, retail, and accounting, a _____ is the value of money that has been used up to produce something, and hence is not available for use anymore. In economics, a _____ is an alternative that is given up as a result of a decision. In business, the _____ may be one of acquisition, in which case the amount of money expended to acquire it is counted as _____.

a. Cost allocation
b. Prime cost
c. Cost of quality
d. Cost

37. _____ is a term in both law and accounting that is based on the economics term of 'market value.' It is also a common basis for assessing damages to be awarded for the loss of or damage to the property, generally in a claim under tort or a contract of insurance.

A _____ is often an estimate of what a willing buyer would pay to a willing seller, both in a free market, for an asset or any piece of property. If such a transaction actually occurs, then the actual transaction price is usually the _____.

a. Shares authorized
b. Fair market value
c. Cash and cash equivalents
d. Disposal tax effect

Chapter 15. Leases

38. A _____ is any one of a variety of different systems, institutions, procedures, social relations and infrastructures whereby persons trade, and goods and services are exchanged, forming part of the economy. It is an arrangement that allows buyers and sellers to exchange things. _____s vary in size, range, geographic scale, location, types and variety of human communities, as well as the types of goods and services traded.
   - a. Perfect competition
   - b. Recession
   - c. Market Failure
   - d. Market

39. _____ is the price at which an asset would trade in a competitive Walrasian auction setting. _____ is often used interchangeably with open _____, fair value or fair _____, although these terms have distinct definitions in different standards, and may differ in some circumstances.

   International Valuation Standards defines _____ as 'the estimated amount for which a property should exchange on the date of valuation between a willing buyer and a willing seller in an arme;s-length transaction after proper marketing wherein the parties had each acted knowledgeably, prudently, and without compulsion.'

   _____ is a concept distinct from market price, which is e;the price at which one can transacte;, while _____ is e;the true underlying valuee; according to theoretical standards.
   - a. Sinking fund
   - b. Market value
   - c. Debtor
   - d. Segregated portfolio company

40. _____ is one of the constituents of a leasing calculus or operation. It describes the future value of a good in terms of percentage of depreciation of its initial value.
   - a. Round-tripping
   - b. Net pay
   - c. 3M Company
   - d. Residual value

41. In accounting, _____ are considered liabilities of the business that are to be settled in cash within the fiscal year or the operating cycle, whichever period is longer.

   For example accounts payable for goods, services or supplies that were purchased for use in the operation of the business and payable within a normal period of time would be _____.

   Bonds, mortgages and loans that are payable over a term exceeding one year would be fixed liabilities.
   - a. Closing entries
   - b. Treasury stock
   - c. Payroll
   - d. Current liabilities

42. In financial accounting, a _____ is defined as an obligation of an entity arising from past transactions or events, the settlement of which may result in the transfer or use of assets, provision of services or other yielding of economic benefits in the future.
   - a. False Claims Act
   - b. Corporate governance
   - c. Vested
   - d. Liability

43. _____ in economics and business is the result of an exchange and from that trade we assign a numerical monetary value to a good, service or asset. If Alice trades Bob 4 apples for an orange, the _____ of an orange is 4 apples. Inversely, the _____ of an apple is 1/4 oranges.

a. Discounts and allowances
b. Transactional Net Margin Method
c. Price discrimination
d. Price

44. _____ is the value on a given date of a future payment or series of future payments, discounted to reflect the time value of money and other factors such as investment risk. _____ calculations are widely used in business and economics to provide a means to compare cash flows at different times on a meaningful 'like to like' basis.

The most commonly applied model of the time value of money is compound interest.

a. Net present value
b. Future value
c. 3M Company
d. Present value

45. An _____ is the price a borrower pays for the use of money they do not own, for instance a small company might borrow from a bank to kick start their business, and the return a lender receives for deferring the use of funds, by lending it to the borrower. _____s are normally expressed as a percentage rate over the period of one year.

_____s targets are also a vital tool of monetary policy and are used to control variables like investment, inflation, and unemployment.

a. Interest rate
b. ABC Television Network
c. AIG
d. AMEX

46. Simply put, _____ is the value of money figuring in a given amount of interest for a given amount of time. For example 100 dollars of todays money held for a year at 5 percent interest is worth 105 dollars, therefore 100 dollars paid now or 105 dollars paid exactly one year from now is the same amount of payment of money with that given intersest at that given amount of time. This notion dates at least to Martín de Azpilcueta of the School of Salamanca.

a. Competition law
b. Collusion
c. Merck ' Co., Inc.
d. Time value of money

47. An _____ is a derivative in which one party exchanges a stream of interest payments for another party's stream of cash flows. They can be used by hedgers to manage their fixed or floating assets and liabilities. They can also be used by speculators to replicate unfunded bond exposures to profit from changes in interest rates.

a. AIG
b. Interest rate swap
c. AMEX
d. ABC Television Network

48. In finance, a _____ is a derivative in which two counterparties agree to exchange one stream of cash flow against another stream. These streams are called the legs of the _____.

The cash flows are calculated over a notional principal amount, which is usually not exchanged between counterparties.

a. Department of the Treasury
b. Controlled Foreign Corporations
c. Total-factor productivity
d. Swap

49. _____s are expenses that change in proportion to the activity of a business. In other words, _____ is the sum of marginal costs. It can also be considered normal costs.

Chapter 15. Leases

a. Cost accounting
b. Quality costs
c. Fixed costs
d. Variable cost

50. _____ are formal records of a business' financial activities.

In British English, including United Kingdom company law, _____ are often referred to as accounts, although the term _____ is also used, particularly by accountants.

_____ provide an overview of a business' financial condition in both short and long term.

a. Notes to the financial statements
b. 3M Company
c. Statement of retained earnings
d. Financial statements

51. _____ is a company's financial statement that indicates how the revenue is transformed into the net income The purpose of the _____ is to show managers and investors whether the company made or lost money during the period being reported.

The important thing to remember about an _____ is that it represents a period of time.

a. ABC Television Network
b. AMEX
c. AIG
d. Income statement

52. _____ is that which is owed; usually referencing assets owed, but the term can also cover moral obligations and other interactions not requiring money. In the case of assets, _____ is a means of using future purchasing power in the present before a summation has been earned. Some companies and corporations use _____ as a part of their overall corporate finance strategy.

a. Lender
b. Debt
c. Loan
d. Debenture

53. The _____ percentage shows how profitable a company's assets are in generating revenue.

_____ can be computed as:

$$ROA = \frac{\text{Net Income - Interest Expense - Interest Tax savings}}{\text{Average Total Assets}}$$

This number tells you what the company can do with what it has, i.e. how many dollars of earnings they derive from each dollar of assets they control. Its a useful number for comparing competing companies in the same industry.

a. Statutory Liquidity Ratio
b. Return on sales
c. Capital employed
d. Return on assets

Chapter 15. Leases

54. _____ is the balance of the amounts of cash being received and paid by a business during a defined period of time, sometimes tied to a specific project. Measurement of _____ can be used

- to evaluate the state or performance of a business or project.
- to determine problems with liquidity. Being profitable does not necessarily mean being liquid. A company can fail because of a shortage of cash, even while profitable.
- to project rate of returns. The time of _____s into and out of projects are used as inputs to financial models such as internal rate of return, and net present value.
- to examine income or growth of a business when it is believed that accrual accounting concepts do not represent economic realities. Alternately, _____ can be used to 'validate' the net income generated by accrual accounting.

_____ as a generic term may be used differently depending on context, and certain _____ definitions may be adapted by analysts and users for their own uses. Common terms include operating _____ and free _____.

   a. Controlling interest
   b. Commercial paper
   c. Flow-through entity
   d. Cash flow

55. In financial accounting, a _____ or Statement of cash flows is a financial statement that shows a company's flow of cash. The money coming into the business is called cash inflow, and money going out from the business is called cash outflow. The statement shows how changes in balance sheet and income accounts affect cash and cash equivalents, and breaks the analysis down to operating, investing, and financing activities.
   a. BMC Software, Inc.
   b. BNSF Railway
   c. 3M Company
   d. Cash flow statement

56. _____, in accrual accounting, is any account where the asset or liability is not realized until a future date (accounting period), e.g. annuities, charges, taxes, income, etc. The _____ item may be carried, dependent on type of deferral, as either an asset or liability.
   a. Payroll
   b. Cash basis accounting
   c. Deferred
   d. Pro forma

57. An _____ is the buying of one company by another. An _____ may be friendly or hostile. In the former case, the companies cooperate in negotiations; in the latter case, the takeover target is unwilling to be bought or the target's board has no prior knowledge of the offer. _____ usually refers to a purchase of a smaller firm by a larger one. Sometimes, however, a smaller firm will acquire management control of a larger or longer established company and keep its name for the combined entity. This is known as a reverse takeover.
   a. AIG
   b. ABC Television Network
   c. Acquisition
   d. AMEX

58. _____ is an accounting concept, meaning a future tax liability or asset, resulting from temporary differences between book (accounting) value of assets and liabilities and their tax value, or timing differences between the recognition of gains and losses in financial statements and their recognition in a tax computation.

Temporary differences are differences between the carrying amount of an asset or liability recognised in the balance sheet and the amount attributed to that asset or liability for tax purposes (the tax base.)

a. Tax refund
b. Deferred tax
c. Deficit
d. Federal tax revenue by state

Chapter 16. Accounting for Income Taxes

1. An _____ is a tax levied on the financial income of people, corporations, or other legal entities. Various _____ systems exist, with varying degrees of tax incidence. Income taxation can be progressive, proportional, or regressive.
    a. Ordinary income
    b. Individual Retirement Arrangement
    c. Income tax
    d. Implied level of government service

2. _____, in accrual accounting, is any account where the asset or liability is not realized until a future date (accounting period), e.g. annuities, charges, taxes, income, etc. The _____ item may be carried, dependent on type of deferral, as either an asset or liability.
    a. Deferred
    b. Payroll
    c. Cash basis accounting
    d. Pro forma

3. _____ is an accounting concept, meaning a future tax liability or asset, resulting from temporary differences between book (accounting) value of assets and liabilities and their tax value, or timing differences between the recognition of gains and losses in financial statements and their recognition in a tax computation.

    Temporary differences are differences between the carrying amount of an asset or liability recognised in the balance sheet and the amount attributed to that asset or liability for tax purposes (the tax base.)

    a. Federal tax revenue by state
    b. Tax refund
    c. Deficit
    d. Deferred tax

4. In business and accounting, _____ are everything of value that is owned by a person or company. It is a claim on the property your income of a borrower. The balance sheet of a firm records the monetary value of the _____ owned by the firm.
    a. Accounts receivable
    b. Assets
    c. Earnings before interest, taxes, depreciation and amortization
    d. Accrual basis accounting

5. In financial accounting, a _____ is defined as an obligation of an entity arising from past transactions or events, the settlement of which may result in the transfer or use of assets, provision of services or other yielding of economic benefits in the future.
    a. Vested
    b. False Claims Act
    c. Liability
    d. Corporate governance

6. _____ is the term used to refer to the standard framework of guidelines for financial accounting used in any given jurisdiction. _____ includes the standards, conventions, and rules accountants follow in recording and summarizing transactions, and in the preparation of financial statements.

    Financial accounting information must be assembled and reported objectively.

    a. Current asset
    b. Generally accepted accounting principles
    c. Long-term liabilities
    d. General ledger

Chapter 16. Accounting for Income Taxes

7. An _____ is a term used in behavioral economics to describe those types of behaviors that impose costs on a person in the long-run that are not taken into account when making decisions in the present. Classical Economics discourages government from creating legislation that targets internalities, because it is assumed that the consumer takes these personal costs into account when paying for the good that causes the _____. For example, cigarettes should be taxed because of the negative consumption externalities that they impose, such as second-hand smoke, not because the smoker harms him or herself by smoking.
   a. Internality
   b. Inventory turnover ratio
   c. Operating budget
   d. Authorised capital

8. The _____ is the United States federal government agency that collects taxes and enforces the internal revenue laws. It is an agency within the U.S. Dept of the treasury responsible for interpretation and application of Federal tax law. The official U.S. Treasury regulations provide (in part):

   The _____ is a bureau of the Department of the Treasury under the immediate direction of the Commissioner of Internal Revenue.

   a. Use tax
   b. Internal Revenue Service
   c. Indirect tax
   d. Income tax

9. In financial accounting, a _____ or statement of financial position is a summary of a person's or organization's balances. Assets, liabilities and ownership equity are listed as of a specific date, such as the end of its financial year. A _____ is often described as a snapshot of a company's financial condition.
   a. Statement of retained earnings
   b. Balance sheet
   c. 3M Company
   d. Financial statements

10. In physics, and more specifically kinematics, _____ is the change in velocity over time. Because velocity is a vector, it can change in two ways: a change in magnitude and/or a change in direction. In one dimension, _____ is the rate at which something speeds up or slows down.
    a. Acceleration
    b. AMEX
    c. ABC Television Network
    d. AIG

11. The _____ is the current method of accelerated asset depreciation required by the United States income tax code. Under _____, all assets are divided into classes which dictate the number of years over which an asset's cost will be recovered.

    Prior to the Accelerated Cost Recovery System (ACRS), most capital purchases were depreciated using a straight line technique, that allowed for the depreciation of the asset over its useful life.

    a. Categorical grants
    b. 3M Company
    c. BMC Software, Inc.
    d. Modified Accelerated Cost Recovery System

12. _____ refers to any one of several methods by which a company, for 'financial accounting' and/or tax purposes, depreciates a fixed asset in such a way that the amount of depreciation taken each year is higher during the earlier years of an assete;s life. For financial accounting purposes, _____ is generally used when an asset is expected to be much more productive during its early years, so that depreciation expense will more accurately represent how much of an assete;s usefulness is being used up each year. For tax purposes, _____ provides a way of deferring corporate income taxes by reducing taxable income in current years, in exchange for increased taxable income in future years.

    a. Indirect tax   b. Effective marginal tax rates

    c. Accelerated depreciation   d. User charge

13. _____ refers to services paid for in advance. Examples include tolls, pay as you go cell phones, and stored-value cards such as gift cards and preloaded credit cards. _____ accounts are assets, and they are increased by debiting the account(s.)

    a. BMC Software, Inc.   b. Prepaid

    c. 3M Company   d. BNSF Railway

14. _____ refers to a business or organization attempting to acquire goods or services to accomplish the goals of the enterprise. Though there are several organizations that attempt to set standards in the _____ process, processes can vary greatly between organizations. Typically the word e;_____e; is not used interchangeably with the word e;procuremente;, since procurement typically includes Expediting, Supplier Quality, and Traffic and Logistics (T'L) in addition to _____.

    a. Free port   b. Consignor

    c. Supply chain   d. Purchasing

15. _____ principle is a cornerstone of accrual accounting together with matching principle. They both determine the accounting period, in which revenues and expenses are recognized. According to the principle, revenues are recognized when they are (1) realized or realizable, and are (2) earned (usually when goods are transferred or services rendered), no matter when cash is received.

    a. BMC Software, Inc.   b. 3M Company

    c. Net realizable value   d. Revenue recognition

16. There are several methods for calculating depreciation, generally based on either the passage of time or the level of activity (or use) of the asset.

_____ is the simplest and most often used technique, in which the company estimates the salvage value of the asset at the end of the period during which it will be used to generate revenues (useful life), and will expense a portion of original cost in equal increments over that period.

    a. Pro forma   b. Closing entries

    c. Current asset   d. Straight-line depreciation

17. The _____ is a business model where a customer must pay a subscription price to have access to the product/service. The model was pioneered by magazines and newspapers, but is now used by many businesses and websites. Rather than selling products individually, a subscription sells periodic (monthly or yearly or seasonal) use or access to a product or service, or, in the case of such non-profit organizations as opera companies or symphony orchestras, it sells tickets to the entire run of five to fifteen scheduled performances for an entire season.

Chapter 16. Accounting for Income Taxes

a. BNSF Railway
b. 3M Company
c. BMC Software, Inc.
d. Subscription business model

18. _____ is generally understood in financial circles as the point at which revenue is recognized, typically through a transaction which involves the exchange of an asset, product, or service for cash or its equivalents.

This approach gives the accounting division a strictly objective basis for changing the books. For example, a homeowner may believe that his house has grown in value during a strong market, or fallen in value during a weak market, but until the house is actually sold for a specific price to a specific buyer, the change in value can only be estimated and is considered unrealized.

a. Total-factor productivity
b. Merck ' Co., Inc.
c. Realization
d. Valuation

19. _____ is a subsection in equity where 'other comprehensive income' is accumulated (summed or 'aggregated'.)

The balance of _____ is presented in the Equity section of the Balance Sheet as is the Retained Earnings balance, which aggregates past and current Earnings, and past and current Dividends.

Other comprehensive income is the difference between net income and comprehensive income and represents the certain gains and losses of the enterprise.

a. Authorised capital
b. Operating budget
c. Inventory turnover ratio
d. Accumulated other comprehensive income

20. _____ is a specific term used in companies' financial reporting from the company-whole point of view. Because that use excludes the effects of changing ownership interest, an economic measure of _____ is necessary for financial analysis from the shareholders' point of view

_____ is defined by the Financial Accounting Standards Board, or FASB, as 'the change in equity [net assets] of a business enterprise during a period from transactions and other events and circumstances from nonowner sources. It includes all changes in equity during a period except those resulting from investments by owners and distributions to owners.'

_____ is the sum of net income and other items that must bypass the income statement because they have not been realized, including items like an unrealized holding gain or loss from available for sale securities and foreign currency translation gains or losses.

a. 3M Company
b. BMC Software, Inc.
c. Comprehensive income
d. BNSF Railway

21. In economics, business, retail, and accounting, a _____ is the value of money that has been used up to produce something, and hence is not available for use anymore. In economics, a _____ is an alternative that is given up as a result of a decision. In business, the _____ may be one of acquisition, in which case the amount of money expended to acquire it is counted as _____.

a. Cost of quality
c. Cost allocation
b. Prime cost
d. Cost

22. _____ is a term used in accounting, economics and finance to spread the cost of an asset over the span of several years.

In simple words we can say that _____ is the reduction in the value of an asset due to usage, passage of time, wear and tear, technological outdating or obsolescence, depletion, inadequacy, rot, rust, decay or other such factors.

In accounting, _____ is a term used to describe any method of attributing the historical or purchase cost of an asset across its useful life, roughly corresponding to normal wear and tear.

a. General ledger
c. Current asset
b. Depreciation
d. Net profit

23. In accounting, _____ has a very specific meaning. It is an outflow of cash or other valuable assets from a person or company to another person or company. This outflow of cash is generally one side of a trade for products or services that have equal or better current or future value to the buyer than to the seller.

a. AMEX
c. ABC Television Network
b. AIG
d. Expense

24. A _____ is the transfer of wealth from one party (such as a person or company) to another. A _____ is usually made in exchange for the provision of goods, services or both, or to fulfill a legal obligation.

The simplest and oldest form of _____ is barter, the exchange of one good or service for another.

a. Payee
c. 3M Company
b. BMC Software, Inc.
d. Payment

25. A _____ is the pinnacle activity involved in selling products or services in return for money or other compensation. It is an act of completion of a commercial activity.

A _____ is completed by the seller, the owner of the goods.

a. High yield stock
c. Tertiary sector of economy
b. Sale
d. Maturity

26. A _____ is a computer application that simulates a paper worksheet. It displays multiple cells that together make up a grid consisting of rows and columns, each cell containing either alphanumeric text or numeric values. A _____ cell may alternatively contain a formula that defines how the contents of that cell is to be calculated from the contents of any other cell (or combination of cells) each time any cell is updated.

a. Linear regression
c. Merck ' Co., Inc.
b. Spreadsheet
d. Mutual fund

Chapter 16. Accounting for Income Taxes

27. In finance, _____ is the process of estimating the potential market value of a financial asset or liability. They can be done on assets (for example, investments in marketable securities such as stocks, options, business enterprises, or intangible assets such as patents and trademarks) or on liabilities (e.g., Bonds issued by a company.) A _____ is required in many contexts including investment analysis, capital budgeting, merger and acquisition transactions, financial reporting, taxable events to determine the proper tax liability, and in litigation.

a. Daybook
b. Vyborg Appeal
c. Disclosure
d. Valuation

28. _____ is the portion of income that is the subject of taxation according to the laws that determine what is income and the taxation rate for that income. Generally, _____ refers to an individual's (or corporation's) gross income, adjusted for various deductions allowable by statute. The main questions put by most individuals in any jurisdiction are 'what makes up my _____' and what tax rates should be applied such that I can work out my tax liability to the state.

a. Taxable income
b. Half-year convention
c. SUTA dumping
d. Reverse Morris trust

29. _____ means the giving out of information, either voluntarily or to be in compliance with legal regulations or workplace rules.

- In Computer security, full _____ means disclosing full information about vulnerabilities.
- In computing, _____ widget
- Journalism, full _____ refers to disclosing the interests of the writer which may bear on the subject being written about, for example, if the writer has worked with an interview subject in the past.

- In law:
    - The law of England and Wales, _____ refers to a process that may form part of legal proceedings, whereby parties inform to other parties the existence of any relevant documents that are, or have been, in their control. This compares with the process known as discovery in the course of legal proceedings in the United States.
    - In U.S. civil procedure (litigation rules for civil cases), _____ is a stage prior to trial. In civil cases, each party must disclose to the opposing party the following: names of witnesses which it may use to support its side, copies of documents (or mere description of these documents) in its control which it may use to support its side, computation of damages claimed, and certain insurance information. _____ is related to, but technically prior to, the discovery stage.
    - In Company law (known as 'corporate law' in the United States), _____ refers to giving out information about public or limited companies or their officers, which might be kept secret if the company was a private company or a partnership.

- In real property transactions, _____ refers to providing to a buyer information known to the seller or broker/agent concerning the condition or other aspects of real property that would affect the property's value or desirability. These rules regarding what information must be disclosed, and whether the information must be disclosed even if a buyer does not ask, vary from one jurisdiction to the next.

a. Disclosure
b. Tax harmonisation
c. Controlled Foreign Corporations
d. Trailing

30. _____ are payments made by a corporation to its shareholder members. It is the portion of corporate profits paid out to stockholders. When a corporation earns a profit or surplus, that money can be put to two uses: it can either be re-invested in the business (called retained earnings), or it can be paid to the shareholders as a dividend.
   a. Dividend payout ratio
   b. Dividends
   c. Dividend stripping
   d. Dividend yield

31. In accounting, _____ are considered liabilities of the business that are to be settled in cash within the fiscal year or the operating cycle, whichever period is longer.

For example accounts payable for goods, services or supplies that were purchased for use in the operation of the business and payable within a normal period of time would be _____.

Bonds, mortgages and loans that are payable over a term exceeding one year would be fixed liabilities.

   a. Payroll
   b. Closing entries
   c. Current liabilities
   d. Treasury stock

32. A _____ or a tax-deductible expense affects a taxpayer's income tax. A _____ represents an expense incurred by a taxpayer. They are variable amounts that you can subtract, or deduct, from your gross income. It is subtracted from gross income when the taxpayer computes his or her income taxes.
   a. Tax avoidance
   b. Tax protester constitutional arguments
   c. Tax incidence
   d. Tax deduction

33. Under U.S. Federal income tax law, a _____ occurs when certain tax-deductible expenses exceed taxable revenues for a taxable year. If a taxpayer is taxed during profitable periods without receiving any tax relief (e.g. a refund) during periods of _____s, an unbalanced tax burden results. Consequently, in some situations, Congress allows taxpayers to use the losses in one year to offset the profits of other years.
   a. Half-year convention
   b. Revenue Procedures
   c. SUTA dumping
   d. Net operating loss

34. _____ methods are means of managing inventory and financial matters involving the money a company ties up within inventory of produced goods, raw materials, parts, components, or feed stocks. FIFO stands for first-in, first-out, meaning that the oldest inventory items are recorded as sold first. LIFO stands for last-in, first-out, meaning that the most recently purchased items are recorded as sold first.
   a. Reorder point
   b. Finished good
   c. 3M Company
   d. FIFO and LIFO accounting

35. In law, _____ refers to the process by which a company (or part of a company) is brought to an end, and the assets and property of the company redistributed. _____ can also be referred to as winding-up or dissolution, although dissolution technically refers to the last stage of _____. The process of _____ also arises when customs, an authority or agency in a country responsible for collecting and safeguarding customs duties, determines the final computation or ascertainment of the duties or drawback accruing on an entry.
   a. 3M Company
   b. Liquidation
   c. BMC Software, Inc.
   d. Bankruptcy protection

Chapter 16. Accounting for Income Taxes

36. _____ is a term used with respect to a retailed product, indicating that the product is in the end of its product lifetime and a vendor will no longer be marketing, selling, or promoting a particular product and may also be limiting or ending support for the product. In the specific case of product sales, the term end-of-sale (EOS) has also been used. The term lifetime, after the last production date, depends on the product and is related to a customer's expected product lifetime.

a. ABC Television Network
b. AMEX
c. AIG
d. End-of-life

37. At its simplest, a company's _____ as it sometimes called, is computed in by multiplying the income before tax number, as reported to shareholders, by the appropriate tax rate. In reality, the computation is typically considerably more complex due to things such as expenses considered not deductible by taxing authorities ('add backs'), the range of tax rates applicable to various levels of income, different tax rates in different jurisdictions, multiple layers of tax on income, and other issues.

Historically, in many places, a revenue-expense method was used, in which the income statement was seen as primary, and the balance sheet as secondary.

a. 3M Company
b. Total Expense Ratio
c. Payroll
d. Tax expense

38. _____ were documents issued by the Committee on Accounting Procedure between 1938 and 1959 on various accounting problems. They were discontinued with the dissolution of the Committee in 1959 under a recommendation from the Special Committee on Research Program. In all, 51 bulletins were issued, however, the lack of binding authority over AICPA's membership reduced the influence of, and compliance with the content of the bulletins.

a. AIG
b. Accounting Research Bulletins
c. Other postemployment benefits
d. ABC Television Network

39. _____ is a financial mechanism in which a debtor obtains the right to delay payments to a creditor, for a defined period of time, in exchange for a charge or fee. Essentially, the party that owes money in the present purchases the right to delay the payment until some future date. The discount, or charge, is simply the difference between the original amount owed in the present and the amount that has to be paid in the future to settle the debt.

a. Risk aversion
b. Discounting
c. Risk adjusted return on capital
d. Discount factor

40. _____ is the value on a given date of a future payment or series of future payments, discounted to reflect the time value of money and other factors such as investment risk. _____ calculations are widely used in business and economics to provide a means to compare cash flows at different times on a meaningful 'like to like' basis.

The most commonly applied model of the time value of money is compound interest.

a. Present value
b. 3M Company
c. Future value
d. Net present value

41. _____ is that which is owed; usually referencing assets owed, but the term can also cover moral obligations and other interactions not requiring money. In the case of assets, _____ is a means of using future purchasing power in the present before a summation has been earned. Some companies and corporations use _____ as a part of their overall corporate finance strategy.

a. Loan
b. Lender
c. Debenture
d. Debt

Chapter 17. Pensions and Other Postretirement Benefits

1. An _____ is a retirement plan account that provides some tax advantages for retirement savings in the United States.

The _____ and related vehicles were created by amendments to the Internal Revenue Code of 1954 (as amended) made by the Employee Retirement Income Security Act of 1974 (ERISA), which enacted (among other things) Internal Revenue Code sections 219 (26 U.S.C. Â§ 219) and 408 (26 U.S.C.

   a. Indirect tax
   b. Equity of condition
   c. Implied level of government service
   d. Individual Retirement Arrangement

2. In financial accounting, a _____ is defined as an obligation of an entity arising from past transactions or events, the settlement of which may result in the transfer or use of assets, provision of services or other yielding of economic benefits in the future.

   a. False Claims Act
   b. Vested
   c. Corporate governance
   d. Liability

3. In economics, a _____ is a type of pension plan in which an employer promises a specified monthly benefit on retirement that is predetermined by a formula based on the employee's earnings history, tenure of service and age, rather than depending on investment returns. It is 'defined' in the sense that the formula for computing the employer's contribution is known in advance. In the United States, 26 U.S.C.

   a. 3M Company
   b. Fixed asset turnover
   c. Defined benefit pension plan
   d. BMC Software, Inc.

4. The _____ is the current method of accelerated asset depreciation required by the United States income tax code. Under _____, all assets are divided into classes which dictate the number of years over which an asset's cost will be recovered.

Prior to the Accelerated Cost Recovery System (ACRS), most capital purchases were depreciated using a straight line technique, that allowed for the depreciation of the asset over its useful life.

   a. Categorical grants
   b. Modified Accelerated Cost Recovery System
   c. BMC Software, Inc.
   d. 3M Company

5. A _____ or a tax-deductible expense affects a taxpayer's income tax. A _____ represents an expense incurred by a taxpayer. They are variable amounts that you can subtract, or deduct, from your gross income. It is subtracted from gross income when the taxpayer computes his or her income taxes.

   a. Tax avoidance
   b. Tax protester constitutional arguments
   c. Tax incidence
   d. Tax deduction

Chapter 17. Pensions and Other Postretirement Benefits

6. _____ means the giving out of information, either voluntarily or to be in compliance with legal regulations or workplace rules.

- In Computer security, full _____ means disclosing full information about vulnerabilities.
- In computing, _____ widget
- Journalism, full _____ refers to disclosing the interests of the writer which may bear on the subject being written about, for example, if the writer has worked with an interview subject in the past.

- In law:
    - The law of England and Wales, _____ refers to a process that may form part of legal proceedings, whereby parties inform to other parties the existence of any relevant documents that are, or have been, in their control. This compares with the process known as discovery in the course of legal proceedings in the United States.
    - In U.S. civil procedure (litigation rules for civil cases), _____ is a stage prior to trial. In civil cases, each party must disclose to the opposing party the following: names of witnesses which it may use to support its side, copies of documents (or mere description of these documents) in its control which it may use to support its side, computation of damages claimed, and certain insurance information. _____ is related to, but technically prior to, the discovery stage.
    - In Company law (known as 'corporate law' in the United States), _____ refers to giving out information about public or limited companies or their officers, which might be kept secret if the company was a private company or a partnership.

- In real property transactions, _____ refers to providing to a buyer information known to the seller or broker/agent concerning the condition or other aspects of real property that would affect the property's value or desirability. These rules regarding what information must be disclosed, and whether the information must be disclosed even if a buyer does not ask, vary from one jurisdiction to the next.

a. Controlled Foreign Corporations
c. Tax harmonisation
b. Trailing
d. Disclosure

7. Most patent law systems require that a patent application disclose a claimed invention in sufficient detail for the notional person skilled in the art to carry out that claimed invention. This requirement is often known as sufficiency of disclosure or enablement, depending on the jurisdiction.

The _____ lies at the heart and origin of patent law. A state or government grants an inventor, or the inventor's assignee, a monopoly for a given period of time in exchange for the inventor disclosing to the public how to make or practice his or her invention. If a patent fails to contain such information, then the bargain is violated, and the patent is unenforceable.

a. Pre-emption right
c. False Claims Act
b. Tax patent
d. Disclosure requirement

8. An _____ is a business professional who deals with the financial impact of risk and uncertainty. They have a deep understanding of financial security systems, their reasons for being, their complexity, their mathematics, and the way they work (Trowbridge 1989, p. 7).

Chapter 17. Pensions and Other Postretirement Benefits

a. Actuary
b. AIG
c. AMEX
d. ABC Television Network

9. In business and accounting, _____ are everything of value that is owned by a person or company. It is a claim on the property your income of a borrower. The balance sheet of a firm records the monetary value of the _____ owned by the firm.

a. Accrual basis accounting
b. Earnings before interest, taxes, depreciation and amortization
c. Accounts receivable
d. Assets

10. In accounting, _____ has a very specific meaning. It is an outflow of cash or other valuable assets from a person or company to another person or company. This outflow of cash is generally one side of a trade for products or services that have equal or better current or future value to the buyer than to the seller.

a. AIG
b. AMEX
c. ABC Television Network
d. Expense

11. A _____ is a computer application that simulates a paper worksheet. It displays multiple cells that together make up a grid consisting of rows and columns, each cell containing either alphanumeric text or numeric values. A _____ cell may alternatively contain a formula that defines how the contents of that cell is to be calculated from the contents of any other cell (or combination of cells) each time any cell is updated.

a. Linear regression
b. Spreadsheet
c. Merck ' Co., Inc.
d. Mutual fund

12. The _____ of 1974 (Pub.L. 93-406, 88 Stat. 829, enacted September 2, 1974) is an American federal statute that establishes minimum standards for pension plans in private industry and provides for extensive rules on the federal income tax effects of transactions associated with employee benefit plans. It was enacted to protect the interests of employee benefit plan participants and their beneficiaries by requiring the disclosure to them of financial and other information concerning the plan; by establishing standards of conduct for plan fiduciaries; and by providing for appropriate remedies and access to the federal courts.

a. Investment Advisers Act of 1940
b. Employee Retirement Income Security Act
c. Operating Lease
d. Exclusive right

13. Employment is a contract between two parties, one being the employer and the other being the _____. An _____ may be defined as: 'A person in the service of another under any contract of hire, express or implied, oral or written, where the employer has the power or right to control and direct the _____ in the material details of how the work is to be performed.' Black's Law Dictionary page 471 (5th ed. 1979.)

a. AIG
b. Employee
c. AMEX
d. ABC Television Network

14. A _____ is a fungible, negotiable instrument representing financial value. they are broadly categorized into debt securities (such as banknotes, bonds and debentures), and equity securities; e.g., common stocks. The company or other entity issuing the _____ is called the issuer.

a. BMC Software, Inc.
b. 3M Company
c. Tracking stock
d. Security

15. In law, vesting is to give an immediately secured right of present or future enjoyment. One has a _____ right to an asset that cannot be taken away by any third party, even though one may not yet possess the asset. When the right, interest or title to the present or future possession of a legal estate can be transferred to any other party, it is termed a _____ interest.
   a. Malpractice
   b. Tax lien
   c. Liability
   d. Vested

16. The _____ is an independent agency of the United States government that was created by the Employee Retirement Income Security Act of 1974 (ERISA) to encourage the continuation and maintenance of voluntary private defined benefit pension plans, provide timely and uninterrupted payment of pension benefits, and keep pension insurance premiums at the lowest level necessary to carry out its operations. Subject to other statutory limitations, the _____ insurance program pays pension benefits up to the maximum guaranteed benefit set by law to participants who retire at age 65 ($54,000 a year as of 2009.) The benefits payable to insured retirees who start their benefits at ages other than 65, or who elect survivor coverage, are adjusted to be equivalent in value.
   a. Financial Crimes Enforcement Network
   b. Pension Benefit Guaranty Corporation
   c. 3M Company
   d. Public Company Accounting Oversight Board

17. _____ is a fee paid on borrowed assets. It is the price paid for the use of borrowed money , or, money earned by deposited funds .Assets that are sometimes lent with _____ include money, shares, consumer goods through hire purchase, major assets such as aircraft, and even entire factories in finance lease arrangements. The _____ is calculated upon the value of the assets in the same manner as upon money.
   a. Insolvency
   b. ABC Television Network
   c. Interest
   d. AIG

18. In economics, business, retail, and accounting, a _____ is the value of money that has been used up to produce something, and hence is not available for use anymore. In economics, a _____ is an alternative that is given up as a result of a decision. In business, the _____ may be one of acquisition, in which case the amount of money expended to acquire it is counted as _____.
   a. Cost allocation
   b. Cost of quality
   c. Prime cost
   d. Cost

19. Discounting is a financial mechanism in which a debtor obtains the right to delay payments to a creditor, for a defined period of time, in exchange for a charge or fee. Essentially, the party that owes money in the present purchases the right to delay the payment until some future date. The _____, or charge, is simply the difference between the original amount owed in the present and the amount that has to be paid in the future to settle the debt.
   a. Discounting
   b. Discount factor
   c. Discount
   d. Risk aversion

20. The _____ is an interest rate a central bank charges depository institutions that borrow reserves from it.

Chapter 17. Pensions and Other Postretirement Benefits

The term _____ has two meanings:

- the same as interest rate; the term 'discount' does not refer to the meaning of the word, but to the purpose of using the quantity, such as computations of present value, e.g. net present value or discounted cash flow

- the annual effective _____, which is the annual interest divided by the capital including that interest; this rate is lower than the interest rate; it corresponds to using the value after a year as the nominal value, and seeing the initial value as the nominal value minus a discount; it is used for Treasury Bills and similar financial instruments

The annual effective _____ is the annual interest divided by the capital including that interest, which is the interest rate divided by 100% plus the interest rate. It is the annual discount factor to be applied to the future cash flow, to find the discount, subtracted from a future value to find the value one year earlier.

For example, suppose there is a government bond that sells for $95 and pays $100 in a year's time.

- a. Convertible bond
- b. Municipal bond
- c. Process time
- d. Discount rate

21. An _____ is the price a borrower pays for the use of money they do not own, for instance a small company might borrow from a bank to kick start their business, and the return a lender receives for deferring the use of funds, by lending it to the borrower. _____s are normally expressed as a percentage rate over the period of one year.

_____s targets are also a vital tool of monetary policy and are used to control variables like investment, inflation, and unemployment.

- a. AMEX
- b. AIG
- c. ABC Television Network
- d. Interest rate

22. A _____ is the transfer of wealth from one party (such as a person or company) to another. A _____ is usually made in exchange for the provision of goods, services or both, or to fulfill a legal obligation.

The simplest and oldest form of _____ is barter, the exchange of one good or service for another.

- a. BMC Software, Inc.
- b. Payee
- c. 3M Company
- d. Payment

23. _____ is a legal term that refers to a holder of property on behalf of a beneficiary. A trust can be set up either to benefit particular persons, or for any charitable purposes (but not generally for non-charitable purposes): typical examples are a will trust for the testator's children and family, a pension trust (to confer benefits on employees and their families), and a charitable trust. In all cases, the _____ may be a person or company, whether or not they are a prospective beneficiary.

212 Chapter 17. Pensions and Other Postretirement Benefits

a. Cash cow
b. Performance measurement
c. Management by exception
d. Trustee

24. _____ is a term used in subtly different ways in a number of fields, including philosophy, physics, statistics, economics, finance, insurance, psychology, sociology, engineering, and information science. It applies to predictions of future events, to physical measurements already made, or to the unknown.

In his seminal work Risk, _____, and Profit University of Chicago economist Frank Knight (1921) established the important distinction between risk and _____:

> '_____ must be taken in a sense radically distinct from the familiar notion of risk, from which it has never been properly separated....

a. ABC Television Network
b. AMEX
c. AIG
d. Uncertainty

25. _____ is a cornerstone of accrual accounting together with the revenue recognition principle. They both determine the accounting period, in which revenues and expenses are recognized. According to the principle, expenses are recognized when obligations are (1) incurred (usually when goods are transferred or services rendered, e.g. sold), and (2) offset against recognized revenues, which were generated from those expenses (related on the cause-and-effect basis), no matter when cash is paid out.

a. Payroll
b. Current liabilities
c. Net sales
d. Matching principle

26. _____ is the process of increasing, or accounting for, an amount over a period of time. Particular instances of the term include:

- _____, the allocation of a lump sum amount to different time periods, particularly for loans and other forms of finance, including related interest or other finance charges.
    - _____ schedule, a table detailing each periodic payment on a loan (typically a mortgage), as generated by an _____ calculator.
    - Negative _____, an _____ schedule where the loan amount actually increases through not paying the full interest
- Amortized analysis, analyzing the execution cost of algorithms over a sequence of operations.
- _____ of capital expenditures of certain assets under accounting rules, particularly intangible assets, in a manner analogous to depreciation.
- _____

a. EBIT
b. Intangible
c. Annuity
d. Amortization

Chapter 17. Pensions and Other Postretirement Benefits

27. _____ are defined as identifiable non-monetary assets that cannot be seen, touched or physically measured, which are created through time and/or effort and that are identifiable as a separate asset. There are two primary forms of intangibles - legal intangibles (such as trade secrets (e.g., customer lists), copyrights, patents, trademarks, and goodwill) and competitive intangibles (such as knowledge activities (know-how, knowledge), collaboration activities, leverage activities, and structural activities.) Legal intangibles are known under the generic term intellectual property and generate legal property rights defensible in a court of law.
   a. ABC Television Network
   b. Overhead
   c. Intangible assets
   d. AIG

28. _____, in accrual accounting, is any account where the asset or liability is not realized until a future date (accounting period), e.g. annuities, charges, taxes, income, etc. The _____ item may be carried, dependent on type of deferral, as either an asset or liability.
   a. Cash basis accounting
   b. Payroll
   c. Pro forma
   d. Deferred

29. _____ methods are means of managing inventory and financial matters involving the money a company ties up within inventory of produced goods, raw materials, parts, components, or feed stocks. FIFO stands for first-in, first-out, meaning that the oldest inventory items are recorded as sold first. LIFO stands for last-in, first-out, meaning that the most recently purchased items are recorded as sold first.
   a. Reorder point
   b. Finished good
   c. 3M Company
   d. FIFO and LIFO accounting

30. In accounting, _____ are considered liabilities of the business that are to be settled in cash within the fiscal year or the operating cycle, whichever period is longer.

For example accounts payable for goods, services or supplies that were purchased for use in the operation of the business and payable within a normal period of time would be _____.

Bonds, mortgages and loans that are payable over a term exceeding one year would be fixed liabilities.

   a. Payroll
   b. Closing entries
   c. Treasury stock
   d. Current liabilities

31. In law, _____ refers to the process by which a company (or part of a company) is brought to an end, and the assets and property of the company redistributed. _____ can also be referred to as winding-up or dissolution, although dissolution technically refers to the last stage of _____. The process of _____ also arises when customs, an authority or agency in a country responsible for collecting and safeguarding customs duties, determines the final computation or ascertainment of the duties or drawback accruing on an entry.
   a. Liquidation
   b. Bankruptcy protection
   c. BMC Software, Inc.
   d. 3M Company

32. In financial accounting, a _____ or statement of financial position is a summary of a person's or organization's balances. Assets, liabilities and ownership equity are listed as of a specific date, such as the end of its financial year. A _____ is often described as a snapshot of a company's financial condition.

a. Financial statements
b. 3M Company
c. Balance sheet
d. Statement of retained earnings

33. _____ in accounting is the process of treating equity investments, usually 20-50%, in associate companies. The investor keeps such equities as an asset. Proportional share of associate company's net income increases the investment, and proportional payment of dividends decreases it.
   a. Out-of-pocket
   b. AIG
   c. Equity method
   d. ABC Television Network

34. In finance, an _____ is a contract between a buyer and a seller that gives the buyer the right--but not the obligation-- to buy or to sell a particular asset (the underlying asset) at a later time at an agreed price. In return for granting the _____, the seller collects a payment (the premium) from the buyer. A call _____ gives the buyer the right to buy the underlying asset; a put _____ gives the buyer of the _____ the right to sell the underlying asset.
   a. AIG
   b. ABC Television Network
   c. AMEX
   d. Option

35. The term _____ or superannuation refers to a pension granted upon retirement. They may be set up by employers, insurance companies, the government or other institutions such as employer associations or trade unions.
   a. Wage
   b. 3M Company
   c. BMC Software, Inc.
   d. Retirement plan

36. _____ is an accounting concept, meaning a future tax liability or asset, resulting from temporary differences between book (accounting) value of assets and liabilities and their tax value, or timing differences between the recognition of gains and losses in financial statements and their recognition in a tax computation.

Temporary differences are differences between the carrying amount of an asset or liability recognised in the balance sheet and the amount attributed to that asset or liability for tax purposes (the tax base.)

   a. Tax refund
   b. Federal tax revenue by state
   c. Deficit
   d. Deferred tax

37. A _____ is a financial instrument aimed at a reduction in greenhouse gas emissions. _____s are measured in metric tons of carbon dioxide-equivalent (_____$_2$e) and may represent six primary categories of greenhouse gases. One _____ represents the reduction of one metric ton of carbon dioxide or its equivalent in other greenhouse gases.
   a. Sustainable development
   b. Mutual fund
   c. General Accounting Office
   d. Carbon offset

38. _____ is a specific term used in companies' financial reporting from the company-whole point of view. Because that use excludes the effects of changing ownership interest, an economic measure of _____ is necessary for financial analysis from the shareholders' point of view

_____ is defined by the Financial Accounting Standards Board, or FASB, as 'the change in equity [net assets] of a business enterprise during a period from transactions and other events and circumstances from nonowner sources. It includes all changes in equity during a period except those resulting from investments by owners and distributions to owners.'

Chapter 17. Pensions and Other Postretirement Benefits 215

_____ is the sum of net income and other items that must bypass the income statement because they have not been realized, including items like an unrealized holding gain or loss from available for sale securities and foreign currency translation gains or losses.

   a. Comprehensive income   b. BNSF Railway
   c. 3M Company   d. BMC Software, Inc.

39. _____ is that which is owed; usually referencing assets owed, but the term can also cover moral obligations and other interactions not requiring money. In the case of assets, _____ is a means of using future purchasing power in the present before a summation has been earned. Some companies and corporations use _____ as a part of their overall corporate finance strategy.

   a. Debenture   b. Debt
   c. Loan   d. Lender

40. In finance, a _____ or accounting ratio is a ratio of two selected numerical values taken from an enterprise's financial statements. There are many standard ratios used to try to evaluate the overall financial condition of a corporation or other organization. _____s may be used by managers within a firm, by current and potential shareholders (owners) of a firm, and by a firm's creditors.

   a. Financial ratio   b. Price/cash flow ratio
   c. Current ratio   d. Return of capital

41. _____ or interest coverage ratio is a measure of a company's ability to honor its debt payments. It may be calculated as either EBIT or EBITDA divided by the total interest payable.

   a. Return of capital   b. Capital recovery factor
   c. Times interest earned   d. Yield Gap

42. The _____ is a financial ratio indicating the relative proportion of equity to all used to finance a company's assets. The two components are often taken from the firm's balance sheet or statement of financial position (so-called book value), but the ratio may also be calculated using market values for both, if the company's equities are publicly traded.

The _____ is especially in Central Europe a very common financial ratio while in the US the debt to _____ is more often used in financial (research) reports.

   a. Equity ratio   b. Average accounting return
   c. Efficiency ratio   d. Earnings yield

43. The Exxon Mobil Corporation is an American oil and gas corporation. It is a direct descendant of John D. Rockefeller's Standard Oil company, formed on November 30, 1999, by the merger of Exxon and Mobil.

_____ is the world's largest publicly traded company when measured by either revenue or market capitalization.

Chapter 17. Pensions and Other Postretirement Benefits

a. Arthur Betz Laffer
b. Abby Joseph Cohen
c. Alan Greenspan
d. ExxonMobil

44. _____ is a subsection in equity where 'other comprehensive income' is accumulated (summed or 'aggregated'.)

The balance of _____ is presented in the Equity section of the Balance Sheet as is the Retained Earnings balance, which aggregates past and current Earnings, and past and current Dividends.

Other comprehensive income is the difference between net income and comprehensive income and represents the certain gains and losses of the enterprise.

a. Authorised capital
b. Inventory turnover ratio
c. Operating budget
d. Accumulated other comprehensive income

45. _____ is a company's financial statement that indicates how the revenue is transformed into the net income The purpose of the _____ is to show managers and investors whether the company made or lost money during the period being reported.

The important thing to remember about an _____ is that it represents a period of time.

a. Income statement
b. AMEX
c. ABC Television Network
d. AIG

46. A _____ is a compensation, usually financial, received by a worker in exchange for their labor.

Compensation in terms of _____s is given to worker and compensation in terms of salary is given to employees. Compensation is a monetary benefits given to employees in returns of the services provided by them.

a. Retirement plan
b. 3M Company
c. BMC Software, Inc.
d. Wage

47. _____ refers to services paid for in advance. Examples include tolls, pay as you go cell phones, and stored-value cards such as gift cards and preloaded credit cards. _____ accounts are assets, and they are increased by debiting the account(s).

a. BNSF Railway
b. BMC Software, Inc.
c. Prepaid
d. 3M Company

Chapter 18. Shareholders' Equity

1. _____ are payments made by a corporation to its shareholder members. It is the portion of corporate profits paid out to stockholders. When a corporation earns a profit or surplus, that money can be put to two uses: it can either be re-invested in the business (called retained earnings), or it can be paid to the shareholders as a dividend.
   - a. Dividends
   - b. Dividend payout ratio
   - c. Dividend stripping
   - d. Dividend yield

2. A _____ or stock divide increases or decreases the number of shares in a public company. The price is adjusted such that the before and after market capitalization of the company remains the same and dilution does not occur. Options and warrants are included.
   - a. 3M Company
   - b. Growth investing
   - c. Stockholder
   - d. Stock split

3. The Exxon Mobil Corporation is an American oil and gas corporation. It is a direct descendant of John D. Rockefeller's Standard Oil company, formed on November 30, 1999, by the merger of Exxon and Mobil.

   _____ is the world's largest publicly traded company when measured by either revenue or market capitalization.
   - a. Abby Joseph Cohen
   - b. Alan Greenspan
   - c. Arthur Betz Laffer
   - d. ExxonMobil

4. _____ is a specific term used in companies' financial reporting from the company-whole point of view. Because that use excludes the effects of changing ownership interest, an economic measure of _____ is necessary for financial analysis from the shareholders' point of view

   _____ is defined by the Financial Accounting Standards Board, or FASB, as 'the change in equity [net assets] of a business enterprise during a period from transactions and other events and circumstances from nonowner sources. It includes all changes in equity during a period except those resulting from investments by owners and distributions to owners.'

   _____ is the sum of net income and other items that must bypass the income statement because they have not been realized, including items like an unrealized holding gain or loss from available for sale securities and foreign currency translation gains or losses.
   - a. BNSF Railway
   - b. 3M Company
   - c. BMC Software, Inc.
   - d. Comprehensive income

5. A sole _____, or simply _____ is a type of business entity which legally has no separate existence from its owner. Hence, the limitations of liability enjoyed by a corporation and limited liability partnerships do not apply to sole proprietors. All debts of the business are debts of the owner.
   - a. Pre-determined overhead rate
   - b. Free cash flow
   - c. Safety stock
   - d. Proprietorship

6. In financial accounting, a _____ or statement of financial position is a summary of a person's or organization's balances. Assets, liabilities and ownership equity are listed as of a specific date, such as the end of its financial year. A _____ is often described as a snapshot of a company's financial condition.

a. 3M Company
b. Statement of retained earnings
c. Financial statements
d. Balance sheet

7. An _____ is a tax levied on the financial income of people, corporations, or other legal entities. Various _____ systems exist, with varying degrees of tax incidence. Income taxation can be progressive, proportional, or regressive.
- a. Implied level of government service
- b. Income tax
- c. Individual Retirement Arrangement
- d. Ordinary income

8. In economics, _____ or _____ goods or real _____ refers to factors of production used to create goods or services that are not themselves significantly consumed (though they may depreciate) in the production process. _____ goods may be acquired with money or financial _____. In finance and accounting, _____ generally refers to financial wealth, especially that used to start or maintain a business.
- a. Vyborg Appeal
- b. Disclosure
- c. Capital
- d. Screening

9. _____, in accrual accounting, is any account where the asset or liability is not realized until a future date (accounting period), e.g. annuities, charges, taxes, income, etc. The _____ item may be carried, dependent on type of deferral, as either an asset or liability.
- a. Pro forma
- b. Payroll
- c. Deferred
- d. Cash basis accounting

10. _____ in accounting is the process of treating equity investments, usually 20-50%, in associate companies. The investor keeps such equities as an asset. Proportional share of associate company's net income increases the investment, and proportional payment of dividends decreases it.
- a. ABC Television Network
- b. Out-of-pocket
- c. AIG
- d. Equity method

11. _____ are generally defined as increases (decreases) in the replacement costs of the assets held during a given period. _____ and losses accrue to the owners of assets and liabilities purely as a result of holding the assets or liabilities over time, without transforming them in any way.

For example, if a company holds bottles of wine in its inventory and that specific wine becomes more expensive on the market, the replacement cost of the wine in the inventory increases as it has become more expensive for the company to replace its current stock of wine.

- a. Par value
- b. Holding gains
- c. Net worth
- d. Fair market value

12. A _____ or transnational corporation (TNC) is a corporation or enterprise that manages production or delivers services in more than one country. It can also be referred to as an international corporation. The first modern _____ is generally thought to be the British East India Company, established in 1600.
- a. Butterfield Bank
- b. MicroStrategy
- c. Multinational corporation
- d. Privately held

13. _____ is typically a 'higher ranking' stock than voting shares, and its terms are negotiated between the corporation and the investor.

Chapter 18. Shareholders' Equity

_____ usually carries no voting rights, but may carry superior priority over common stock in the payment of dividends and upon liquidation. _____ may carry a dividend that is paid out prior to any dividends being paid to common stock holders.

- a. Restricted stock
- b. Cash flow
- c. Gross income
- d. Preferred stock

14. _____ is a subsection in equity where 'other comprehensive income' is accumulated (summed or 'aggregated'.)

The balance of _____ is presented in the Equity section of the Balance Sheet as is the Retained Earnings balance, which aggregates past and current Earnings, and past and current Dividends.

Other comprehensive income is the difference between net income and comprehensive income and represents the certain gains and losses of the enterprise.

- a. Inventory turnover ratio
- b. Authorised capital
- c. Operating budget
- d. Accumulated other comprehensive income

15. _____ is the process of increasing, or accounting for, an amount over a period of time. Particular instances of the term include:

- _____, the allocation of a lump sum amount to different time periods, particularly for loans and other forms of finance, including related interest or other finance charges.
    - _____ schedule, a table detailing each periodic payment on a loan (typically a mortgage), as generated by an _____ calculator.
    - Negative _____, an _____ schedule where the loan amount actually increases through not paying the full interest
- Amortized analysis, analyzing the execution cost of algorithms over a sequence of operations.
- _____ of capital expenditures of certain assets under accounting rules, particularly intangible assets, in a manner analogous to depreciation.
- _____

- a. Annuity
- b. EBIT
- c. Intangible
- d. Amortization

16. In monetary economics _____ can refer either to a particular _____, for example British Pounds or United States Dollars, or, to the coins and banknotes of a particular _____, which actually form only a small part of the monetary base of a nation's money supply. The other part of a nation's money supply consists of money deposited in banks (sometimes called deposit money), ownership of which can be transferred by means of checks (cheques in the United Kingdom and Australia) or other forms of money transfer such as credit and debit cards. Deposit money and _____ are 'money' in the sense that both are acceptable as a means of exchange, but money need not necessarily be '_____'.

- a. 3M Company
- b. BMC Software, Inc.
- c. Currency
- d. BNSF Railway

17. In accounting, _____ are considered liabilities of the business that are to be settled in cash within the fiscal year or the operating cycle, whichever period is longer.

For example accounts payable for goods, services or supplies that were purchased for use in the operation of the business and payable within a normal period of time would be _____.

Bonds, mortgages and loans that are payable over a term exceeding one year would be fixed liabilities.

a. Treasury stock
b. Payroll
c. Closing entries
d. Current liabilities

18. In financial accounting, a _____ is defined as an obligation of an entity arising from past transactions or events, the settlement of which may result in the transfer or use of assets, provision of services or other yielding of economic benefits in the future.

a. False Claims Act
b. Corporate governance
c. Liability
d. Vested

19. The term _____ or superannuation refers to a pension granted upon retirement. They may be set up by employers, insurance companies, the government or other institutions such as employer associations or trade unions.

a. Wage
b. BMC Software, Inc.
c. 3M Company
d. Retirement plan

20. A _____ is a fungible, negotiable instrument representing financial value. they are broadly categorized into debt securities (such as banknotes, bonds and debentures), and equity securities; e.g., common stocks. The company or other entity issuing the _____ is called the issuer.

a. Tracking stock
b. 3M Company
c. BMC Software, Inc.
d. Security

21. A _____ is a computer application that simulates a paper worksheet. It displays multiple cells that together make up a grid consisting of rows and columns, each cell containing either alphanumeric text or numeric values. A _____ cell may alternatively contain a formula that defines how the contents of that cell is to be calculated from the contents of any other cell (or combination of cells) each time any cell is updated.

a. Spreadsheet
b. Mutual fund
c. Linear regression
d. Merck ' Co., Inc.

Chapter 18. Shareholders' Equity

22. _____ means the giving out of information, either voluntarily or to be in compliance with legal regulations or workplace rules.

- In Computer security, full _____ means disclosing full information about vulnerabilities.
- In computing, _____ widget
- Journalism, full _____ refers to disclosing the interests of the writer which may bear on the subject being written about, for example, if the writer has worked with an interview subject in the past.

- In law:
    - The law of England and Wales, _____ refers to a process that may form part of legal proceedings, whereby parties inform to other parties the existence of any relevant documents that are, or have been, in their control. This compares with the process known as discovery in the course of legal proceedings in the United States.
    - In U.S. civil procedure (litigation rules for civil cases), _____ is a stage prior to trial. In civil cases, each party must disclose to the opposing party the following: names of witnesses which it may use to support its side, copies of documents (or mere description of these documents) in its control which it may use to support its side, computation of damages claimed, and certain insurance information. _____ is related to, but technically prior to, the discovery stage.
    - In Company law (known as 'corporate law' in the United States), _____ refers to giving out information about public or limited companies or their officers, which might be kept secret if the company was a private company or a partnership.

- In real property transactions, _____ refers to providing to a buyer information known to the seller or broker/agent concerning the condition or other aspects of real property that would affect the property's value or desirability. These rules regarding what information must be disclosed, and whether the information must be disclosed even if a buyer does not ask, vary from one jurisdiction to the next.

a. Disclosure
c. Trailing
b. Controlled Foreign Corporations
d. Tax harmonisation

23. A _____ or reacquired stock is stock which is bought back by the issuing company, reducing the amount of outstanding stock on the open market ('open market' including insiders' holdings).

Stock repurchases are often used as a tax-efficient method to put cash into shareholders' hands, rather than pay dividends. Sometimes, companies do this when they feel that their stock is undervalued on the open market.

a. Treasury stock
c. Cost of goods sold
b. Net profit
d. Matching principle

24. _____ is a concept whereby a person's financial liability is limited to a fixed sum, most commonly the value of a person's investment in a company or partnership with _____. A shareholder in a limited company is not personally liable for any of the debts of the company, other than for the value of his investment in that company. The same is true for the members of a _____ partnership and the limited partners in a limited partnership.

a. Due diligence
c. Joint venture
b. Limited liability
d. Burden of proof

25. A _____ is a type of business entity in which partners (owners) share with each other the profits or losses of the business undertaking in which all have invested. _____s are often favored over corporations for taxation purposes, as the _____ structure does not generally incur a tax on profits before it is distributed to the partners (i.e. there is no dividend tax levied.) However, depending on the _____ structure and the jurisdiction in which it operates, owners of a _____ may be exposed to greater personal liability than they would as shareholders of a corporation.

    a. Resource Conservation and Recovery Act
    b. National Information Infrastructure Protection Act
    c. Partnership
    d. Corporate governance

26. _____ is an accounting concept, meaning a future tax liability or asset, resulting from temporary differences between book (accounting) value of assets and liabilities and their tax value, or timing differences between the recognition of gains and losses in financial statements and their recognition in a tax computation.

Temporary differences are differences between the carrying amount of an asset or liability recognised in the balance sheet and the amount attributed to that asset or liability for tax purposes (the tax base.)

    a. Federal tax revenue by state
    b. Deferred tax
    c. Deficit
    d. Tax refund

27. _____ is the imposition of two or more taxes on the same income (in the case of income taxes), asset (in the case of capital taxes), or financial transaction (in the case of sales taxes.) It refers to two distinct situations:

- taxation of dividend income without relief or credit for taxes paid by the company paying the dividend on the income from which the dividend is paid. This arises in the so-called 'classical' system of corporate taxation, used in the United States.
- taxation by two or more countries of the same income, asset or transaction, for example income paid by an entity of one country to a resident of a different country. The double liability is often mitigated by tax treaties between countries.

It is not unusual for a business or individual who is resident in one country to make a taxable gain (earnings, profits) in another. This person may find that he is obliged by domestic laws to pay tax on that gain locally and pay again in the country in which the gain was made. Since this is inequitable, many nations make bilateral _____ agreements with each other.

    a. Federal Unemployment Tax Act
    b. Carbon tax
    c. Double taxation
    d. Tax shelter

28. _____, also referred to simply as a 'public offering' or 'flotation,' is when a company issues common stock or shares to the public for the first time. They are often issued by smaller, younger companies seeking capital to expand, but can also be done by large privately-owned companies looking to become publicly traded.

In an _____ the issuer may obtain the assistance of an underwriting firm, which helps it determine what type of security to issue (common or preferred), best offering price and time to bring it to market.

    a. Initial public offering
    b. Intergenerational equity
    c. Insolvency
    d. AT'T Wireless Services, Inc.

Chapter 18. Shareholders' Equity

29. _____, in law and economics, is a form of risk management primarily used to hedge against the risk of a contingent loss. _____ is defined as the equitable transfer of the risk of a loss, from one entity to another, in exchange for a premium, and can be thought of as a guaranteed small loss to prevent a large, possibly devastating loss. An insurer is a company selling the _____; an insured is the person or entity buying the _____.

    a. AMEX
    b. AIG
    c. ABC Television Network
    d. Insurance

30. A _____ is a partnership in which some or all partners (depending on the jurisdiction) have limited liability. It therefore exhibits elements of partnerships and corporations. In an _____ one partner is not responsible or liable for another partner's misconduct or negligence.

    a. Financial Accounting Standards Board
    b. Dow Jones ' Company
    c. Privately held
    d. Limited liability partnership

31. The _____ (acronym of National Association of Securities Dealers Automated Quotations) is an American stock exchange. It is the largest electronic screen-based equity securities trading market in the United States. With approximately 3,800 companies, it has more trading volume per hour than any other stock exchange in the world.

    a. Variance
    b. Sustainability measurement
    c. Sale of goods
    d. NASDAQ

32. _____ is an equity (stock) exchange located at 11 Wall Street in lower Manhattan, New York, USA.) It is the largest stock exchange in the world by dollar value of its listed companies' securities. As of October 2008, the combined capitalization of all domestic _____ listed companies was US$10.1 trillion.

    a. BNSF Railway
    b. New York Stock Exchange
    c. 3M Company
    d. BMC Software, Inc.

33. The term _____ company refers to the ownership of a business company in two different ways: first, referring to ownership by non-governmental organizations; and second, referring to ownership of the company's stock by a relatively small number of holders who do not trade the stock publicly on the stock market. Less ambiguous terms for a _____ company are unquoted company and unlisted company.

Though less visible than their publicly traded counterparts, private companies have a major importance in the world's economy.

    a. Privately held
    b. Fannie Mae
    c. HFMA
    d. Freddie Mac

34. The U.S. _____ is an independent agency of the United States government which holds primary responsibility for enforcing the federal securities laws and regulating the securities industry, the nation's stock and options exchanges, and other electronic securities markets. The SEC was created by section 4 of the Securities Exchange Act of 1934 (now codified as 15 U.S.C. ÂÂ§ 78d and commonly referred to as the 1934 Act.)

    a. 3M Company
    b. BMC Software, Inc.
    c. BNSF Railway
    d. Securities and Exchange Commission

35. A _____, (formerly a securities exchange) is a corporation or mutual organization which provides 'trading' facilities for stock brokers and traders, to trade stocks and other securities. _____s also provide facilities for the issue and redemption of securities as well as other financial instruments and capital events including the payment of income and dividends. The securities traded on a _____ include: shares issued by companies, unit trusts, derivatives, pooled investment products and bonds.
   a. 3M Company
   b. Stock Exchange
   c. BMC Software, Inc.
   d. BNSF Railway

36. In business and accounting, _____ are everything of value that is owned by a person or company. It is a claim on the property your income of a borrower. The balance sheet of a firm records the monetary value of the _____ owned by the firm.
   a. Earnings before interest, taxes, depreciation and amortization
   b. Accounts receivable
   c. Accrual basis accounting
   d. Assets

37. _____ is a legally declared inability or impairment of ability of an individual or organization to pay its creditors. Creditors may file a _____ petition against a debtor ('involuntary _____') in an effort to recoup a portion of what they are owed or initiate a restructuring. In the majority of cases, however, _____ is initiated by the debtor (a 'voluntary _____' that is filed by the bankrupt individual or organization.)
   a. Bankruptcy protection
   b. BMC Software, Inc.
   c. Bankruptcy
   d. 3M Company

38. In economics, business, retail, and accounting, a _____ is the value of money that has been used up to produce something, and hence is not available for use anymore. In economics, a _____ is an alternative that is given up as a result of a decision. In business, the _____ may be one of acquisition, in which case the amount of money expended to acquire it is counted as _____.
   a. Cost of quality
   b. Cost allocation
   c. Prime cost
   d. Cost

39. Initial _____, also referred to simply as a '_____' or 'flotation,' is when a company issues common stock or shares to the public for the first time. They are often issued by smaller, younger companies seeking capital to expand, but can also be done by large privately-owned companies looking to become publicly traded.

In an Ipublic offering the issuer may obtain the assistance of an underwriting firm, which helps it determine what type of security to issue (common or preferred), best offering price and time to bring it to market.

   a. Gross income
   b. Public offering
   c. Restricted stock
   d. Commercial paper

40. The _____ are the primary rules governing the management of a corporation in the United States and Canada, and are filed with a state or other regulatory agency. The equivalent in the United Kingdom and various other countries is Articles of Association.

A corporation's _____ generally provide information such as:

- The corporation's name, which has to be unique from any other corporation in that jurisdiction. As part of the corporation's name, certain words such as 'incorporated', 'limited', 'corporation', (or their abbreviations) or some equivalent term in countries whose language is not English, are usually required as part of the name as a 'flag' to indicate to persons doing business with the organization that it is a corporation as opposed to an individual or partnership (with unlimited liability.) In some cases, certain types of names are prohibited except by special permission, such as words implying the corporation is a government agency or has powers to act in ways it is not otherwise allowed.
- The name of the person(s) organizing the corporation (usually members of the board of directors.)
- Whether the corporation is a stock corporation or a non-stock corporation.
- Whether the corporation's existence is permanent or limited for a specific period of time. Generally the rule is that a corporation existence is forever, or until (1) it stops paying the yearly corporate renewal fees or otherwise fails to do something required to continue its existence such as file certain paperwork each year; or (2) it files a request to 'wind up and dissolve.'
- In some cases, a corporation must state the purposes for which it is formed. Some jurisdictions permit a general statement such as 'any lawful purpose' but some require explicit specifications.
- If a non-stock corporation, whether it is for profit or non-profit. However, some jurisdictions differentiate by 'for profit' or 'non profit' and some by 'stock or non-stock'.
- In the United States, if a corporation is to be organized as a non-profit, to be recognized as such by the Internal Revenue Service, such as for eligibility for tax exemption, certain specific wording must be included stating no part of the assets of the corporation are to benefit the members.
- If a stock corporation, the number of shares the corporation is authorized to issue, or the maximum amount in a specific currency of stock that may be issued, e.g. a maximum of $25,000.
- The number and names of the corporation's initial Board of Directors (though this is optional in most cases.)
- The initial director(s) of the corporation (in some cases the incorporator or the registered agent must be a director, if not an attorney or another corporation.)
- The location of the corporation's 'registered office' - the location at which legal papers can be served to the corporation if necessary. Some states further require the designation of a Registered Agent: a person to whom such papers could be delivered.

Most states permit a corporation to be formed by one person; in some cases (such as non-profit corporations) it may require three or five or more. This change has come about as a result of Delaware liberalizing its corporation rules to allow corporations to bo formed by one person, and states not wanting to lose corporate charters to Delaware had to revise their rules as a result.

a. Exclusive right
c. Express warranty
b. Articles of incorporation
d. Employee Retirement Income Security Act

41. A _____ is a body of elected or appointed members who jointly oversee the activities of a company or organization. The body sometimes has a different name, such as board of trustees, board of governors, board of managers, or executive board. It is often simply referred to as 'the board.'

Chapter 18. Shareholders' Equity

A board's activities are determined by the powers, duties, and responsibilities delegated to it or conferred on it by an authority outside itself.

a. Consumer protection laws
b. Hospital Survey and Construction Act
c. Chief Financial Officers Act of 1990
d. Board of Directors

42. _____ is a form of corporation equity ownership represented in the securities. It is a stock whose dividends are based on market fluctuations. It is dangerous in comparison to preferred shares and some other investment options, in that in the event of bankruptcy, _____ investors receive their funds after preferred stock holders, bondholders, creditors, etc. On the other hand, common shares on average perform better than preferred shares or bonds over time.

a. Stock split
b. Common stock
c. 3M Company
d. Growth investing

43. A _____ is a right to acquire certain property in preference to any other person. It usually refers to property newly coming into existence. A right to acquire existing property in preference to any other person is usually referred to as a right of first refusal.

In practice, the most common form of _____ is the right of existing shareholders to acquire newly issued shares issued by a company in a rights issue, a usually but not always public offering.

a. Fiduciary
b. Corporate governance
c. Pre-emption right
d. Disclosure requirement

44. _____ is a fee paid on borrowed assets. It is the price paid for the use of borrowed money, or, money earned by deposited funds .Assets that are sometimes lent with _____ include money, shares, consumer goods through hire purchase, major assets such as aircraft, and even entire factories in finance lease arrangements. The _____ is calculated upon the value of the assets in the same manner as upon money.

a. Insolvency
b. ABC Television Network
c. Interest
d. AIG

45. _____ is the state or fact of exclusive rights and control over property, which may be an object, land/real estate or intellectual property. An _____ right is also referred to as title.

_____ is the key building block in the development of the capitalist socio-economic system.

a. Encumbrance
b. Administrative proceeding
c. ABC Television Network
d. Ownership

46. _____ is one of a series of accounting transactions dealing with the billing of customers who owe money to a person, company or organization for goods and services that have been provided to the customer. In most business entities this is typically done by generating an invoice and mailing or electronically delivering it to the customer, who in turn must pay it within an established timeframe called credit or payment terms.

An example of a common payment term is Net 30, meaning payment is due in the amount of the invoice 30 days from the date of invoice.

Chapter 18. Shareholders' Equity

a. Accrued revenue
c. Adjusting entries
b. Accrual
d. Accounts receivable

47. In finance, a _____ is a type of bond that can be converted into shares of stock in the issuing company, usually at some pre-announced ratio. It is a hybrid security with debt- and equity-like features. Although it typically has a low coupon rate, the holder is compensated with the ability to convert the bond to common stock, usually at a substantial discount to the stock's market value.

a. Zero-coupon bond
c. Coupon rate
b. Zero-coupon
d. Convertible bond

48. _____, in finance and accounting, means stated value or face value. From this comes the expressions at par (at the _____), over par (over _____) and under par (under _____).

_____ is a nominal value of a security which is determined by an issuer company at a minimum price. _____ of an equity (a stock) is a somewhat archaic concept. The _____ of a stock was the share price upon initial offering; the issuing company promised not to issue further shares below _____, so investors could be confident that no one else was receiving a more favorable issue price. This was far more important in unregulated equity markets than in the regulated markets that exist today.

a. Par value
c. Restructuring
b. Creditor
d. Net worth

49. The _____ is a business model where a customer must pay a subscription price to have access to the product/service. The model was pioneered by magazines and newspapers, but is now used by many businesses and websites. Rather than selling products individually, a subscription sells periodic (monthly or yearly or seasonal) use or access to a product or service, or, in the case of such non-profit organizations as opera companies or symphony orchestras, it sells tickets to the entire run of five to fifteen scheduled performances for an entire season.

a. BMC Software, Inc.
c. BNSF Railway
b. 3M Company
d. Subscription business model

50. _____, also called fair price (in a commonplace conflation of the two distinct concepts), is a concept used in finance and economics, defined as a rational and unbiased estimate of the potential market price of a good, service, or asset, taking into account such objective factors as:

- acquisition/production/distribution costs, replacement costs, or costs of close substitutes
- actual utility at a given level of development of social productive capability
- supply vs. demand

and subjective factors such as

- risk characteristics
- cost of capital
- individually perceived utility

Chapter 18. Shareholders' Equity

In accounting, _____ is used as an estimate of the market value of an asset (or liability) for which a market price cannot be determined (usually because there is no established market for the asset.) Under GAAP (FAS 157), _____ is the amount at which the asset could be bought or sold in a current transaction between willing parties, or transferred to an equivalent party, other than in a liquidation sale. This is used for assets whose carrying value is based on mark-to-market valuations; for assets carried at historical cost, the _____ of the asset is not used. One example of where _____ is an issue is a College kitchen with a cost of $2 million which was built 5 years ago.

    a. BNSF Railway
    b. BMC Software, Inc.
    c. 3M Company
    d. Fair value

51. _____ in economics and business is the result of an exchange and from that trade we assign a numerical monetary value to a good, service or asset. If Alice trades Bob 4 apples for an orange, the _____ of an orange is 4 apples. Inversely, the _____ of an apple is 1/4 oranges.

    a. Price discrimination
    b. Price
    c. Transactional Net Margin Method
    d. Discounts and allowances

52. _____ is that which is owed; usually referencing assets owed, but the term can also cover moral obligations and other interactions not requiring money. In the case of assets, _____ is a means of using future purchasing power in the present before a summation has been earned. Some companies and corporations use _____ as a part of their overall corporate finance strategy.

    a. Loan
    b. Debt
    c. Lender
    d. Debenture

53. The phrase _____, according to the Organization for Economic Co-operation and Development, refers to 'creative work undertaken on a systematic basis in order to increase the stock of knowledge, including knowledge of man, culture and society, and the use of this stock of knowledge to devise new applications [sic]'

New product design and development is more than often a crucial factor in the survival of a company. In an industry that is fast changing, firms must continually revise their design and range of products. This is necessary due to continuous technology change and development as well as other competitors and the changing preference of customers.

    a. Research and development
    b. BMC Software, Inc.
    c. 3M Company
    d. BNSF Railway

54. A _____ is any one of a variety of different systems, institutions, procedures, social relations and infrastructures whereby persons trade, and goods and services are exchanged, forming part of the economy. It is an arrangement that allows buyers and sellers to exchange things. _____s vary in size, range, geographic scale, location, types and variety of human communities, as well as the types of goods and services traded.

    a. Perfect competition
    b. Market Failure
    c. Recession
    d. Market

Chapter 18. Shareholders' Equity

55. _____ methods are means of managing inventory and financial matters involving the money a company ties up within inventory of produced goods, raw materials, parts, components, or feed stocks. FIFO stands for first-in, first-out, meaning that the oldest inventory items are recorded as sold first. LIFO stands for last-in, first-out, meaning that the most recently purchased items are recorded as sold first.
   a. 3M Company
   b. FIFO and LIFO accounting
   c. Reorder point
   d. Finished good

56. In law, _____ refers to the process by which a company (or part of a company) is brought to an end, and the assets and property of the company redistributed. _____ can also be referred to as winding-up or dissolution, although dissolution technically refers to the last stage of _____. The process of _____ also arises when customs, an authority or agency in a country responsible for collecting and safeguarding customs duties, determines the final computation or ascertainment of the duties or drawback accruing on an entry.
   a. BMC Software, Inc.
   b. 3M Company
   c. Bankruptcy protection
   d. Liquidation

57. In finance, an _____ is a contract between a buyer and a seller that gives the buyer the right--but not the obligation-- to buy or to sell a particular asset (the underlying asset) at a later time at an agreed price. In return for granting the _____, the seller collects a payment (the premium) from the buyer. A call _____ gives the buyer the right to buy the underlying asset; a put _____ gives the buyer of the _____ the right to sell the underlying asset.
   a. ABC Television Network
   b. AMEX
   c. AIG
   d. Option

58. An _____ is the buying of one company by another. An _____ may be friendly or hostile. In the former case, the companies cooperate in negotiations; in the latter case, the takeover target is unwilling to be bought or the target's board has no prior knowledge of the offer. _____ usually refers to a purchase of a smaller firm by a larger one. Sometimes, however, a smaller firm will acquire management control of a larger or longer established company and keep its name for the combined entity. This is known as a reverse takeover.
   a. AMEX
   b. AIG
   c. ABC Television Network
   d. Acquisition

59. A budget _____ occurs when an entity spends more money than it takes in. The opposite of a budget _____ is a budget surplus. Debt is essentially an accumulated flow of _____s.
   a. Land value taxation
   b. Progressive tax
   c. Windfall profits tax
   d. Deficit

60.

The key date to remember for dividend paying stocks is the _____. The Record Date, or Date of Record determines the _____, when you must own the stock.

In order to receive the upcoming dividend payment pay-out you must already own or you must purchase the stock prior to the _____.

   a. Ex-dividend date
   b. AMEX
   c. ABC Television Network
   d. AIG

61. _____ is a payment of a dividend to stockholders that exceeds the company's retained earnings. Once retained earnings is depleted, capital accounts such as additional paid-in capital are decreased to make up for the remaining dividend to be paid to stockholders. When a _____ occurs, it is considered to be a return of investment instead of profits.
   a. Trade name
   b. Redemption value
   c. Liquidating dividend
   d. Fund accounting

62. _____ is any physical or virtual entity that is owned by an individual or jointly by a group of individuals. An owner of _____ has the right to consume, sell, rent, mortgage, transfer and exchange his or her _____. Important widely-recognized types of _____ include real _____, personal _____ (other physical possessions), and intellectual _____ (rights over artistic creations, inventions, etc.), although the latter is not always as widely recognized or enforced.
   a. Primary authority
   b. Property
   c. Fiduciary
   d. Disclosure requirement

63. In accounting, _____ or carrying value is the value of an asset according to its balance sheet account balance. For assets, the value is based on the original cost of the asset less any depreciation, amortization or impairment costs made against the asset. Traditionally, a company's _____ is its total assets minus intangible assets and liabilities.
   a. Matching principle
   b. Depreciation
   c. Generally accepted accounting principles
   d. Book value

64. _____ is the price at which an asset would trade in a competitive Walrasian auction setting. _____ is often used interchangeably with open _____, fair value or fair _____, although these terms have distinct definitions in different standards, and may differ in some circumstances.

International Valuation Standards defines _____ as 'the estimated amount for which a property should exchange on the date of valuation between a willing buyer and a willing seller in an arme;s-length transaction after proper marketing wherein the parties had each acted knowledgeably, prudently, and without compulsion.'

_____ is a concept distinct from market price, which is e;the price at which one can transacte;, while _____ is e;the true underlying valuee; according to theoretical standards.

   a. Sinking fund
   b. Debtor
   c. Segregated portfolio company
   d. Market value

65. On a stock exchange, a _____ or reverse split is the opposite of a stock split, i.e. a stock merge - a reduction in the number of shares and an accompanying increase in the share price. The ratio is also reversed: 1-for-2, 1-for-3 and so on.

There is a stigma attached to doing this so it is not initiated without very good reason.

   a. Cost of capital
   b. Public good
   c. Discount rate
   d. Reverse stock split

66. The _____ is a financial ratio indicating the relative proportion of equity to all used to finance a company's assets. The two components are often taken from the firm's balance sheet or statement of financial position (so-called book value), but the ratio may also be calculated using market values for both, if the company's equities are publicly traded.

The _____ is especially in Central Europe a very common financial ratio while in the US the debt to _____ is more often used in financial (research) reports.

a. Efficiency ratio
b. Equity ratio
c. Average accounting return
d. Earnings yield

67. _____, also known as property, plant, and equipment (PP&E), is a term used in accountancy for assets and property which cannot easily be converted into cash. This can be compared with current assets such as cash or bank accounts, which are described as liquid assets. In most cases, only tangible assets are referred to as fixed.

a. Minority interest
b. Bankruptcy prediction
c. Fixed asset
d. Subledger

Chapter 19. Share-Based Compensation and Earnings Per Share

1. _____ is typically a 'higher ranking' stock than voting shares, and its terms are negotiated between the corporation and the investor.

_____ usually carries no voting rights, but may carry superior priority over common stock in the payment of dividends and upon liquidation. _____ may carry a dividend that is paid out prior to any dividends being paid to common stock holders.

   a. Preferred stock   b. Restricted stock
   c. Cash flow   d. Gross income

2. In finance, an _____ is a contract between a buyer and a seller that gives the buyer the right--but not the obligation-- to buy or to sell a particular asset (the underlying asset) at a later time at an agreed price. In return for granting the _____, the seller collects a payment (the premium) from the buyer. A call _____ gives the buyer the right to buy the underlying asset; a put _____ gives the buyer of the _____ the right to sell the underlying asset.
   a. ABC Television Network   b. AIG
   c. AMEX   d. Option

3. _____ refers to stock of a company that is not fully transferable until certain conditions have been met. Upon satisfaction of those conditions, the stock becomes transferable by the person holding the award.

Another type of _____ is a form of compensation granted by a company. Typically, the conditions that allow the shares to be transferred are a period of time, when they vest. However, those restrictions can also be some sort of performance condition, such as the company reaching earnings per share goals or financial targets. _____ is becoming a more prominent form of employee compensation, particularly to executives.

   a. Capital structure   b. Gross income
   c. Flow-through entity   d. Restricted stock

4. _____, in accrual accounting, is any account where the asset or liability is not realized until a future date (accounting period), e.g. annuities, charges, taxes, income, etc. The _____ item may be carried, dependent on type of deferral, as either an asset or liability.
   a. Pro forma   b. Deferred
   c. Payroll   d. Cash basis accounting

5. The _____ is a private, not-for-profit organization whose primary purpose is to develop generally accepted accounting principles (GAAP) within the United States in the public's interest. The Securities and Exchange Commission (SEC) designated the _____ as the organization responsible for setting accounting standards for public companies in the U.S. It was created in 1973, replacing the Accounting Principles Board and the Committee on Accounting Procedure of the American Institute of Certified Public Accountants. The _____'s mission is 'to establish and improve standards of financial accounting and reporting for the guidance and education of the public, including issuers, auditors, and users of financial information.'

The _____ is not a governmental body.

   a. Public company   b. Fannie Mae
   c. Financial Accounting Standards Board   d. Governmental Accounting Standards Board

Chapter 19. Share-Based Compensation and Earnings Per Share

6. _____, also called fair price (in a commonplace conflation of the two distinct concepts), is a concept used in finance and economics, defined as a rational and unbiased estimate of the potential market price of a good, service, or asset, taking into account such objective factors as:

- acquisition/production/distribution costs, replacement costs, or costs of close substitutes
- actual utility at a given level of development of social productive capability
- supply vs. demand

and subjective factors such as

- risk characteristics
- cost of capital
- individually perceived utility

In accounting, _____ is used as an estimate of the market value of an asset (or liability) for which a market price cannot be determined (usually because there is no established market for the asset.) Under GAAP (FAS 157), _____ is the amount at which the asset could be bought or sold in a current transaction between willing parties, or transferred to an equivalent party, other than in a liquidation sale. This is used for assets whose carrying value is based on mark-to-market valuations; for assets carried at historical cost, the _____ of the asset is not used. One example of where _____ is an issue is a College kitchen with a cost of $2 million which was built 5 years ago.

a. 3M Company
b. Fair value
c. BMC Software, Inc.
d. BNSF Railway

7. In business and accounting, _____ are everything of value that is owned by a person or company. It is a claim on the property your income of a borrower. The balance sheet of a firm records the monetary value of the _____ owned by the firm.

a. Accounts receivable
b. Accrual basis accounting
c. Earnings before interest, taxes, depreciation and amortization
d. Assets

8. In economics, business, retail, and accounting, a _____ is the value of money that has been used up to produce something, and hence is not available for use anymore. In economics, a _____ is an alternative that is given up as a result of a decision. In business, the _____ may be one of acquisition, in which case the amount of money expended to acquire it is counted as _____.

a. Cost allocation
b. Cost
c. Prime cost
d. Cost of quality

9. _____ is an accounting concept, meaning a future tax liability or asset, resulting from temporary differences between book (accounting) value of assets and liabilities and their tax value, or timing differences between the recognition of gains and losses in financial statements and their recognition in a tax computation.

Temporary differences are differences between the carrying amount of an asset or liability recognised in the balance sheet and the amount attributed to that asset or liability for tax purposes (the tax base.)

a. Deficit
b. Tax refund
c. Deferred tax
d. Federal tax revenue by state

10. An _____ is a tax levied on the financial income of people, corporations, or other legal entities. Various _____ systems exist, with varying degrees of tax incidence. Income taxation can be progressive, proportional, or regressive.
    a. Individual Retirement Arrangement
    b. Implied level of government service
    c. Ordinary income
    d. Income tax

11. In financial accounting, a _____ is defined as an obligation of an entity arising from past transactions or events, the settlement of which may result in the transfer or use of assets, provision of services or other yielding of economic benefits in the future.
    a. False Claims Act
    b. Vested
    c. Corporate governance
    d. Liability

12. _____ is one of the four Ps of the marketing mix. The other three aspects are product, promotion, and place. It is also a key variable in microeconomic price allocation theory.
    a. Price
    b. Target costing
    c. Cost-plus pricing
    d. Pricing

13. Employment is a contract between two parties, one being the employer and the other being the _____. An _____ may be defined as: 'A person in the service of another under any contract of hire, express or implied, oral or written, where the employer has the power or right to control and direct the _____ in the material details of how the work is to be performed.' Black's Law Dictionary page 471 (5th ed. 1979.)
    a. ABC Television Network
    b. AMEX
    c. Employee
    d. AIG

14. A _____ is any one of a variety of different systems, institutions, procedures, social relations and infrastructures whereby persons trade, and goods and services are exchanged, forming part of the economy. It is an arrangement that allows buyers and sellers to exchange things. _____s vary in size, range, geographic scale, location, types and variety of human communities, as well as the types of goods and services traded.
    a. Market
    b. Perfect competition
    c. Recession
    d. Market Failure

15. _____ is an economic concept with commonplace familiarity. It is the price that a good or service is offered at, or will fetch, in the marketplace. It is of interest mainly in the study of microeconomics.
    a. Transfer agent
    b. Market price
    c. Financial instruments
    d. Spot rate

16. _____ is that which is owed; usually referencing assets owed, but the term can also cover moral obligations and other interactions not requiring money. In the case of assets, _____ is a means of using future purchasing power in the present before a summation has been earned. Some companies and corporations use _____ as a part of their overall corporate finance strategy.
    a. Loan
    b. Debt
    c. Lender
    d. Debenture

Chapter 19. Share-Based Compensation and Earnings Per Share   235

17. _____ in economics and business is the result of an exchange and from that trade we assign a numerical monetary value to a good, service or asset. If Alice trades Bob 4 apples for an orange, the _____ of an orange is 4 apples. Inversely, the _____ of an apple is 1/4 oranges.

   a. Price
   b. Price discrimination
   c. Transactional Net Margin Method
   d. Discounts and allowances

18. A _____ or reacquired stock is stock which is bought back by the issuing company, reducing the amount of outstanding stock on the open market ('open market' including insiders' holdings).

   Stock repurchases are often used as a tax-efficient method to put cash into shareholders' hands, rather than pay dividends. Sometimes, companies do this when they feel that their stock is undervalued on the open market.

   a. Cost of goods sold
   b. Net profit
   c. Matching principle
   d. Treasury stock

19. In accounting, _____ has a very specific meaning. It is an outflow of cash or other valuable assets from a person or company to another person or company. This outflow of cash is generally one side of a trade for products or services that have equal or better current or future value to the buyer than to the seller.

   a. AMEX
   b. AIG
   c. ABC Television Network
   d. Expense

20. In economics, _____ or _____ goods or real _____ refers to factors of production used to create goods or services that are not themselves significantly consumed (though they may depreciate) in the production process. _____ goods may be acquired with money or financial _____. In finance and accounting, _____ generally refers to financial wealth, especially that used to start or maintain a business.

   a. Vyborg Appeal
   b. Disclosure
   c. Screening
   d. Capital

21. _____ is a specific term used in companies' financial reporting from the company-whole point of view. Because that use excludes the effects of changing ownership interest, an economic measure of _____ is necessary for financial analysis from the shareholders' point of view

   _____ is defined by the Financial Accounting Standards Board, or FASB, as 'the change in equity [net assets] of a business enterprise during a period from transactions and other events and circumstances from nonowner sources. It includes all changes in equity during a period except those resulting from investments by owners and distributions to owners.'

   _____ is the sum of net income and other items that must bypass the income statement because they have not been realized, including items like an unrealized holding gain or loss from available for sale securities and foreign currency translation gains or losses.

   a. BNSF Railway
   b. BMC Software, Inc.
   c. Comprehensive income
   d. 3M Company

22. _____ are the earnings returned on the initial investment amount.

In the US, the Financial Accounting Standards Board (FASB) requires companies' income statements to report _____ for each of the major categories of the income statement: continuing operations, discontinued operations, extraordinary items, and net income.

The _____ formula does not include preferred dividends for categories outside of continued operations and net income.

a. Earnings per share
b. Earnings yield
c. Average accounting return
d. Invested capital

23. The _____ founded on April 1, 2001 is the successor of the International Accounting Standards Committee (IASC) founded in June 1973 in London. It is responsible for developing the International Financial Reporting Standards (new name for the International Accounting Standards issued after 2001), and promoting the use and application of these standards.

The _____ is an independent, privately-funded accounting standard-setter based in London, UK.

a. Institute of Management Accountants
b. Emerging technologies
c. International Accounting Standards Board
d. Information Systems Audit and Control Association

24. In accounting, _____ are considered liabilities of the business that are to be settled in cash within the fiscal year or the operating cycle, whichever period is longer.

For example accounts payable for goods, services or supplies that were purchased for use in the operation of the business and payable within a normal period of time would be _____.

Bonds, mortgages and loans that are payable over a term exceeding one year would be fixed liabilities.

a. Closing entries
b. Treasury stock
c. Payroll
d. Current liabilities

25. _____ is a company's earnings per share (EPS) calculated using fully diluted shares outstanding. _____ indicates a 'worst case' scenario, one in which everyone who could have received stock without purchasing it directly for the full market value did so.

To find _____, basic EPS is calculated for each of the categories on the income statement first. Then each of the dilutive securities are ranked based on their effects, from most dilutive to least dilutive and antidilutive. Then the basic EPS number is diluted one by one by applying each one, skipping any instruments that have an antidilutive effect.

a. Return on assets Du Pont
b. Cash conversion cycle
c. Financial ratio
d. Diluted Earnings Per Share

Chapter 19. Share-Based Compensation and Earnings Per Share

26. In finance, _____ refers to the way a corporation finances its assets through some combination of equity, debt, or hybrid securities. A firm's _____ is then the composition or 'structure' of its liabilities. For example, a firm that sells $20 billion in equity and $80 billion in debt is said to be 20% equity-financed and 80% debt-financed.

   a. Flow-through entity   b. Restricted stock
   c. Gross income   d. Capital structure

27. _____ is a form of corporation equity ownership represented in the securities. It is a stock whose dividends are based on market fluctuations. It is dangerous in comparison to preferred shares and some other investment options, in that in the event of bankruptcy, _____ investors receive their funds after preferred stock holders, bondholders, creditors, etc. On the other hand, common shares on average perform better than preferred shares or bonds over time.

   a. Growth investing   b. Stock split
   c. Common stock   d. 3M Company

28. _____ are payments made by a corporation to its shareholder members. It is the portion of corporate profits paid out to stockholders. When a corporation earns a profit or surplus, that money can be put to two uses: it can either be re-invested in the business (called retained earnings), or it can be paid to the shareholders as a dividend.

   a. Dividend stripping   b. Dividend payout ratio
   c. Dividend yield   d. Dividends

29. A _____ or stock divide increases or decreases the number of shares in a public company. The price is adjusted such that the before and after market capitalization of the company remains the same and dilution does not occur. Options and warrants are included.

   a. Stockholder   b. Stock split
   c. 3M Company   d. Growth investing

30. _____ are formal records of a business' financial activities.

In British English, including United Kingdom company law, _____ are often referred to as accounts, although the term _____ is also used, particularly by accountants.

_____ provide an overview of a business' financial condition in both short and long term.

   a. Statement of retained earnings   b. 3M Company
   c. Notes to the financial statements   d. Financial statements

31. _____ is a company's financial statement that indicates how the revenue is transformed into the net income The purpose of the _____ is to show managers and investors whether the company made or lost money during the period being reported.

The important thing to remember about an _____ is that it represents a period of time.

   a. AMEX   b. Income statement
   c. ABC Television Network   d. AIG

32. In finance, a _____ is a type of bond that can be converted into shares of stock in the issuing company, usually at some pre-announced ratio. It is a hybrid security with debt- and equity-like features. Although it typically has a low coupon rate, the holder is compensated with the ability to convert the bond to common stock, usually at a substantial discount to the stock's market value.
   a. Zero-coupon
   b. Zero-coupon bond
   c. Coupon rate
   d. Convertible bond

33. A _____ is a fungible, negotiable instrument representing financial value. they are broadly categorized into debt securities (such as banknotes, bonds and debentures), and equity securities; e.g., common stocks. The company or other entity issuing the _____ is called the issuer.
   a. 3M Company
   b. Tracking stock
   c. Security
   d. BMC Software, Inc.

34. A mutual shareholder or _____ is an individual or company (including a corporation) that legally owns one or more shares of stock in a joint stock company. A company's shareholders collectively own that company. Thus, the typical goal of such companies is to enhance shareholder value.
   a. 3M Company
   b. Stockholder
   c. Growth investing
   d. Stock split

35. In finance, a _____ is a debt security, in which the authorized issuer owes the holders a debt and, depending on the terms of the _____, is obliged to pay interest (the coupon) and/or to repay the principal at a later date, termed maturity. It is a formal contract to repay borrowed money with interest at fixed intervals.

Thus a _____ is like a loan: the issuer is the borrower, the _____ holder is the lender, and the coupon is the interest.

   a. Zero-coupon bond
   b. Coupon rate
   c. Revenue bonds
   d. Bond

36. Discounting is a financial mechanism in which a debtor obtains the right to delay payments to a creditor, for a defined period of time, in exchange for a charge or fee. Essentially, the party that owes money in the present purchases the right to delay the payment until some future date. The _____, or charge, is simply the difference between the original amount owed in the present and the amount that has to be paid in the future to settle the debt.
   a. Risk aversion
   b. Discount
   c. Discounting
   d. Discount factor

37. A _____ is a bond bought at a price lower than its face value, with the face value repaid at the time of maturity. It does not make periodic interest payments, or so-called 'coupons,' hence the term _____. Investors earn return from the compounded interest all paid at maturity plus the difference between the discounted price of the bond and its par value.
   a. Municipal bond
   b. Callable bond
   c. Premium bond
   d. Zero-coupon bond

Chapter 19. Share-Based Compensation and Earnings Per Share

38. _____ means the giving out of information, either voluntarily or to be in compliance with legal regulations or workplace rules.

- In Computer security, full _____ means disclosing full information about vulnerabilities.
- In computing, _____ widget
- Journalism, full _____ refers to disclosing the interests of the writer which may bear on the subject being written about, for example, if the writer has worked with an interview subject in the past.

- In law:
    - The law of England and Wales, _____ refers to a process that may form part of legal proceedings, whereby parties inform to other parties the existence of any relevant documents that are, or have been, in their control. This compares with the process known as discovery in the course of legal proceedings in the United States.
    - In U.S. civil procedure (litigation rules for civil cases), _____ is a stage prior to trial. In civil cases, each party must disclose to the opposing party the following: names of witnesses which it may use to support its side, copies of documents (or mere description of these documents) in its control which it may use to support its side, computation of damages claimed, and certain insurance information. _____ is related to, but technically prior to, the discovery stage.
    - In Company law (known as 'corporate law' in the United States), _____ refers to giving out information about public or limited companies or their officers, which might be kept secret if the company was a private company or a partnership.

- In real property transactions, _____ refers to providing to a buyer information known to the seller or broker/agent concerning the condition or other aspects of real property that would affect the property's value or desirability. These rules regarding what information must be disclosed, and whether the information must be disclosed even if a buyer does not ask, vary from one jurisdiction to the next.

a. Tax harmonisation
c. Trailing
b. Controlled Foreign Corporations
d. Disclosure

39. _____ methods are means of managing inventory and financial matters involving the money a company ties up within inventory of produced goods, raw materials, parts, components, or feed stocks. FIFO stands for first-in, first-out, meaning that the oldest inventory items are recorded as sold first. LIFO stands for last-in, first-out, meaning that the most recently purchased items are recorded as sold first.

a. Finished good
c. Reorder point
b. 3M Company
d. FIFO and LIFO accounting

40. In law, _____ refers to the process by which a company (or part of a company) is brought to an end, and the assets and property of the company redistributed. _____ can also be referred to as winding-up or dissolution, although dissolution technically refers to the last stage of _____. The process of _____ also arises when customs, an authority or agency in a country responsible for collecting and safeguarding customs duties, determines the final computation or ascertainment of the duties or drawback accruing on an entry.

a. BMC Software, Inc.
c. Bankruptcy protection
b. Liquidation
d. 3M Company

41. A _____ is a contract conferring a right on one person to possess property belonging to another person (called a landlord or lessor) to the exclusion of the owner landlord. It is a rental agreement between landlord and tenant. The relationship between the tenant and the landlord is called a tenancy, and the right to possession by the tenant is sometimes called a leasehold interest.
   a. Lease
   b. Federal Sentencing Guidelines
   c. Model Code of Professional Responsibility
   d. Robinson-Patman Act

42. The term _____ is a term applied to practices that are perfunctory, or seek to satisfy the minimum requirements or to conform to a convention or doctrine. It has different meanings in different fields.

In accounting, _____ earnings are those earnings of companies in addition to actual earnings calculated under the Generally Accepted Accounting Principles (GAAP) in their quarterly and yearly financial reports.

   a. Pro forma
   b. Payroll
   c. Treasury stock
   d. Bottom line

43. _____ is the fraction of net income a firm pays to its stockholders in dividends:

The part of the earnings not paid to investors is left for investment to provide for future earnings growth. Investors seeking high current income and limited capital growth prefer companies with high _____. However investors seeking capital growth may prefer lower payout ratio because capital gains are taxed at a lower rate.

   a. Dividend payout ratio
   b. Dividend stripping
   c. Dividends
   d. Dividend yield

44. _____ in accounting is the process of treating equity investments, usually 20-50%, in associate companies. The investor keeps such equities as an asset. Proportional share of associate company's net income increases the investment, and proportional payment of dividends decreases it.
   a. Equity method
   b. ABC Television Network
   c. Out-of-pocket
   d. AIG

45. Simply put, _____ is the value of money figuring in a given amount of interest for a given amount of time. For example 100 dollars of todays money held for a year at 5 percent interest is worth 105 dollars, therefore 100 dollars paid now or 105 dollars paid exactly one year from now is the same amount of payment of money with that given intersest at that given amount of time. This notion dates at least to Martín de Azpilcueta of the School of Salamanca.
   a. Time value of money
   b. Collusion
   c. Merck ' Co., Inc.
   d. Competition law

Chapter 20. Accounting Changes and Error Corrections 241

1. In mathematics, two elements x and y of a set partially ordered by a relation ≤ are said to be _____ if and only if x ≤ y or y ≤ x if and only if x < y or y < x or y = x. For example, two sets are _____ with respect to inclusion if and only if one is a subset of the other.

In a classification of mathematical objects such as topological spaces, two criteria are said to be _____ when the objects that obey one criterion constitute a subset of the objects that obey the other one.

a. Scientific Research and Experimental Development Tax Incentive Program
b. Consumption
c. Database auditing
d. Comparable

2. A _____ proof is a mathematical proof that a particular theory is consistent. The early development of mathematical proof theory was driven by the desire to provide finitary _____ proofs for all of mathematics as part of Hilbert's program. Hilbert's program was strongly impacted by incompleteness theorems, which showed that sufficiently strong proof theories cannot prove their own _____

a. Consistency
b. Monte Carlo methods
c. Daybook
d. Consumption

3. _____ is an acronym for First In, First Out, an abstraction in ways of organizing and manipulation of data relative to time and prioritization. This expression describes the principle of a queue processing technique or servicing conflicting demands by ordering process by first-come, first-served (FCFS) behaviour: what comes in first is handled first, what comes in next waits until the first is finished, etc.

Thus it is analogous to the behaviour of persons queueing (or 'standing in line', in common American parlance), where the persons leave the queue in the order they arrive, or waiting one's turn at a traffic control signal.

a. Risk management
b. FIFO
c. Kanban
d. Trademark

4. _____ methods are means of managing inventory and financial matters involving the money a company ties up within inventory of produced goods, raw materials, parts, components, or feed stocks. FIFO stands for first-in, first-out, meaning that the oldest inventory items are recorded as sold first. LIFO stands for last-in, first-out, meaning that the most recently purchased items are recorded as sold first.

a. Finished good
b. 3M Company
c. Reorder point
d. FIFO and LIFO accounting

5. _____ is that which is owed; usually referencing assets owed, but the term can also cover moral obligations and other interactions not requiring money. In the case of assets, _____ is a means of using future purchasing power in the present before a summation has been earned. Some companies and corporations use _____ as a part of their overall corporate finance strategy.

a. Loan
b. Lender
c. Debt
d. Debenture

6. Employment is a contract between two parties, one being the employer and the other being the _____. An _____ may be defined as: 'A person in the service of another under any contract of hire, express or implied, oral or written, where the employer has the power or right to control and direct the _____ in the material details of how the work is to be performed.' Black's Law Dictionary page 471 (5th ed. 1979).

a. AMEX
b. Employee
c. ABC Television Network
d. AIG

7. A _____ is a compensation, usually financial, received by a worker in exchange for their labor.

Compensation in terms of _____s is given to worker and compensation in terms of salary is given to employees. Compensation is a monetary benefits given to employees in returns of the services provided by them.

a. 3M Company
b. Retirement plan
c. Wage
d. BMC Software, Inc.

8. An _____ is a term used in behavioral economics to describe those types of behaviors that impose costs on a person in the long-run that are not taken into account when making decisions in the present. Classical Economics discourages government from creating legislation that targets internalities, because it is assumed that the consumer takes these personal costs into account when paying for the good that causes the _____. For example, cigarettes should be taxed because of the negative consumption externalities that they impose, such as second-hand smoke, not because the smoker harms him or herself by smoking.

a. Operating budget
b. Internality
c. Inventory turnover ratio
d. Authorised capital

9. The _____ is the main body of domestic statutory tax law of the United States organized topically, including laws covering the income tax, payroll taxes, gift taxes, estate taxes and statutory excise taxes. The _____ is published as Title 26 of the United States Code (USC), and is also known as the internal revenue title.

a. Equity of condition
b. Ordinary income
c. Income tax
d. Internal Revenue Code

10. _____ is the corporate management term for the act of partially dismantling or otherwise reorganizing a company for the purpose of making it more profitable. Also known as corporate _____, debt _____ and financial _____.

_____ is often done as part of a bankruptcy or of a strategic takeover by another firm, such as a leveraged buyout by a private equity firm.

a. Fair market value
b. Net worth
c. Payback period
d. Restructuring

11. _____ is a specific term used in companies' financial reporting from the company-whole point of view. Because that use excludes the effects of changing ownership interest, an economic measure of _____ is necessary for financial analysis from the shareholders' point of view

_____ is defined by the Financial Accounting Standards Board, or FASB, as 'the change in equity [net assets] of a business enterprise during a period from transactions and other events and circumstances from nonowner sources. It includes all changes in equity during a period except those resulting from investments by owners and distributions to owners.'

Chapter 20. Accounting Changes and Error Corrections 243

_____ is the sum of net income and other items that must bypass the income statement because they have not been realized, including items like an unrealized holding gain or loss from available for sale securities and foreign currency translation gains or losses.

a. BMC Software, Inc.
b. 3M Company
c. BNSF Railway
d. Comprehensive income

12. _____ is a company's financial statement that indicates how the revenue is transformed into the net income The purpose of the _____ is to show managers and investors whether the company made or lost money during the period being reported.

The important thing to remember about an _____ is that it represents a period of time.

a. ABC Television Network
b. Income statement
c. AIG
d. AMEX

13. _____ means the giving out of information, either voluntarily or to be in compliance with legal regulations or workplace rules.

- In Computer security, full _____ means disclosing full information about vulnerabilities.
- In computing, _____ widget
- Journalism, full _____ refers to disclosing the interests of the writer which may bear on the subject being written about, for example, if the writer has worked with an interview subject in the past.

- In law:
  o The law of England and Wales, _____ refers to a process that may form part of legal proceedings, whereby parties inform to other parties the existence of any relevant documents that are, or have been, in their control. This compares with the process known as discovery in the course of legal proceedings in the United States.
  o In U.S. civil procedure (litigation rules for civil cases), _____ is a stage prior to trial. In civil cases, each party must disclose to the opposing party the following: names of witnesses which it may use to support its side, copies of documents (or mere description of these documents) in its control which it may use to support its side, computation of damages claimed, and certain insurance information. _____ is related to, but technically prior to, the discovery stage.
  o In Company law (known as 'corporate law' in the United States), _____ refers to giving out information about public or limited companies or their officers, which might be kept secret if the company was a private company or a partnership.

- In real property transactions, _____ refers to providing to a buyer information known to the seller or broker/agent concerning the condition or other aspects of real property that would affect the property's value or desirability. These rules regarding what information must be disclosed, and whether the information must be disclosed even if a buyer does not ask, vary from one jurisdiction to the next.

a. Controlled Foreign Corporations
b. Trailing
c. Tax harmonisation
d. Disclosure

14. _____ are formal records of a business' financial activities.

In British English, including United Kingdom company law, _____ are often referred to as accounts, although the term _____ is also used, particularly by accountants.

_____ provide an overview of a business' financial condition in both short and long term.

a. Notes to the financial statements
b. Statement of retained earnings
c. 3M Company
d. Financial statements

15. A _____ is a fungible, negotiable instrument representing financial value. they are broadly categorized into debt securities (such as banknotes, bonds and debentures), and equity securities; e.g., common stocks. The company or other entity issuing the _____ is called the issuer.

a. Tracking stock
b. BMC Software, Inc.
c. Security
d. 3M Company

16. In financial accounting, a _____ or statement of financial position is a summary of a person's or organization's balances. Assets, liabilities and ownership equity are listed as of a specific date, such as the end of its financial year. A _____ is often described as a snapshot of a company's financial condition.

a. Statement of retained earnings
b. Financial statements
c. 3M Company
d. Balance sheet

17. A _____ is the pinnacle activity involved in selling products or services in return for money or other compensation. It is an act of completion of a commercial activity.

A _____ is completed by the seller, the owner of the goods.

a. Sale
b. Maturity
c. Tertiary sector of economy
d. High yield stock

18. In accounting/accountancy, _____ are journal entries usually made at the end of an accounting period to allocate income and expenditure to the period in which they actually occurred. The revenue recognition principle is the basis of making _____ that pertain to unearned and accrued revenues under accrual-basis accounting. They are sometimes called Balance Day adjustments because they are made on balance day.

a. Adjusting entries
b. Accrued expense
c. Earnings before interest, taxes, depreciation and amortization
d. Accrual

19. _____, in accrual accounting, is any account where the asset or liability is not realized until a future date (accounting period), e.g. annuities, charges, taxes, income, etc. The _____ item may be carried, dependent on type of deferral, as either an asset or liability.

Chapter 20. Accounting Changes and Error Corrections

a. Pro forma
c. Payroll
b. Cash basis accounting
d. Deferred

20. _____ is an accounting concept, meaning a future tax liability or asset, resulting from temporary differences between book (accounting) value of assets and liabilities and their tax value, or timing differences between the recognition of gains and losses in financial statements and their recognition in a tax computation.

Temporary differences are differences between the carrying amount of an asset or liability recognised in the balance sheet and the amount attributed to that asset or liability for tax purposes (the tax base.)

a. Federal tax revenue by state
c. Tax refund
b. Deficit
d. Deferred tax

21. In business and accounting, _____ are everything of value that is owned by a person or company. It is a claim on the property your income of a borrower. The balance sheet of a firm records the monetary value of the _____ owned by the firm.

a. Earnings before interest, taxes, depreciation and amortization
c. Assets
b. Accrual basis accounting
d. Accounts receivable

22. An _____ is a tax levied on the financial income of people, corporations, or other legal entities. Various _____ systems exist, with varying degrees of tax incidence. Income taxation can be progressive, proportional, or regressive.

a. Individual Retirement Arrangement
c. Income tax
b. Implied level of government service
d. Ordinary income

23. In financial accounting, a _____ is defined as an obligation of an entity arising from past transactions or events, the settlement of which may result in the transfer or use of assets, provision of services or other yielding of economic benefits in the future.

a. False Claims Act
c. Liability
b. Vested
d. Corporate governance

24. Under the average-cost method, it is assumed that the cost of inventory is based on the _____ of the goods available for sale during the period. _____ is computed by dividing the total cost of goods available for sale by the total units available for sale. This gives a weighted-average unit cost that is applied to the units in the ending inventory.

a. ABC Television Network
c. Ending inventory
b. AIG
d. Average cost

25. Under the _____, it is assumed that the cost of inventory is based on the average cost of the goods available for sale during the period. Average cost is computed by dividing the total cost of goods available for sale by the total units available for sale. This gives a weighted-average unit cost that is applied to the units in the ending inventory.

a. AMEX
c. Average-cost method
b. AIG
d. ABC Television Network

26. In economics, business, retail, and accounting, a _____ is the value of money that has been used up to produce something, and hence is not available for use anymore. In economics, a _____ is an alternative that is given up as a result of a decision. In business, the _____ may be one of acquisition, in which case the amount of money expended to acquire it is counted as _____.
   a. Prime cost
   b. Cost allocation
   c. Cost
   d. Cost of quality

27. The doctrine of _____ in the common law of contracts excuses performance of a duty, where that duty has become unfeasibly difficult or expensive for the party who was to perform. It is similar in some respects to the doctrine of impossibility because it is triggered by the occurrence of a condition, the nonoccurrence of which was a basic assumption of the contract. The major difference between impossibility and _____, however, is that while impossibility excuses performance where the contractual duty cannot physically be performed, the doctrine of _____ comes into play where performance is still physically possible, but would be very burdensome for the party whose performance is due.
   a. Impracticability
   b. Operating Lease
   c. Employee Retirement Income Security Act
   d. Investment Advisers Act of 1940

28. _____ in accounting is the process of treating equity investments, usually 20-50%, in associate companies. The investor keeps such equities as an asset. Proportional share of associate company's net income increases the investment, and proportional payment of dividends decreases it.
   a. AIG
   b. Out-of-pocket
   c. ABC Television Network
   d. Equity method

29. The _____ founded on April 1, 2001 is the successor of the International Accounting Standards Committee (IASC) founded in June 1973 in London. It is responsible for developing the International Financial Reporting Standards (new name for the International Accounting Standards issued after 2001), and promoting the use and application of these standards.

The _____ is an independent, privately-funded accounting standard-setter based in London, UK.

   a. International Accounting Standards Board
   b. Institute of Management Accountants
   c. Emerging technologies
   d. Information Systems Audit and Control Association

30. In physics, and more specifically kinematics, _____ is the change in velocity over time. Because velocity is a vector, it can change in two ways: a change in magnitude and/or a change in direction. In one dimension, _____ is the rate at which something speeds up or slows down.
   a. AMEX
   b. AIG
   c. ABC Television Network
   d. Acceleration

31. _____ refers to any one of several methods by which a company, for 'financial accounting' and/or tax purposes, depreciates a fixed asset in such a way that the amount of depreciation taken each year is higher during the earlier years of an assete;s life. For financial accounting purposes, _____ is generally used when an asset is expected to be much more productive during its early years, so that depreciation expense will more accurately represent how much of an assete;s usefulness is being used up each year. For tax purposes, _____ provides a way of deferring corporate income taxes by reducing taxable income in current years, in exchange for increased taxable income in future years.
   a. Indirect tax
   b. User charge
   c. Accelerated depreciation
   d. Effective marginal tax rates

Chapter 20. Accounting Changes and Error Corrections

32. _____ is the process of increasing, or accounting for, an amount over a period of time. Particular instances of the term include:

- _____, the allocation of a lump sum amount to different time periods, particularly for loans and other forms of finance, including related interest or other finance charges.
    - _____ schedule, a table detailing each periodic payment on a loan (typically a mortgage), as generated by an _____ calculator.
    - Negative _____, an _____ schedule where the loan amount actually increases through not paying the full interest
- Amortized analysis, analyzing the execution cost of algorithms over a sequence of operations.
- _____ of capital expenditures of certain assets under accounting rules, particularly intangible assets, in a manner analogous to depreciation.
- _____

a. Intangible
c. EBIT
b. Amortization
d. Annuity

33. The _____ is a private, not-for-profit organization whose primary purpose is to develop generally accepted accounting principles (GAAP) within the United States in the public's interest. The Securities and Exchange Commission (SEC) designated the _____ as the organization responsible for setting accounting standards for public companies in the U.S. It was created in 1973, replacing the Accounting Principles Board and the Committee on Accounting Procedure of the American Institute of Certified Public Accountants. The _____'s mission is 'to establish and improve standards of financial accounting and reporting for the guidance and education of the public, including issuers, auditors, and users of financial information.'

The _____ is not a governmental body.

a. Financial Accounting Standards Board
c. Governmental Accounting Standards Board
b. Fannie Mae
d. Public company

34. In accounting, _____ are considered liabilities of the business that are to be settled in cash within the fiscal year or the operating cycle, whichever period is longer.

For example accounts payable for goods, services or supplies that were purchased for use in the operation of the business and payable within a normal period of time would be _____.

Bonds, mortgages and loans that are payable over a term exceeding one year would be fixed liabilities.

a. Payroll
c. Treasury stock
b. Closing entries
d. Current liabilities

35. _____ is a term used in accounting, economics and finance to spread the cost of an asset over the span of several years.

In simple words we can say that _____ is the reduction in the value of an asset due to usage, passage of time, wear and tear, technological outdating or obsolescence, depletion, inadequacy, rot, rust, decay or other such factors.

In accounting, _____ is a term used to describe any method of attributing the historical or purchase cost of an asset across its useful life, roughly corresponding to normal wear and tear.

   a. Current asset
   b. Net profit
   c. General ledger
   d. Depreciation

36. The _____ is the current method of accelerated asset depreciation required by the United States income tax code. Under _____, all assets are divided into classes which dictate the number of years over which an asset's cost will be recovered.

Prior to the Accelerated Cost Recovery System (ACRS), most capital purchases were depreciated using a straight line technique, that allowed for the depreciation of the asset over its useful life.

   a. Modified Accelerated Cost Recovery System
   b. 3M Company
   c. BMC Software, Inc.
   d. Categorical grants

37. _____ is a demonstration of a process -- such as a variable, term, or object -- relative in terms of the specific process or set of validation tests used to determine its presence and quantity. Properties described in this manner must be sufficiently accessible, so that persons other than the definer may independently measure or test for them at will. An _____ is generally designed to model a conceptual definition.

   a. AIG
   b. ABC Television Network
   c. AMEX
   d. Operational definition

38. There are several methods for calculating depreciation, generally based on either the passage of time or the level of activity (or use) of the asset.

_____ is the simplest and most often used technique, in which the company estimates the salvage value of the asset at the end of the period during which it will be used to generate revenues (useful life), and will expense a portion of original cost in equal increments over that period.

   a. Pro forma
   b. Current asset
   c. Closing entries
   d. Straight-line depreciation

39. _____ (or _____ Financial Services), formerly known as _____, is a United States bank that was previously the wholly owned financial services arm of General Motors. _____ Financial Services provide a suite of financial programs including insurance and mortgage operations in approximately 40 countries around the world. In 2008, the firm provided financing to 75 percent of the 6,450 GM dealers.

   a. BNSF Railway
   b. 3M Company
   c. GMAC
   d. BMC Software, Inc.

Chapter 20. Accounting Changes and Error Corrections

40. A _____ is a computer application that simulates a paper worksheet. It displays multiple cells that together make up a grid consisting of rows and columns, each cell containing either alphanumeric text or numeric values. A _____ cell may alternatively contain a formula that defines how the contents of that cell is to be calculated from the contents of any other cell (or combination of cells) each time any cell is updated.
   a. Spreadsheet
   c. Merck ' Co., Inc.
   b. Linear regression
   d. Mutual fund

41. The _____ is one of the basic financial statements as per Generally Accepted Accounting Principles, and it explains the changes in a company's retained earnings over the reporting period. It breaks down changes affecting the account, such as profits or losses from operations, dividends paid, and any other items charged or credited to retained earnings. A retained earnings statement is required by Generally Accepted Accounting Principles whenever comparative balance sheets and income statements are presented.
   a. Financial statements
   c. 3M Company
   b. Statement of retained earnings
   d. Notes to the financial statements

42. _____ is equal to the income that a firm has after subtracting costs and expenses from the total revenue. _____ can be distributed among holders of common stock as a dividend or held by the firm as retained earnings.

The items deducted will typically include tax expense, financing expense (interest expense), and minority interest. Likewise, preferred stock dividends will be subtracted too, though they are not an expense.

   a. Long-term liabilities
   c. Generally accepted accounting principles
   b. Net income
   d. Matching principle

43. In accounting, _____ has a very specific meaning. It is an outflow of cash or other valuable assets from a person or company to another person or company. This outflow of cash is generally one side of a trade for products or services that have equal or better current or future value to the buyer than to the seller.
   a. AIG
   c. ABC Television Network
   b. AMEX
   d. Expense

44. _____ is the calculated approximation of a result which is usable even if input data may be incomplete or uncertain.

In statistics, see _____ theory, estimator.

In mathematics, approximation or _____ typically means finding upper or lower bounds of a quantity that cannot readily be computed precisely and is also an educated guess .

   a. ABC Television Network
   c. AMEX
   b. AIG
   d. Estimation

45. A _____ estate is an ownership interest in land in which a lessee or a tenant holds real property by some form of title from a lessor or landlord.

_____ is a form of property tenure where one party buys the right to occupy land or a building for a given length of time. As lease is a legal estate, _____ estate can be bought and sold on the open market.

a. 3M Company
c. Leasehold
b. Liquidation value
d. Real Estate Investment Trust

Chapter 21. The Statement of Cash Flows Revisited

1. In financial accounting, a _____ or Statement of cash flows is a financial statement that shows a company's flow of cash. The money coming into the business is called cash inflow, and money going out from the business is called cash outflow. The statement shows how changes in balance sheet and income accounts affect cash and cash equivalents, and breaks the analysis down to operating, investing, and financing activities.
   a. Cash flow statement
   b. 3M Company
   c. BNSF Railway
   d. BMC Software, Inc.

2. _____ is the balance of the amounts of cash being received and paid by a business during a defined period of time, sometimes tied to a specific project. Measurement of _____ can be used

   - to evaluate the state or performance of a business or project.
   - to determine problems with liquidity. Being profitable does not necessarily mean being liquid. A company can fail because of a shortage of cash, even while profitable.
   - to project rate of returns. The time of _____s into and out of projects are used as inputs to financial models such as internal rate of return, and net present value.
   - to examine income or growth of a business when it is believed that accrual accounting concepts do not represent economic realities. Alternately, _____ can be used to 'validate' the net income generated by accrual accounting.

   _____ as a generic term may be used differently depending on context, and certain _____ definitions may be adapted by analysts and users for their own uses. Common terms include operating _____ and free _____.

   a. Commercial paper
   b. Flow-through entity
   c. Controlling interest
   d. Cash flow

3. In economics, _____ or _____ goods or real _____ refers to factors of production used to create goods or services that are not themselves significantly consumed (though they may depreciate) in the production process. _____ goods may be acquired with money or financial _____. In finance and accounting, _____ generally refers to financial wealth, especially that used to start or maintain a business.
   a. Screening
   b. Capital
   c. Disclosure
   d. Vyborg Appeal

4. _____ is a type of lease - the other being an operating lease. A _____ effectively allows a firm to finance the purchase of an asset, even if, strictly speaking, the firm never acquires the asset. Typically, a _____ will give the lessee control over an asset for a large proportion of the asset's useful life, providing them the benefits and risks of ownership.
   a. 3M Company
   b. Profitability index
   c. Debt ratio
   d. Finance lease

5. A _____ is a contract conferring a right on one person to possess property belonging to another person (called a landlord or lessor) to the exclusion of the owner landlord. It is a rental agreement between landlord and tenant. The relationship between the tenant and the landlord is called a tenancy, and the right to possession by the tenant is sometimes called a leasehold interest.
   a. Federal Sentencing Guidelines
   b. Robinson-Patman Act
   c. Lease
   d. Model Code of Professional Responsibility

6. In financial accounting, a _____ or statement of financial position is a summary of a person's or organization's balances. Assets, liabilities and ownership equity are listed as of a specific date, such as the end of its financial year. A _____ is often described as a snapshot of a company's financial condition.
   a. 3M Company
   b. Financial statements
   c. Statement of retained earnings
   d. Balance sheet

7. _____ are the most liquid assets found within the asset portion of a company's balance sheet. Cash equivalents are assets that are readily convertible into cash, such as money market holdings, short-term government bonds or Treasury bills, marketable securities and commercial paper. _____ are distinguished from other investments through their short-term existence; they mature within 3 months whereas short-term investments are 12 months or less, and long-term investments are any investments that mature in excess of 12 months.
   a. Par value
   b. Debtor
   c. Cash and cash equivalents
   d. Payback period

8. A _____ or reacquired stock is stock which is bought back by the issuing company, reducing the amount of outstanding stock on the open market ('open market' including insiders' holdings).

Stock repurchases are often used as a tax-efficient method to put cash into shareholders' hands, rather than pay dividends. Sometimes, companies do this when they feel that their stock is undervalued on the open market.

   a. Matching principle
   b. Cost of goods sold
   c. Net profit
   d. Treasury stock

9. The term _____, derived from the distinctive T shape, is frequently used when discussing or analyzing accounting or business transactions. _____s are used to represent general ledger accounts.

Typically one or more Ts are drawn on a white board or blank piece of paper. A general ledger account name or number is then written above each T. Debit entries are recorded on the left side of the 'T' and credit entries are recorded on the right side of the 'T'.

   a. 3M Company
   b. BMC Software, Inc.
   c. BNSF Railway
   d. T account

10. The _____ was a predecessor of the Accounting Principles Board, itself a predecessor to the Financial Accounting Standards Board in the United States. Its formation and activities were early efforts to rationalize and legitimize the reporting of business performance. However, it is widely regarded as having failed.
   a. Price variance
   b. Lump sum
   c. Consolidated financial statements
   d. Committee on Accounting Procedure

11. _____ means the giving out of information, either voluntarily or to be in compliance with legal regulations or workplace rules.

- In Computer security, full _____ means disclosing full information about vulnerabilities.
- In computing, _____ widget
- Journalism, full _____ refers to disclosing the interests of the writer which may bear on the subject being written about, for example, if the writer has worked with an interview subject in the past.

- In law:
    - The law of England and Wales, _____ refers to a process that may form part of legal proceedings, whereby parties inform to other parties the existence of any relevant documents that are, or have been, in their control. This compares with the process known as discovery in the course of legal proceedings in the United States.
    - In U.S. civil procedure (litigation rules for civil cases), _____ is a stage prior to trial. In civil cases, each party must disclose to the opposing party the following: names of witnesses which it may use to support its side, copies of documents (or mere description of these documents) in its control which it may use to support its side, computation of damages claimed, and certain insurance information. _____ is related to, but technically prior to, the discovery stage.
    - In Company law (known as 'corporate law' in the United States), _____ refers to giving out information about public or limited companies or their officers, which might be kept secret if the company was a private company or a partnership.

- In real property transactions, _____ refers to providing to a buyer information known to the seller or broker/agent concerning the condition or other aspects of real property that would affect the property's value or desirability. These rules regarding what information must be disclosed, and whether the information must be disclosed even if a buyer does not ask, vary from one jurisdiction to the next.

a. Controlled Foreign Corporations
b. Trailing
c. Tax harmonisation
d. Disclosure

12. The Exxon Mobil Corporation is an American oil and gas corporation. It is a direct descendant of John D. Rockefeller's Standard Oil company, formed on November 30, 1999, by the merger of Exxon and Mobil.

_____ is the world's largest publicly traded company when measured by either revenue or market capitalization.

a. Abby Joseph Cohen
b. ExxonMobil
c. Arthur Betz Laffer
d. Alan Greenspan

13. In economics, the concept of the _____ refers to the decision-making time frame of a firm in which at least one factor of production is fixed. Costs which are fixed in the _____ have no impact on a firms decisions. For example a firm can raise output by increasing the amount of labour through overtime.

a. Long-run
b. 3M Company
c. BMC Software, Inc.
d. Short-run

14. A _____ is the pinnacle activity involved in selling products or services in return for money or other compensation. It is an act of completion of a commercial activity.

A _____ is completed by the seller, the owner of the goods.

   a. Maturity
   b. Sale
   c. Tertiary sector of economy
   d. High yield stock

15. A _____ is a computer application that simulates a paper worksheet. It displays multiple cells that together make up a grid consisting of rows and columns, each cell containing either alphanumeric text or numeric values. A _____ cell may alternatively contain a formula that defines how the contents of that cell is to be calculated from the contents of any other cell (or combination of cells) each time any cell is updated.
   a. Linear regression
   b. Spreadsheet
   c. Mutual fund
   d. Merck ' Co., Inc.

16. _____ is equal to the income that a firm has after subtracting costs and expenses from the total revenue. _____ can be distributed among holders of common stock as a dividend or held by the firm as retained earnings.

The items deducted will typically include tax expense, financing expense (interest expense), and minority interest. Likewise, preferred stock dividends will be subtracted too, though they are not an expense.

   a. Net income
   b. Generally accepted accounting principles
   c. Matching principle
   d. Long-term liabilities

17. _____ of something is, in finance, the adding together of interest or different investments over a period of time such as atoms (1 - the act or process of accruing; 2 - the amount that accrues.) It holds specific meanings in accounting and payroll.

_____, in accounting, describes the accounting method known as _____ basis, whereby revenues and expenses are recognized when they are accrued, i.e. accumulated (earned or incurred), regardless when the actual cash is received or paid out.

   a. Accrual
   b. Assets
   c. Earnings before interest, taxes, depreciation and amortization
   d. Accounts receivable

18. _____ is a method of accounting whereby economic activities (rather than cash flow) of financial events are considered, because of two complementary principles, which (together) determine the point, at which expenses and revenues are recognized. According to revenue recognition principle, revenues are realized when earned, whether or not they are received in cash.
   a. Accrual
   b. Accrued revenue
   c. Earnings before interest, taxes, depreciation and amortization
   d. Accrual basis accounting

Chapter 21. The Statement of Cash Flows Revisited 255

19. _____ refers to a business or organization attempting to acquire goods or services to accomplish the goals of the enterprise. Though there are several organizations that attempt to set standards in the _____ process, processes can vary greatly between organizations. Typically the word e;_____e; is not used interchangeably with the word e;procuremente;, since procurement typically includes Expediting, Supplier Quality, and Traffic and Logistics (T'L) in addition to _____.

a. Free port
b. Consignor
c. Purchasing
d. Supply chain

20. In business and accounting, _____ are everything of value that is owned by a person or company. It is a claim on the property your income of a borrower. The balance sheet of a firm records the monetary value of the _____ owned by the firm.

a. Earnings before interest, taxes, depreciation and amortization
b. Accounts receivable
c. Accrual basis accounting
d. Assets

21. A _____ is a habit, a preparation, a state of readiness, or a tendency to act in a specified way.

The terms dispositional belief and occurrent belief refer, in the former case, to a belief that is held in the mind but not currently being considered, and in the latter case, to a belief that is currently being considered by the mind.

In Bourdieu's theory of fields _____s are the natural tendencies of each individual to take on a certain position in any field.

a. 3M Company
b. BMC Software, Inc.
c. BNSF Railway
d. Disposition

22. _____ is any physical or virtual entity that is owned by an individual or jointly by a group of individuals. An owner of _____ has the right to consume, sell, rent, mortgage, transfer and exchange his or her _____. Important widely-recognized types of _____ include real _____, personal _____ (other physical possessions), and intellectual _____ (rights over artistic creations, inventions, etc.), although the latter is not always as widely recognized or enforced.

a. Disclosure requirement
b. Fiduciary
c. Primary authority
d. Property

23. _____, also known as property, plant, and equipment (PP&E), is a term used in accountancy for assets and property which cannot easily be converted into cash. This can be compared with current assets such as cash or bank accounts, which are described as liquid assets. In most cases, only tangible assets are referred to as fixed.

a. Bankruptcy prediction
b. Minority interest
c. Fixed asset
d. Subledger

24. A _____ is a fungible, negotiable instrument representing financial value. they are broadly categorized into debt securities (such as banknotes, bonds and debentures), and equity securities; e.g., common stocks. The company or other entity issuing the _____ is called the issuer.

a. Security
b. Tracking stock
c. BMC Software, Inc.
d. 3M Company

25. An _____ is the buying of one company by another. An _____ may be friendly or hostile. In the former case, the companies cooperate in negotiations; in the latter case, the takeover target is unwilling to be bought or the target's board has no prior knowledge of the offer. _____ usually refers to a purchase of a smaller firm by a larger one. Sometimes, however, a smaller firm will acquire management control of a larger or longer established company and keep its name for the combined entity. This is known as a reverse takeover.
   a. AIG
   b. Acquisition
   c. ABC Television Network
   d. AMEX

26. _____ is a demonstration of a process -- such as a variable, term, or object -- relative in terms of the specific process or set of validation tests used to determine its presence and quantity. Properties described in this manner must be sufficiently accessible, so that persons other than the definer may independently measure or test for them at will. An _____ is generally designed to model a conceptual definition.
   a. Operational definition
   b. AMEX
   c. ABC Television Network
   d. AIG

27. _____ is a form of corporation equity ownership represented in the securities. It is a stock whose dividends are based on market fluctuations. It is dangerous in comparison to preferred shares and some other investment options, in that in the event of bankruptcy, _____ investors receive their funds after preferred stock holders, bondholders, creditors, etc. On the other hand, common shares on average perform better than preferred shares or bonds over time.
   a. 3M Company
   b. Growth investing
   c. Common stock
   d. Stock split

28. A _____ is the transfer of wealth from one party (such as a person or company) to another. A _____ is usually made in exchange for the provision of goods, services or both, or to fulfill a legal obligation.

The simplest and oldest form of _____ is barter, the exchange of one good or service for another.

   a. Payee
   b. Payment
   c. 3M Company
   d. BMC Software, Inc.

29. _____ are payments made by a corporation to its shareholder members. It is the portion of corporate profits paid out to stockholders. When a corporation earns a profit or surplus, that money can be put to two uses: it can either be re-invested in the business (called retained earnings), or it can be paid to the shareholders as a dividend.
   a. Dividend stripping
   b. Dividend yield
   c. Dividend payout ratio
   d. Dividends

30. In finance, a _____ is a type of bond that can be converted into shares of stock in the issuing company, usually at some pre-announced ratio. It is a hybrid security with debt- and equity-like features. Although it typically has a low coupon rate, the holder is compensated with the ability to convert the bond to common stock, usually at a substantial discount to the stock's market value.
   a. Zero-coupon bond
   b. Coupon rate
   c. Zero-coupon
   d. Convertible bond

Chapter 21. The Statement of Cash Flows Revisited

31. Discounting is a financial mechanism in which a debtor obtains the right to delay payments to a creditor, for a defined period of time, in exchange for a charge or fee. Essentially, the party that owes money in the present purchases the right to delay the payment until some future date. The _____, or charge, is simply the difference between the original amount owed in the present and the amount that has to be paid in the future to settle the debt.
   a. Discount factor
   b. Risk aversion
   c. Discount
   d. Discounting

32. The _____ is an interest rate a central bank charges depository institutions that borrow reserves from it.

   The term _____ has two meanings:

   - the same as interest rate; the term 'discount' does not refer to the meaning of the word, but to the purpose of using the quantity, such as computations of present value, e.g. net present value or discounted cash flow

   - the annual effective _____, which is the annual interest divided by the capital including that interest; this rate is lower than the interest rate; it corresponds to using the value after a year as the nominal value, and seeing the initial value as the nominal value minus a discount; it is used for Treasury Bills and similar financial instruments

   The annual effective _____ is the annual interest divided by the capital including that interest, which is the interest rate divided by 100% plus the interest rate. It is the annual discount factor to be applied to the future cash flow, to find the discount, subtracted from a future value to find the value one year earlier.

   For example, suppose there is a government bond that sells for $95 and pays $100 in a year's time.

   a. Discount rate
   b. Process time
   c. Convertible bond
   d. Municipal bond

33. In finance, an _____ is a contract between a buyer and a seller that gives the buyer the right--but not the obligation-- to buy or to sell a particular asset (the underlying asset) at a later time at an agreed price. In return for granting the _____, the seller collects a payment (the premium) from the buyer. A call _____ gives the buyer the right to buy the underlying asset; a put _____ gives the buyer of the _____ the right to sell the underlying asset.
   a. AIG
   b. AMEX
   c. ABC Television Network
   d. Option

34. A _____ is any one of a variety of different systems, institutions, procedures, social relations and infrastructures whereby persons trade, and goods and services are exchanged, forming part of the economy. It is an arrangement that allows buyers and sellers to exchange things. _____s vary in size, range, geographic scale, location, types and variety of human communities, as well as the types of goods and services traded.
   a. Perfect competition
   b. Recession
   c. Market Failure
   d. Market

35. _____ are formal records of a business' financial activities.

258   *Chapter 21. The Statement of Cash Flows Revisited*

In British English, including United Kingdom company law, _____ are often referred to as accounts, although the term _____ is also used, particularly by accountants.

_____ provide an overview of a business' financial condition in both short and long term.

a. 3M Company
b. Financial statements
c. Notes to the financial statements
d. Statement of retained earnings

36. _____ is a company's financial statement that indicates how the revenue is transformed into the net income The purpose of the _____ is to show managers and investors whether the company made or lost money during the period being reported.

The important thing to remember about an _____ is that it represents a period of time.

a. AMEX
b. AIG
c. ABC Television Network
d. Income statement

37. A _____ has several related meanings:

- a daily record of events or business; a private _____ is usually referred to as a diary.
- a newspaper or other periodical, in the literal sense of one published each day;
- many publications issued at stated intervals, such as magazines, or scholarly academic _____s, or the record of the transactions of a society, are often called _____s. Although _____ is sometimes used, erroneously, as a synonym for 'magazine,' in academic use, a _____ refers to a serious, scholarly publication, most often peer-reviewed. A non-scholarly magazine written for an educated audience about an industry or an area of professional activity is usually called a professional magazine.

The word 'journalist' for one whose business is writing for the public press has been in use since the end of the 17th century.

Open access _____s are scholarly _____s that are available to the reader without financial or other barrier other than access to the internet itself. Some are subsidized, and some require payment on behalf of the author. Subsidized _____s are financed by an academic institution or a government information center.

a. Journal
b. BMC Software, Inc.
c. 3M Company
d. BNSF Railway

38. In financial accounting and finance, _____ is the portion of receivables that can no longer be collected, typically from accounts receivable or loans. _____ in accounting is considered an expense.

There are two methods to account for _____:

1. Direct write off method (Non - GAAP)

Chapter 21. The Statement of Cash Flows Revisited 259

A receivable which is not considered collectible is charged directly to the income statement.

1. Allowance method (GAAP)

An estimate is made at the end of each fiscal year of the amount of _____. This is then accumulated in a provision which is then used to reduce specific receivable accounts as and when necessary.

a. Tax expense
b. Total Expense Ratio
c. 3M Company
d. Bad debt

39. _____, in accrual accounting, (e.g. advance payment received from a client) is, according to revenue recognition, revenue not earned until the delivery of goods or services, which until then, is still owed to the payer, hence remaining a liability.

_____, sometimes referred to as deferred revenue or unearned revenue, shares characteristics with accrued expense with the difference that a liability to be covered latter is cash received FROM a counterpart, while goods or services are to be delivered in a latter period, when such income item is earned, the related revenue item is recognized, and the same amount is deducted from deferred revenues.

a. Deferred income
b. Treasury stock
c. Matching principle
d. Gross sales

40. _____ is that which is owed; usually referencing assets owed, but the term can also cover moral obligations and other interactions not requiring money. In the case of assets, _____ is a means of using future purchasing power in the present before a summation has been earned. Some companies and corporations use _____ as a part of their overall corporate finance strategy.

a. Lender
b. Debt
c. Loan
d. Debenture

41. In accounting, _____ has a very specific meaning. It is an outflow of cash or other valuable assets from a person or company to another person or company. This outflow of cash is generally one side of a trade for products or services that have equal or better current or future value to the buyer than to the seller.

a. Expense
b. AMEX
c. AIG
d. ABC Television Network

42. In economic models, the _____ time frame assumes no fixed factors of production. Firms can enter or leave the marketplace, and the cost (and availability) of land, labor, raw materials, and capital goods can be assumed to vary. In contrast, in the short-run time frame, certain factors are assumed to be fixed, because there is not sufficient time for them to change.

a. BMC Software, Inc.
b. Short-run
c. 3M Company
d. Long-run

43. The term _____ describes a reduction in recognized value. In accounting terminology, it refers to recognition of the reduced or zero value of an asset. In income tax statements, it refers to a reduction of taxable income as recognition of certain expenses required to produce the income.

a. Write-off
b. Current asset
c. Payroll
d. Salvage value

44. In economics, business, retail, and accounting, a _____ is the value of money that has been used up to produce something, and hence is not available for use anymore. In economics, a _____ is an alternative that is given up as a result of a decision. In business, the _____ may be one of acquisition, in which case the amount of money expended to acquire it is counted as _____.

a. Prime cost
b. Cost of quality
c. Cost
d. Cost allocation

45. In financial accounting, _____ or cost of sales includes the direct costs attributable to the production of the goods sold by a company. This amount includes the materials cost used in creating the goods along with the direct labor costs used to produce the good. It excludes indirect expenses such as distribution costs and sales force costs.

a. Cost of goods sold
b. 3M Company
c. FIFO and LIFO accounting
d. Reorder point

46. _____ is a term used in accounting, economics and finance to spread the cost of an asset over the span of several years.

In simple words we can say that _____ is the reduction in the value of an asset due to usage, passage of time, wear and tear, technological outdating or obsolescence, depletion, inadequacy, rot, rust, decay or other such factors.

In accounting, _____ is a term used to describe any method of attributing the historical or purchase cost of an asset across its useful life, roughly corresponding to normal wear and tear.

a. Net profit
b. Current asset
c. Depreciation
d. General ledger

47. In finance, a _____ is a debt security, in which the authorized issuer owes the holders a debt and, depending on the terms of the _____, is obliged to pay interest (the coupon) and/or to repay the principal at a later date, termed maturity. It is a formal contract to repay borrowed money with interest at fixed intervals.

Thus a _____ is like a loan: the issuer is the borrower, the _____ holder is the lender, and the coupon is the interest.

a. Revenue bonds
b. Bond
c. Zero-coupon bond
d. Coupon rate

48. _____, in law and economics, is a form of risk management primarily used to hedge against the risk of a contingent loss. _____ is defined as the equitable transfer of the risk of a loss, from one entity to another, in exchange for a premium, and can be thought of as a guaranteed small loss to prevent a large, possibly devastating loss. An insurer is a company selling the _____; an insured is the person or entity buying the _____.

a. AMEX
b. ABC Television Network
c. AIG
d. Insurance

Chapter 21. The Statement of Cash Flows Revisited

49. _____ is a fee paid on borrowed assets. It is the price paid for the use of borrowed money, or, money earned by deposited funds. Assets that are sometimes lent with _____ include money, shares, consumer goods through hire purchase, major assets such as aircraft, and even entire factories in finance lease arrangements. The _____ is calculated upon the value of the assets in the same manner as upon money.
   a. Insolvency
   b. AIG
   c. ABC Television Network
   d. Interest

50. _____ relates to the cost of borrowing money. It is the price that a lender charges a borrower for the use of the lender's money. _____ is different from OPEX and CAPEX, for it relates to the capital structure of a company.
   a. AIG
   b. Interest expense
   c. Interest
   d. ABC Television Network

51. An _____ is a tax levied on the financial income of people, corporations, or other legal entities. Various _____ systems exist, with varying degrees of tax incidence. Income taxation can be progressive, proportional, or regressive.
   a. Implied level of government service
   b. Income tax
   c. Individual Retirement Arrangement
   d. Ordinary income

52. At its simplest, a company's _____ as it sometimes called, is computed in by multiplying the income before tax number, as reported to shareholders, by the appropriate tax rate. In reality, the computation is typically considerably more complex due to things such as expenses considered not deductible by taxing authorities ('add backs'), the range of tax rates applicable to various levels of income, different tax rates in different jurisdictions, multiple layers of tax on income, and other issues.

Historically, in many places, a revenue-expense method was used, in which the income statement was seen as primary, and the balance sheet as secondary.

   a. Payroll
   b. Total Expense Ratio
   c. Tax expense
   d. 3M Company

53. _____, in accrual accounting, is any account where the asset or liability is not realized until a future date (accounting period), e.g. annuities, charges, taxes, income, etc. The _____ item may be carried, dependent on type of deferral, as either an asset or liability.
   a. Cash basis accounting
   b. Payroll
   c. Pro forma
   d. Deferred

54. In the global money market, _____ is an unsecured promissory note with a fixed maturity of one to 270 days. _____ is a money-market security issued (sold) by large banks and corporations to get money to meet short term debt obligations (for example, payroll), and is only backed by an issuing bank or corporation's promise to pay the face amount on the maturity date specified on the note. Since it is not backed by collateral, only firms with excellent credit ratings from a recognized rating agency will be able to sell their _____ at a reasonable price.
   a. Controlling interest
   b. Flow-through entity
   c. Gross profit margin
   d. Commercial paper

55. _____s are cash, evidence of an ownership interest in an entity or deliver, cash or another _____.

_____s can be categorized by form depending on whether they are cash instruments or derivative instruments:

- Cash instruments are _____s whose value is determined directly by markets. They can be divided into securities, which are readily transferable, and other cash instruments such as loans and deposits, where both borrower and lender have to agree on a transfer.
- Derivative instruments are _____s which derive their value from the value and characteristics of one or more underlying assets. They can be divided into exchange-traded derivatives and over-the-counter (OTC) derivatives.

Alternatively, _____s can be categorized by 'asset class' depending on whether they are equity based (reflecting ownership of the issuing entity) or debt based (reflecting a loan the investor has made to the issuing entity.) If it is debt, it can be further categorised into short term (less than one year) or long term.

Foreign Exchange instruments and transactions are neither debt nor equity based and belong in their own category.

a. Mark-to-market
c. Market price
b. Financial instrument
d. Financial instruments

56. _____ are cash, evidence of an ownership interest in an entity, or a contractual right to receive, or deliver, cash or another financial instrument.

_____ can be categorized by form depending on whether they are cash instruments or derivative instruments:

- Cash instruments are _____ whose value is determined directly by markets. They can be divided into securities, which are readily transferable, and other cash instruments such as loans and deposits, where both borrower and lender have to agree on a transfer.
- Derivative instruments are _____ which derive their value from the value and characteristics of one or more underlying assets. They can be divided into exchange-traded derivatives and over-the-counter (OTC) derivatives.

Alternatively, _____ can be categorized by 'asset class' depending on whether they are equity based (reflecting ownership of the issuing entity) or debt based (reflecting a loan the investor has made to the issuing entity.) If it is debt, it can be further categorised into short term (less than one year) or long term.

Foreign Exchange instruments and transactions are neither debt nor equity based and belong in their own category.

a. Market liquidity
c. Transfer agent
b. Spot rate
d. Financial instruments

Chapter 21. The Statement of Cash Flows Revisited

57. In finance, the _____ is the global financial market for short-term borrowing and lending. It provides short-term liquidity funding for the global financial system. The _____ is where short-term obligations such as Treasury bills, commercial paper and bankers' acceptances are bought and sold.

   a. Money market
   b. Restructuring
   c. Securitization
   d. Segregated portfolio company

58. Treasury securities are government debt issued by the United States Department of the Treasury through the Bureau of the Public Debt. They are the debt financing instruments of the U.S. Federal government, and they are often referred to simply as Treasuries or Treasurys. There are four types of marketable treasury securities: _____, Treasury notes, Treasury bonds, and Treasury Inflation Protected Securities (TIPS.)

   _____ mature in one year or less. Like zero-coupon bonds, they do not pay interest prior to maturity; instead they are sold at a discount of the par value to create a positive yield to maturity. Many regard _____ as the least risky investment available to U.S. investors.

   a. BNSF Railway
   b. Treasury bills
   c. BMC Software, Inc.
   d. 3M Company

59. A _____ is a time deposit, a financial product commonly offered to consumers by banks, thrift institutions, and credit unions.

   They are similar to savings accounts in that they are insured and thus virtually risk-free; they are 'money in the bank' (_____s are insured by the FDIC for banks or by the NCUA for credit unions.) They are different from savings accounts in that the _____ has a specific, fixed term (often three months, six months, or one to five years), and, usually, a fixed interest rate.

   a. Reserve requirement
   b. Prime rate
   c. Transactional account
   d. Certificate of deposit

60. _____ is a specific term used in companies' financial reporting from the company-whole point of view. Because that use excludes the effects of changing ownership interest, an economic measure of _____ is necessary for financial analysis from the shareholders' point of view

   _____ is defined by the Financial Accounting Standards Board, or FASB, as 'the change in equity [net assets] of a business enterprise during a period from transactions and other events and circumstances from nonowner sources. It includes all changes in equity during a period except those resulting from investments by owners and distributions to owners.'

   _____ is the sum of net income and other items that must bypass the income statement because they have not been realized, including items like an unrealized holding gain or loss from available for sale securities and foreign currency translation gains or losses.

   a. BNSF Railway
   b. Comprehensive income
   c. 3M Company
   d. BMC Software, Inc.

Chapter 21. The Statement of Cash Flows Revisited

61. _____ are the earnings returned on the initial investment amount.

In the US, the Financial Accounting Standards Board (FASB) requires companies' income statements to report _____ for each of the major categories of the income statement: continuing operations, discontinued operations, extraordinary items, and net income.

The _____ formula does not include preferred dividends for categories outside of continued operations and net income.

a. Invested capital
b. Earnings yield
c. Average accounting return
d. Earnings per share

62. An _____ is a lease whose term is short compared to the useful life of the asset or piece of equipment (an airliner, a ship etc.) being leased. An _____ is commonly used to acquire equipment on a relatively short-term basis.

a. Operating lease
b. Express warranty
c. Issued shares
d. Employee Retirement Income Security Act

63. _____ is the process of increasing, or accounting for, an amount over a period of time. Particular instances of the term include:

- _____, the allocation of a lump sum amount to different time periods, particularly for loans and other forms of finance, including related interest or other finance charges.
    - _____ schedule, a table detailing each periodic payment on a loan (typically a mortgage), as generated by an _____ calculator.
    - Negative _____, an _____ schedule where the loan amount actually increases through not paying the full interest
- Amortized analysis, analyzing the execution cost of algorithms over a sequence of operations.
- _____ of capital expenditures of certain assets under accounting rules, particularly intangible assets, in a manner analogous to depreciation.
- _____

a. Annuity
b. Intangible
c. EBIT
d. Amortization

64. A _____ is the dividend paid to common stock owners from the profits of the company. Like other dividends, the payout is in the form of cash or other like stock. The law may regulate the size of the _____ particularly when the payout is a cash distribution tantamount to a liquidation.

a. Foreign Corrupt Practices Act
b. Disclosure requirement
c. Common stock dividend
d. Due diligence

65. In accounting, _____ are considered liabilities of the business that are to be settled in cash within the fiscal year or the operating cycle, whichever period is longer.

For example accounts payable for goods, services or supplies that were purchased for use in the operation of the business and payable within a normal period of time would be _____.

Bonds, mortgages and loans that are payable over a term exceeding one year would be fixed liabilities.

a. Closing entries
b. Payroll
c. Treasury stock
d. Current liabilities

66. In financial accounting, a _____ is defined as an obligation of an entity arising from past transactions or events, the settlement of which may result in the transfer or use of assets, provision of services or other yielding of economic benefits in the future.
a. Corporate governance
b. False Claims Act
c. Vested
d. Liability

67. _____ is one of a series of accounting transactions dealing with the billing of customers who owe money to a person, company or organization for goods and services that have been provided to the customer. In most business entities this is typically done by generating an invoice and mailing or electronically delivering it to the customer, who in turn must pay it within an established timeframe called credit or payment terms.

An example of a common payment term is Net 30, meaning payment is due in the amount of the invoice 30 days from the date of invoice.

a. Adjusting entries
b. Accrual
c. Accounts receivable
d. Accrued revenue

68. _____ in accounting is the process of treating equity investments, usually 20-50%, in associate companies. The investor keeps such equities as an asset. Proportional share of associate company's net income increases the investment, and proportional payment of dividends decreases it.
a. Out-of-pocket
b. ABC Television Network
c. AIG
d. Equity method

69. _____ or interest coverage ratio is a measure of a company's ability to honor its debt payments. It may be calculated as either EBIT or EBITDA divided by the total interest payable.

a. Capital recovery factor
b. Yield Gap
c. Return of capital
d. Times interest earned

70. The _____ is a financial ratio indicating the relative proportion of equity to all used to finance a company's assets. The two components are often taken from the firm's balance sheet or statement of financial position (so-called book value), but the ratio may also be calculated using market values for both, if the company's equities are publicly traded.

The _____ is especially in Central Europe a very common financial ratio while in the US the debt to _____ is more often used in financial (research) reports.

a. Earnings yield
b. Efficiency ratio
c. Average accounting return
d. Equity ratio

71. The _____ percentage shows how profitable a company's assets are in generating revenue.

_____ can be computed as:

$$ROA = \frac{\text{Net Income - Interest Expense - Interest Tax savings}}{\text{Average Total Assets}}$$

This number tells you what the company can do with what it has, i.e. how many dollars of earnings they derive from each dollar of assets they control. Its a useful number for comparing competing companies in the same industry.

a. Return on sales
b. Capital employed
c. Statutory Liquidity Ratio
d. Return on assets

72. A _____ is a hedge of the exposure to the variability of cash flow that

1. is attributable to a particular risk associated with a recognized asset or liability. Such as all or some future interest payments on variable rate debt or a highly probable forecast transaction and
2. could affect profit or loss

a. Cash flow hedge
b. Currency risk
c. 3M Company
d. Credit risk

73. _____, also called fair price (in a commonplace conflation of the two distinct concepts), is a concept used in finance and economics, defined as a rational and unbiased estimate of the potential market price of a good, service, or asset, taking into account such objective factors as:

- acquisition/production/distribution costs, replacement costs, or costs of close substitutes
- actual utility at a given level of development of social productive capability
- supply vs. demand

and subjective factors such as

- risk characteristics
- cost of capital
- individually perceived utility

Chapter 21. The Statement of Cash Flows Revisited

In accounting, _____ is used as an estimate of the market value of an asset (or liability) for which a market price cannot be determined (usually because there is no established market for the asset.) Under GAAP (FAS 157), _____ is the amount at which the asset could be bought or sold in a current transaction between willing parties, or transferred to an equivalent party, other than in a liquidation sale. This is used for assets whose carrying value is based on mark-to-market valuations; for assets carried at historical cost, the _____ of the asset is not used. One example of where _____ is an issue is a College kitchen with a cost of $2 million which was built 5 years ago.

a. BNSF Railway
b. BMC Software, Inc.
c. 3M Company
d. Fair value

74. An _____ is the price a borrower pays for the use of money they do not own, for instance a small company might borrow from a bank to kick start their business, and the return a lender receives for deferring the use of funds, by lending it to the borrower. _____s are normally expressed as a percentage rate over the period of one year.

_____s targets are also a vital tool of monetary policy and are used to control variables like investment, inflation, and unemployment.

a. Interest rate
b. ABC Television Network
c. AMEX
d. AIG

75. Procter is a surname, and may also refer to:

- Bryan Waller Procter (pseud. Barry Cornwall), English poet
- Goodwin Procter, American law firm
- _____, consumer products multinational

a. Welfare
b. Screening
c. Markup
d. Procter ' Gamble

76. _____ is a concept that denotes the precise probability of specific eventualities. Technically, the notion of _____ is independent from the notion of value and, as such, eventualities may have both beneficial and adverse consequences. However, in general usage the convention is to focus only on potential negative impact to some characteristic of value that may arise from a future event.

a. Discounting
b. Risk adjusted return on capital
c. Risk
d. Discount factor

77. In monetary economics _____ can refer either to a particular _____, for example British Pounds or United States Dollars, or, to the coins and banknotes of a particular _____, which actually form only a small part of the monetary base of a nation's money supply. The other part of a nation's money supply consists of money deposited in banks (sometimes called deposit money), ownership of which can be transferred by means of checks (cheques in the United Kingdom and Australia) or other forms of money transfer such as credit and debit cards. Deposit money and _____ are 'money' in the sense that both are acceptable as a means of exchange, but money need not necessarily be '_____'.

a. 3M Company
b. Currency
c. BNSF Railway
d. BMC Software, Inc.

78. _____ is a form of risk that arises from the change in price of one currency against another. Whenever investors or companies have assets or business operations across national borders, they face _____ if their positions are not hedged.

- Transaction risk is the risk that exchange rates will change unfavourably over time. It can be hedged against using forward currency contracts;
- Translation risk is an accounting risk, proportional to the amount of assets held in foreign currencies. Changes in the exchange rate over time will render a report inaccurate, and so assets are usually balanced by borrowings in that currency.

The exchange risk associated with a foreign denominated instrument is a key element in foreign investment. This risk flows from differential monetary policy and growth in real productivity, which results in differential inflation rates.

a. Credit risk
b. 3M Company
c. Market risk
d. Currency risk

79. Most patent law systems require that a patent application disclose a claimed invention in sufficient detail for the notional person skilled in the art to carry out that claimed invention. This requirement is often known as sufficiency of disclosure or enablement, depending on the jurisdiction.

The _____ lies at the heart and origin of patent law. A state or government grants an inventor, or the inventor's assignee, a monopoly for a given period of time in exchange for the inventor disclosing to the public how to make or practice his or her invention. If a patent fails to contain such information, then the bargain is violated, and the patent is unenforceable.

a. Pre-emption right
b. False Claims Act
c. Tax patent
d. Disclosure requirement

80. The _____ , established in 1848, is the world's oldest futures and options exchange. More than 50 different options and futures contracts are traded by over 3,600 _____ members through open outcry and eTrading. Volumes at the exchange in 2003 were a record breaking 454 million contracts.

a. Chicago Board of Trade
b. BMC Software, Inc.
c. 3M Company
d. BNSF Railway

81. The _____ (often called 'the Chicago Merc,' or 'the Merc') is an American financial and commodity derivative exchange based in Chicago. The _____ was founded in 1898 as the Chicago Butter and Egg Board. Originally, the exchange was a non-profit organization.

a. 3M Company
b. Financial Crimes Enforcement Network
c. Public Company Accounting Oversight Board
d. Chicago Mercantile Exchange

82. _____ are standards and interpretations adopted by the International Accounting Standards Board (IASB.)

Chapter 21. The Statement of Cash Flows Revisited

Many of the standards forming part of _____ are known by the older name of International Accounting Standards (IAS.) IAS were issued between 1973 and 2001 by the board of the International Accounting Standards Committee (IASC.)

a. Out-of-pocket
b. ABC Television Network
c. AIG
d. International Financial Reporting Standards

83. An _____ is a derivative in which one party exchanges a stream of interest payments for another party's stream of cash flows. They can be used by hedgers to manage their fixed or floating assets and liabilities. They can also be used by speculators to replicate unfunded bond exposures to profit from changes in interest rates.

a. AMEX
b. AIG
c. ABC Television Network
d. Interest rate swap

84. In finance, a _____ is a derivative in which two counterparties agree to exchange one stream of cash flow against another stream. These streams are called the legs of the _____.

The cash flows are calculated over a notional principal amount, which is usually not exchanged between counterparties.

a. Controlled Foreign Corporations
b. Total-factor productivity
c. Swap
d. Department of the Treasury

85. _____ is the process of comparing the cost, cycle time, productivity, or quality of a specific process or method to another that is widely considered to be an industry standard or best practice. Essentially, _____ provides a snapshot of the performance of your business and helps you understand where you are in relation to a particular standard. The result is often a business case for making changes in order to make improvements.

a. 3M Company
b. Benchmarking
c. BMC Software, Inc.
d. Strategic business unit

86. A _____, also referred to as a note payable in accounting, is a contract where one party (the maker or issuer) makes an unconditional promise in writing to pay a sum of money to the other (the payee), either at a fixed or determinable future time or on demand of the payee, under specific terms. They differ from IOUs in that they contain a specific promise to pay, rather than simply acknowledging that a debt exists.

The terms of a note typically include the principal amount, the interest rate if any, and the maturity date.

a. 3M Company
b. Promissory note
c. BNSF Railway
d. BMC Software, Inc.

87. _____ are generally defined as increases (decreases) in the replacement costs of the assets held during a given period. _____ and losses accrue to the owners of assets and liabilities purely as a result of holding the assets or liabilities over time, without transforming them in any way.

For example, if a company holds bottles of wine in its inventory and that specific wine becomes more expensive on the market, the replacement cost of the wine in the inventory increases as it has become more expensive for the company to replace its current stock of wine.

a. Par value
b. Holding gains
c. Net worth
d. Fair market value

88. _____ is the state or fact of exclusive rights and control over property, which may be an object, land/real estate or intellectual property. An _____ right is also referred to as title.

_____ is the key building block in the development of the capitalist socio-economic system.

a. Ownership
b. ABC Television Network
c. Administrative proceeding
d. Encumbrance

89. The term _____ or superannuation refers to a pension granted upon retirement. They may be set up by employers, insurance companies, the government or other institutions such as employer associations or trade unions.

a. Wage
b. Retirement plan
c. BMC Software, Inc.
d. 3M Company

90. _____ is the risk of loss due to a debtor's non-payment of a loan or other line of credit (either the principal or interest (coupon) or both)

Most lenders employ their own models (credit scorecards) to rank potential and existing customers according to risk, and then apply appropriate strategies. With products such as unsecured personal loans or mortgages, lenders charge a higher price for higher risk customers and vice versa. With revolving products such as credit cards and overdrafts, risk is controlled through the setting of credit limits.

a. 3M Company
b. Currency risk
c. Market risk
d. Credit risk

91. _____ principle is a cornerstone of accrual accounting together with matching principle. They both determine the accounting period, in which revenues and expenses are recognized. According to the principle, revenues are recognized when they are (1) realized or realizable, and are (2) earned (usually when goods are transferred or services rendered), no matter when cash is received.

a. BMC Software, Inc.
b. 3M Company
c. Net realizable value
d. Revenue recognition

92. _____ is the risk (variability in value) borne by an interest-bearing asset, such as a loan or a bond, due to variability of interest rates. In general, as rates rise, the price of a fixed rate bond will fall, and vice versa. _____ is commonly measured by the bond's duration.

a. Interest rate risk
b. AMEX
c. AIG
d. ABC Television Network

Chapter 21. The Statement of Cash Flows Revisited

93. A _____ is a financial instrument aimed at a reduction in greenhouse gas emissions. _____s are measured in metric tons of carbon dioxide-equivalent (_____$_2$e) and may represent six primary categories of greenhouse gases. One _____ represents the reduction of one metric ton of carbon dioxide or its equivalent in other greenhouse gases.

a. Sustainable development
b. Mutual fund
c. General Accounting Office
d. Carbon offset

94. _____ is the value on a given date of a future payment or series of future payments, discounted to reflect the time value of money and other factors such as investment risk. _____ calculations are widely used in business and economics to provide a means to compare cash flows at different times on a meaningful 'like to like' basis.

The most commonly applied model of the time value of money is compound interest.

a. Net present value
b. 3M Company
c. Present value
d. Future value

95. _____ are financial statements that factor the holding company's subsidiaries into its aggregated accounting figure. It is a representation of how the holding company is doing as a group. The consolidated accounts should provide a true and fair view of the financial and operating conditions of the group.

a. Replacement cost
b. Consolidated financial statements
c. Redemption value
d. Committee on Accounting Procedure

Chapter 1

1. d	2. d	3. d	4. a	5. a	6. d	7. d	8. d	9. c	10. d
11. d	12. b	13. a	14. d	15. d	16. b	17. c	18. d	19. a	20. a
21. d	22. d	23. b	24. b	25. c	26. b	27. a	28. d	29. d	30. d
31. b	32. d	33. c	34. b	35. d	36. b	37. c	38. a	39. d	40. c
41. a	42. c	43. b	44. d	45. d	46. d	47. d	48. d	49. c	50. a
51. a	52. c	53. b	54. c	55. c	56. c	57. a	58. d	59. b	60. d
61. a	62. d	63. b	64. d	65. c	66. d	67. b	68. b	69. c	70. d
71. d	72. d	73. b	74. d	75. c	76. b	77. d	78. d	79. c	80. d
81. b	82. d	83. a	84. d	85. c	86. a	87. d	88. a	89. b	90. b
91. d	92. d	93. c	94. c	95. d	96. c	97. d	98. d	99. d	100. b
101. b	102. d								

Chapter 2

1. d	2. d	3. a	4. d	5. d	6. c	7. c	8. c	9. c	10. c
11. a	12. d	13. a	14. a	15. b	16. d	17. a	18. d	19. b	20. d
21. b	22. a	23. b	24. a	25. c	26. d	27. b	28. a	29. c	30. d
31. d	32. a	33. b	34. b	35. d	36. b	37. d	38. d	39. b	40. a
41. d	42. a	43. d	44. d	45. c	46. b	47. d	48. a	49. d	50. a
51. d	52. a	53. a	54. c	55. a	56. c	57. d	58. a	59. d	

Chapter 3

1. c	2. b	3. b	4. b	5. b	6. d	7. c	8. c	9. d	10. a
11. c	12. d	13. d	14. c	15. d	16. d	17. c	18. c	19. d	20. d
21. a	22. a	23. d	24. c	25. d	26. d	27. a	28. d	29. d	30. b
31. d	32. d	33. d	34. c	35. a	36. d	37. a	38. a	39. c	40. b
41. d	42. c	43. a	44. d	45. d	46. d	47. c	48. d	49. a	50. d
51. a	52. a	53. d	54. d	55. d	56. b	57. c	58. a	59. d	60. b
61. b	62. d	63. b	64. d	65. b	66. c	67. d	68. d	69. b	70. d
71. d	72. d	73. c	74. a	75. d	76. d				

Chapter 4

1. a	2. b	3. b	4. a	5. c	6. d	7. c	8. d	9. d	10. b
11. a	12. d	13. b	14. c	15. a	16. d	17. d	18. d	19. d	20. d
21. b	22. a	23. d	24. d	25. c	26. d	27. c	28. d	29. b	30. d
31. b	32. d	33. d	34. d	35. b	36. a	37. d	38. d	39. a	40. d
41. d	42. d	43. d	44. b	45. a	46. c	47. d	48. d	49. b	50. d
51. b	52. d	53. c	54. b	55. c	56. d	57. d	58. d	59. d	60. d
61. b	62. d	63. d	64. b						

Chapter 5

1. b	2. d	3. a	4. a	5. b	6. d	7. c	8. b	9. d	10. c
11. d	12. d	13. c	14. d	15. a	16. d	17. b	18. a	19. c	20. a
21. a	22. c	23. a	24. b	25. a	26. b	27. d	28. c	29. b	30. d
31. b	32. d	33. b	34. b	35. d	36. d	37. a	38. d	39. d	40. d
41. d	42. a	43. a	44. a	45. b					

ANSWER KEY

Chapter 6
1. d	2. c	3. d	4. d	5. d	6. d	7. a	8. a	9. d	10. d
11. d	12. d	13. d	14. b	15. a	16. d	17. d	18. a	19. d	20. d
21. c	22. d	23. c	24. c	25. a	26. c	27. d	28. d	29. b	30. a
31. a	32. a	33. c							

Chapter 7
1. d	2. b	3. d	4. d	5. c	6. d	7. d	8. b	9. d	10. c
11. d	12. d	13. a	14. d	15. b	16. d	17. d	18. d	19. d	20. d
21. d	22. d	23. d	24. d	25. c	26. d	27. d	28. b	29. c	30. b
31. d	32. d	33. d	34. b	35. d	36. d	37. a	38. d	39. d	40. c
41. b	42. d	43. c	44. a	45. d	46. d	47. d	48. c	49. d	50. d
51. a	52. c	53. d	54. d	55. c	56. b	57. d	58. d	59. d	60. d
61. d	62. d								

Chapter 8
1. d	2. b	3. d	4. d	5. d	6. a	7. b	8. b	9. b	10. d
11. a	12. b	13. d	14. b	15. d	16. b	17. c	18. c	19. c	20. c
21. a	22. d	23. b	24. d	25. a	26. c	27. a	28. d	29. d	30. a
31. d	32. d	33. d	34. b	35. d	36. d	37. a	38. d	39. d	40. d

Chapter 9
1. d	2. a	3. a	4. b	5. c	6. b	7. b	8. d	9. d	10. b
11. d	12. c	13. d	14. d	15. c	16. c	17. d	18. a	19. a	20. d
21. b	22. b	23. d	24. d	25. d	26. d	27. a	28. c	29. d	30. d
31. d	32. b	33. d	34. b	35. a	36. d	37. d	38. b	39. c	40. a
41. d	42. a	43. d	44. d	45. d	46. d	47. d	48. d		

Chapter 10
1. a	2. d	3. c	4. d	5. c	6. d	7. d	8. d	9. a	10. b
11. d	12. c	13. d	14. d	15. d	16. d	17. b	18. b	19. d	20. b
21. b	22. a	23. b	24. b	25. b	26. d	27. d	28. d	29. b	30. c
31. d	32. d	33. c	34. d	35. d	36. d	37. d	38. a	39. c	40. c
41. b	42. d	43. d	44. a	45. d	46. d	47. d	48. b	49. a	50. d
51. d	52. b	53. b	54. d	55. d					

Chapter 11
1. d	2. d	3. d	4. a	5. b	6. d	7. d	8. d	9. c	10. b
11. b	12. a	13. a	14. d	15. d	16. b	17. d	18. d	19. a	20. b
21. d	22. a	23. b	24. c	25. b	26. a	27. b	28. d	29. d	30. b
31. b	32. d	33. d	34. a	35. d	36. d				

Chapter 12

1. b	2. c	3. d	4. d	5. d	6. c	7. b	8. a	9. d	10. c
11. d	12. c	13. d	14. a	15. d	16. a	17. b	18. b	19. d	20. d
21. b	22. b	23. b	24. b	25. b	26. b	27. c	28. d	29. c	30. d
31. d	32. d	33. d	34. d	35. c	36. d	37. a	38. d	39. d	40. a
41. c	42. d	43. a	44. d	45. c	46. c	47. b	48. b	49. d	

Chapter 13

1. b	2. d	3. d	4. d	5. d	6. a	7. c	8. b	9. d	10. d
11. d	12. d	13. a	14. a	15. d	16. d	17. c	18. a	19. d	20. d
21. d	22. d	23. d	24. d	25. d	26. b	27. d	28. d	29. d	30. d
31. d	32. d	33. b	34. a	35. a	36. d	37. d	38. c	39. c	40. d
41. d	42. d	43. d	44. c	45. c	46. c	47. d	48. b	49. d	50. c
51. d	52. d	53. d	54. c	55. d	56. d	57. a	58. d	59. d	60. b
61. d									

Chapter 14

1. c	2. a	3. d	4. d	5. b	6. c	7. d	8. d	9. d	10. d
11. a	12. a	13. d	14. b	15. d	16. d	17. d	18. b	19. a	20. c
21. b	22. d	23. d	24. d	25. d	26. d	27. b	28. d	29. d	30. c
31. b	32. b	33. a	34. d	35. d	36. b	37. d	38. d	39. d	40. b
41. d	42. d	43. b	44. b	45. b	46. a	47. d	48. d	49. d	50. d
51. d	52. c	53. a	54. a	55. c	56. d	57. d	58. d	59. d	60. d
61. d	62. d	63. d	64. d	65. d	66. b	67. b	68. d	69. a	70. d
71. d	72. d	73. a	74. d	75. c					

Chapter 15

1. b	2. a	3. a	4. b	5. a	6. d	7. d	8. d	9. d	10. a
11. a	12. d	13. d	14. a	15. c	16. c	17. c	18. d	19. d	20. c
21. d	22. d	23. d	24. d	25. d	26. a	27. d	28. d	29. a	30. b
31. b	32. a	33. d	34. b	35. c	36. d	37. b	38. d	39. b	40. d
41. d	42. d	43. d	44. d	45. a	46. d	47. b	48. d	49. d	50. d
51. d	52. b	53. d	54. d	55. d	56. c	57. c	58. b		

Chapter 16

1. c	2. a	3. d	4. b	5. c	6. b	7. a	8. b	9. b	10. a
11. d	12. c	13. b	14. d	15. d	16. d	17. d	18. c	19. d	20. c
21. d	22. b	23. d	24. d	25. b	26. b	27. d	28. a	29. a	30. b
31. c	32. d	33. d	34. d	35. b	36. d	37. d	38. b	39. b	40. a
41. d									

ANSWER KEY

Chapter 17
1. d	2. d	3. c	4. b	5. d	6. d	7. d	8. a	9. d	10. d
11. b	12. b	13. b	14. d	15. d	16. b	17. c	18. d	19. c	20. d
21. d	22. d	23. d	24. d	25. d	26. d	27. c	28. d	29. d	30. d
31. a	32. c	33. c	34. d	35. d	36. d	37. d	38. a	39. b	40. a
41. c	42. a	43. d	44. d	45. a	46. d	47. c			

Chapter 18
1. a	2. d	3. d	4. d	5. d	6. d	7. b	8. c	9. c	10. d
11. b	12. c	13. d	14. d	15. d	16. c	17. d	18. c	19. d	20. d
21. a	22. a	23. a	24. b	25. c	26. b	27. c	28. a	29. d	30. d
31. d	32. b	33. a	34. d	35. b	36. d	37. c	38. d	39. b	40. b
41. d	42. b	43. c	44. c	45. d	46. d	47. d	48. a	49. d	50. d
51. b	52. b	53. a	54. d	55. b	56. d	57. d	58. d	59. d	60. a
61. c	62. b	63. d	64. d	65. d	66. b	67. c			

Chapter 19
1. a	2. d	3. d	4. b	5. c	6. b	7. d	8. b	9. c	10. d
11. d	12. d	13. c	14. a	15. b	16. b	17. a	18. d	19. d	20. d
21. c	22. a	23. c	24. d	25. d	26. d	27. c	28. d	29. b	30. d
31. b	32. d	33. c	34. b	35. d	36. b	37. d	38. d	39. d	40. b
41. a	42. a	43. a	44. a	45. a					

Chapter 20
1. d	2. a	3. b	4. d	5. c	6. b	7. c	8. b	9. d	10. d
11. d	12. b	13. d	14. d	15. c	16. d	17. a	18. a	19. d	20. d
21. c	22. c	23. c	24. d	25. c	26. c	27. a	28. d	29. a	30. d
31. c	32. b	33. a	34. d	35. d	36. a	37. d	38. d	39. c	40. a
41. b	42. b	43. d	44. d	45. c					

Chapter 21
1. a	2. d	3. b	4. d	5. c	6. d	7. c	8. d	9. d	10. d
11. d	12. b	13. d	14. b	15. b	16. a	17. a	18. d	19. c	20. d
21. d	22. d	23. c	24. a	25. b	26. a	27. c	28. b	29. d	30. d
31. c	32. a	33. d	34. d	35. b	36. d	37. a	38. d	39. a	40. b
41. a	42. d	43. a	44. c	45. a	46. c	47. b	48. d	49. d	50. b
51. b	52. c	53. d	54. d	55. b	56. d	57. a	58. b	59. d	60. b
61. d	62. a	63. d	64. c	65. d	66. d	67. c	68. d	69. d	70. d
71. d	72. a	73. d	74. a	75. d	76. c	77. b	78. d	79. d	80. a
81. d	82. d	83. d	84. c	85. b	86. b	87. b	88. a	89. b	90. d
91. d	92. a	93. d	94. c	95. b					

www.ingramcontent.com/pod-product-compliance
Lightning Source LLC
Chambersburg PA
CBHW080546230426
43663CB00015B/2722